PINSTRIPES AND REDS:

An American Ambassador Caught Between the State
Department and the Romanian Communists, 1981-1985

David B. Funderburk

With a Foreword by Congressman Philip M. Crane

Selous Foundation Press, Washington, D.C.

The printing of this book was made possible by the generosity of the Selous Foundation and the following individuals: H.J. Casey, Mrs. Ellen C. Garwood, H.E. King, and Edgar Uihlein.

The photographs are credited in the order in which they appear: William Edwards, William Edwards, William Edwards, no credit, no credit, William Edwards, White House photo, White House photo, State Department photo, no credit, William Edwards, William Edwards, William Edwards, White House photo, White House photo, White House photo, William Edwards, William Edwards, William Edwards, no credit, William Edwards, William Edwards.

Inquiries and book orders should be addressed to Pinstripes & Reds, Post Office Box 1124, Dunn, N.C. 28334. Telephone 919-893-3342.

Library of Congress Catalogue Card Number 87-82566
ISBN: 0-944273-01-7

Printed in the United States of America
Edwards & Broughton Company, Raleigh, N.C.

JACKET DESIGNED BY BRITT FUNDERBURK

For my wife, Betty

Contents

Charts on pages 6, 22 and 23

Illustrations follow pages 55 and 127

Acknowledgments

Many people contributed to this story about Communism, the State Department, and the Reagan Administration. Because the theme of the book shows many State Department policymakers or pinstripers and Romanian Communists or Reds in an unflattering light, some would rather not be associated with it. Particularly with regard to individuals living in Communist Romania, I have left out the names of many who were helpful so their lives would not become more miserable.

Despite whatever experience and background I had in Romania, and in local North Carolina Republican politics, without the strong support of Senator Jesse Helms I would not have had the opportunity to serve as U.S. ambassador to Romania between 1981 and 1985. I am grateful to Senator Helms for providing me with this opportunity.

I also owe a debt of gratitude to President Reagan, whose administration I was proud to have served. The Reagan Administration has done more than any other to rebuild America's defenses in support of freedom, to give conservatives a foot in the door of government, and to restore traditional values, despite a dearth of conservative appointments.

I am grateful to those in the U.S. Embassy, Bucharest, who assisted me and did much of the work in finding out the truth about the Romanian regime and Soviet-Romanian relations. One of them is Frank Corry, my Deputy Chief of Mission (DCM), whose patience and meticulous research helped uncover the true situation. USA Colonel Franklin Mastro, chief Defense Attache, discovered a great deal of value in exposure of the situation, because he did not pull punches or limit investigative undertakings. Others were also helpful, in particular Public Information Officer William Edwards. Edwards, who often traveled with me, recorded for this book and posterity a superb photographic account of happenings in

Romania. Edwards and Cultural Affairs Officer Ernest Latham helped in the task of meeting the people and getting out the positive word about America. There were others who deserve recognition, but suffice it to say that I appreciate what they have contributed to a greater awareness of the actual problems we face in Eastern Europe.

Carter Wrenn and Tom Ellis of the National Congressional Club were very helpful. Others at the National Congressional Club assisted in typing the manuscript including: Weebie Berryhill, Leigh Lineberger, Virgie Anderson, Catherine Maynor, Angela Pearce, Dawn Eubanks, Judy Hassler, Kathy Davis, Saralee Gould, and Kathryn Carpenter. I am thankful for a grant given me to complete the book by the Coalition for Freedom, and for the support of the Coalition's Carter Wrenn and Robert Holding.

Both Ion Ratiu, President of the World Union of Free Romanians and publisher of the *Free Romanian* newspaper (London), and Ion Mihai Pacepa, former Deputy Director of the Romanian Securitate (CIE), read the manuscript and offered suggestions for its improvement. Ratiu provided me with helpful information, especially regarding the pre-World War II internal situation in Transylvania.

U.S. Representative Philip Crane was kind enough to write a foreword for the book. Congressman Crane has helped lead the fight against Most-Favored-Nation (MFN) status for Communist countries that engage in slave labor and religious persecution. Due in part to his efforts, the Generalized System of Preferences (GSP)—an aspect of MFN—was removed from Romania in January of 1987, and both houses of Congress voted in mid 1987 to suspend MFN for six months.

Boyd Cathey, senior editor of *Southern Partisan,* read the manuscript. Dr. Magnus Krynski of Duke University offered advice for developing a more realistic U.S. policy toward Eastern Europe.

The Selous Foundation's officers volunteered to sponsor the book and ensure its publication. Ralph Galliano of Selous was supportive throughout, and helped raise the funds for publication. I am indebted to H. J. Casey, Mrs. Ellen C. Garwood, and Edgar Uihlein for their financial contributions which made possible the printing of the book, which was done excellently by Henry Hagwood and colleagues at Edwards and Broughton Co.

Finally I owe my family members more than I can say. Individuals in the Foreign Service make real sacrifices, especially if they have family, friends, and roots in the United States. As a political appointee whose home is North Carolina, I missed being estranged from family, friends, and things back home that are dear. Less than one year after my appointment as ambassador, both my father, Dr. Guy B. Funderburk, and my mother, Mrs. Vesta Young Funderburk, died without ever having the chance to visit the post of my assignment. My mother had in fact planned a trip to Romania that would have taken place had she not died a week earlier. One year after arriving in Bucharest, my son, Britt (who designed the cover for this book), had to return to the states to attend boarding school because there was no English-language, non-Communist high school in Romania. This was not a desired or easy solution for a close-knit family. But through it all, my wife, Betty, and daughter, Deana, stayed with me and provided the family support needed to carry on. They made tremendous sacrifices by living in a tragic, depressing environment for almost four years.

This work was written in large part because of my deep involvement with Romania and Romanians. It is my special hope that the true plight of the Romanian people (and others) under Communism, will be better understood through this work. Much needs to be done in order to save what is left of Romanian history, traditions, and distinctiveness. And the desire of Romanians for freedom and Western orientation must be supported by those of us in the Free World. There are hundreds of Romanians who have helped me in better understanding the reality behind the scenes and who have expressed their firm commitment for freedom, for the Romanian nation, and against the pervasive Communist tyranny. My wife, son, and I learned a great deal living with the Mircea Tatos family in 1971 and 1972. I cannot mention all of those who are still in Romania, for obvious reasons. I am grateful for the sacrifices of those such as Paul Cernovodeanu, Dinu Giurescu, Teodor Popescu, Vasile Talos, Ion Stanciu, Nicu Gheorghita, Paul Negrut, and a great national patriot from Oltenia. I have not forgotten the note handed to me by an elderly lady in a Baptist church in Romania, paraphrasing a Bible passage: be "a thorn in the flesh" of the [Communist] rulers.

I am indebted to all of the people who helped me in this endeavor. The views, opinions, and statements, however, are mine, and have not been approved by and do not represent the official views of the State Department or the U.S. Government.

Foreword

Since 1975, we have conducted trade with the Socialist Republic of Romania under the provisions of the Jackson-Vanik Amendment to the Trade Act, which links the assignment of Most-Favored Nation (MFN) status to the establishment of free and open emigration procedures. Time and time again, we have been presented with substantial evidence that the Romanian government harasses and persecutes those who try to emigrate. Time and time again, President after President has chosen to overlook these violations of the basic principles of human rights and to accord the Romanians MFN status, citing Romanian "assurances" that progress would be made. Time and time again, these assurances turn out to be tragically empty promises.

In the period in which Romania has enjoyed preferential trade status with the United States, the Romanian government has attempted to silence critics of the regime. In July, 1978, General Ion Pacepa, former Deputy Director of the CIE (Romanian intelligence service) and special advisor to President Ceausescu, was instructed personally by Ceausescu to conduct secret assassinations by mailing plastic explosives to exiles critical of the Ceausescu regime. Pacepa refused and defected. Since his 1978 defection, he has been the target of at least seven assassination attempts. Paul Goma, the dissident writer expelled to France in 1977, was targeted for assassination in 1982. His would-be assassin, Matei Haiducu, revealed to the French secret service the details of his mission. In 1980, West Germany arrested a man who spied on Romanian emigrants for Romanian intelligence; in February 1981, parcel bombs were sent to the homes of prominent Romanian exiles in Paris and Cologne, injuring two of them and a police bomb expert; in July 1981, Emil Georgescu, an outspoken Romanian program editor at Radio Free Europe was stabbed 22 times. Other Radio Free Europe personnel who have been beaten or targeted for assassination include Monica Lovinescu and Sergious Manoliu. Many more cases can be found during the period in which Romania enjoyed MFN status.

The abuse of religious rights, harassment of emigrant applicants, and assassination of critics of the regime continue unabated. Yet, the U.S. government declines to speak out forcefully. To remain silent while these gross violations of fundamental human rights continue is unconscionable. To my mind, these abuses far outweigh the token gestures of cooperation with which the Romanian government has been forthcoming.

Yet, Romania is often considered to be one of the success stories of the State Department's foreign policy: a country against which the U.S. has supposedly used the "leverage" of MFN to move the Romanians away from the Soviet Union and reduce the number of human rights violations. In Congressional testimony, the State Department cites the increased number of applications for emigration to the U.S., West Germany, and Israel, the fact that Romania went to the boycotted 1984 Olympics, and Romania's condemnation of the Soviet invasion of Afghanistan as evidence of the success of the U.S. MFN policy. These "successes" are used to convince the President that MFN treatment of Romania should continue.

However, a simple glance at the map of Eastern Europe will tell us how much "leverage" we actually have in encouraging Romanian independence from the Soviet Union. The geostrategic reality is that this country has no open access to the West. It is completely surrounded by the Soviet Union, Bulgaria, Hungary, and Yugoslavia; countries which have absolutely no tolerance of actions contrary to the wishes of Moscow. A basic review of the governmental structure of that country will also reveal how much "leverage" we actually have in reducing the overall emigration problem, the overall religious persecution, and systematic repression of critics of the government. The political reality is that the government of this country is a totalitarian dictatorship run by the Communist regime of Nicolae Ceausescu. This man has personally ordered the assassination of critics of his regime, has allowed Bibles to be turned into toilet paper, and runs a police state where cars are randomly stopped and trunks inspected, armed military personnel thoroughly search anyone coming into or going out of the country, and citizens are required by law to report to the police any contact they have had with foreigners within 24 hours.

Former Ambassador to Romania, David Funderburk, is a welcomed voice in the attempt to open the eyes of the American people to the reality of Romania. In his book, *Pinstripes and Reds: An American Ambassador Caught Between the State Department and Romanian Communists, 1981-1985,* he skillfully explains how one of the most despotic tyrannies of this century deceives the American government into legitimizing Romania's inhumane and anti-religious domestic policies by the continual granting of Most-Favored Nation trading status, while, at the same time, the U.S. ignores the many alarming characteristics of Romania's foreign policy. At the heart of this deception is the State Department's policy of differentiation, by which the U.S. rewards Romania's facade of an independent foreign policy in hopes of weakening the iron hold of the Soviet Union over the Eastern bloc.

It is Funderburk's personal accounts of U.S. policy toward Romania which expose the naiveté of this well-intended, but misguided, policy and forces a serious reevaluation of the U.S. position *vis-à-vis* Romania. His account of the Romanian government's repression of religion, oppression of dissidents, and support of terrorism is eye-opening. One is led to ask how it is possible to believe that a policy of differentiation outweighs the loss of credibility which our great nation attempts to hold as a nation based upon the tenets of freedom and liberty. Funderburk provides the answer through his examination of the accommodating attitude of the elite group of State Department personnel who run their own agenda regarding U.S. policy toward Romania.

David Funderburk is perhaps the most qualified individual to tell the story of the inside workings of U.S. foreign policy toward Romania. A Fulbright Fellow to Romania during the years before MFN was granted, and a USIA staff officer in Romania in 1975, he had both a solid academic background and personal experiences to understand the true policies of the Romanian government. However, as the U.S. Ambassador to Romania for nearly four years, he found himself pursuing the foreign policies of his President while being constantly undermined by both the pinstripers of the State Department who were running their own foreign policy and the Reds of Communist Romania.

Philip M. Crane
Washington, D.C.
March, 1987

Prologue

Collaboration between the State Department and Communist regimes has been going on for some time. A few writers have addressed traditional problems associated with the State Department: an old boy network of elitists; an entrenched bureaucracy not subject to public opinion or presidential directives; a lack of sympathy for putting American interests first; and a tendency toward internationalism, detentism, and compromise with Communists. Others have written about the State Department held view of Communism and Western democracy being moral equivalents. And a few have described the ways in which U.S. diplomats have carried out policies benefitting Communists.

Few political appointees, much less conservative ones, have ever been posted to a Communist country where such collaboration could be witnessed and recorded. As President Reagan's ambassador to Communist Romania, I saw firsthand the pinstripers and Reds working together. This account endeavors to detail: what is wrong at the State Department; the reality of Nicolae Ceausescu's regime in Romania; and how the two help each other. Highlighted are the frustrations of an ambassador caught between the State Department and the Romanian Communists; and the record of American leaders dealing with a Stalinist boss. In addition to a lengthy meeting with President Reagan, sessions are described that involved Romanian Communist leaders with the Vice President, Cabinet officers, Congressmen, and other leading American policymakers. Especially disturbing is the record of top American officials playing the State Department collaboration game with Ceausescu. The end result of the Communist-State convergence of interests is a benefit for Moscow and its satellite regime in Bucharest, but not for the people of Romania or for U.S. national interests.

A measure of realism in U.S. foreign policy that emphasizes both

U.S. national security interests and the interests of our pro-freedom
allies behind the Iron Curtain, is desperately needed. Some ideas
are advanced in this work for rectifying the unsatisfactory Washington policy *vis-à-vis* Eastern Europe. The experience reflected
is concentrated in one East European Communist country and its
dealings with the U.S. government. The U.S.-Romania case, however, symbolizes and touches on all of U.S. policy with the Soviet
Bloc in East Europe, and on what is lacking in U.S. defense of freedom and Western values. In terms of the Communist threat to the
whole Free World, its applicability goes beyond the European Affairs regional bureau at the State Department.

My association with Romania and selection as ambassador
resulted from a background in Romanian-East European studies,
and in politics.

My studies at Wake Forest University under Professor Keith Hit-
chins first interested me in the world of Eastern Europe and Romania in particular. Romanian language study on the West Coast, and
several grants for research gave me the opportunity to live in Romania during the early and mid 1970s.

Involvement in local Republican politics and friendship with Senator Jesse Helms, led the Reagan Administration to consider me
for a top position in the government.* Senator Helms took my application to the White House, and penned in a letter to Secretary
of State Alexander Haig: "This one means a lot to me!" Many other
Senators, organizations, and individuals backed my nomination.**

With the State Department unenthusiastic about getting a political conservative, anti-Communist, as ambassador, several zigs and

---

* My name was originally submitted for positions in the European Affairs Bu-
  reau and the East European Affairs Office at the State Department, with an
  ambassadorship down the line on a list of preferences.
** Endorsements included those of Senators Thad Cochran, Jeremiah Denton,
   John East, Paula Hawkins, Mack Mattingly, and Strom Thurmond; the Her-
   itage Foundation; and General John B. Hirt, Dr. William A. Brady, Dr.
   Nicholas G. Bountress, Dr. James J. Farsolas, Professor Demetrius
   Dvoichenko-Markov, Dr. Zane Mason, Dr. Michael Preda, Dr. John Basil,
   Dr. Mary Ellen Fischer, Dr. Elmer L. Puryear, John Neiman, Wayne James
   Payne, and Carol Woodfin. Others including Larry Godwin, Mike McLeod,
   Jerry McManis, Randy Gregory, and Louis March telephoned support to appropriate Washington offices. Clint Fuller in Senator Helms's office, Tom Fet-
   zer of Senator East's office and Terry Edmondson of the National Congressional Club, contacted Wendy Borcherdt of the White House Personnel Office,
   who said my application was considered for "the most viable non-career post
   to go to a non-career person."

zags occurred before the result was final. In April 1981, Jack Shaw of the State Department's Personnel section told then Assistant Secretary of State for European Affairs Lawrence Eagleburger, that I was no crazie just because I was being sponsored by Helms. Eagleburger responded by saying: "put it in writing!" When Shaw told Eagleburger it was important to put me in a top State position, Eagleburger responded in four letter Anglo Saxon words. Shaw told me that my chances for the ambassadorship were good because the administration was prepared to do something for Helms.*

A telephone call to me from President Reagan at my home in Buies Creek, North Carolina, came on June 24, 1981. The President asked me to serve as his ambassador to Romania. I replied that I would be greatly honored as there was no one I would rather work for than him. It was a dream come true for the son of a school teacher from the small town of Aberdeen, North Carolina.

There were more hurdles to jump, however, before the ambassadorship became a reality. For a conservative seeking higher office, there is no end to the critical examination by the media, press, and the liberals of the government and Congress. The obligatory background investigations provided those who were opposed to my nomination an opportunity to try to derail it. Two main concerns surfaced: Romanian government *agrément* (formal approval), and my book *If the Blind Lead the Blind.*

What would the Romanian Communist government say about one who had written a book highly critical of Communism? By diplomatic protocol, the government of a country such as Romania has the opportunity to pass judgment on a proposed nomination for ambassador by extending or not extending *agrément*. Since all of this takes place behind the scenes, I was informed on August 11th by the State Department that Romania had favorably returned *agrément*

---

*Two names actually went to the White House regarding the ambassadorial post: mine and that of a career Foreign Service officer who had Russian language qualifications and East European Affairs Office experience. That other person, Robert L. Barry, was a member of the leadership network of Henry Kissinger and his protégé Lawrence Eagleburger. Barry was eventually appointed ambassador to Bulgaria, next-door to Romania, from which he occasionally sent cables second-guessing my analysis of the situation in Romania. More recently, Barry headed the American delegation at the Stockholm "Conference on Confidence and Security Building Measures and Disarmament" in Europe. On a September 21, 1986, television newscast, Barry said the U.S. did not give up too much because the U.S. military was not dissatisfied with the ultimate East-West security agreement.

to President Reagan. This apparently indicated that the government of Romania wanted to get the Reagan Administration's relations with Romania off to a good start in the tradition of the personal presidential relationships and visits of Nixon, Ford and Carter with Romanian President Nicolae Ceausescu. The usual timetable was that after *agrément* the President would make the official nomination, Senate hearings would be held, and the swearing in and departure from Washington to the post of assignment would all take place in a month or two. In the meantime an ambassadorial training seminar was held at the State Department and Foreign Service Institute during the last week of August.

As it turned out, liberals in the press and Congress were more interested in putting fire to a conservative who had written a book critical of Communism, than was the Communist government in question. While I got periodic reports of the book, *If the Blind Lead the Blind*, causing problems during the in-house State Department investigation, the press brought it out in the open.

Senator Joseph Biden apparently got a copy of the book from Wendy Fox of *The Charlotte Observer*. It was a matter of Senator Paul Tsongas wanting this one to repay Jesse Helms more than Biden did. Thus Biden gave the copy to his friend Tsongas, who took the lead in the inquisition. In the manner of Helms putting holds on "liberal" State Department nominations which he opposed, Tsongas determined to send a message to Helms and other conservatives. Caught in the middle of this Foreign Relations Committee skirmish, my little book was reviewed virtually word for word in the press and in Senate hearings.

The Senate Foreign Relations Committee hearing was chaired by Senator Charles Percy, who along with the other Senators present, spoke well of me. The hearing ended on a positive note, and it seemed to be over. Hours later I was informed that Senator Tsongas, who had not been present, wanted to question me. Another hearing was set up, so that Tsongas could grill me on the book. Line after line was pulled out of the book, to indicate that someone with my anti-Communist feelings would not necessarily be the right one to represent the United States in a Communist country.

In the aftermath of the second hearing, Senator Tsongas held up my nomination for a few days to give me some of the medicine Senator Helms gave to Tsongas's favorites. The "other" Senator from Massachusetts invited me to his office, pointedly noting that perhaps I should not sit on the couch where the ill-fated nomination of conservative Ernest Lefever was crushed. He said that I seemed more reasonable and open-minded than the book would indicate. In our conversation, Tsongas pointed out that as one opposed to Communism, we were not too far apart on that subject.

Initially my nomination was included with a list of several other ambassadorial nominees to be voted on by simultaneous voice vote. My name was separated from the others, and no vote was made on my nomination at that time. Senator Helms met with Senator Howard Baker who agreed to set a firm date for a roll call vote on my nomination. Baker told Tsongas he could have his day in court by spending some time on the Senate floor reading my book and airing his objections, but that he would have to end his hold on the nomination.

On October 1st the Senate voted on it. Before the vote, Tsongas and Senator Edward Kennedy were rounding up Senators on the floor to convince them to vote against me. Tsongas showed Senator Mark Hatfield the book on the Senate floor with the result being that Hatfield was the only Republican not to vote for my nomination. Hatfield voted "present," while two Republicans, Warren Rudman and S.I. Hayakawa, were absent. Senator Helms in a moving speech defended my nomination saying that "Funderburk's sin is that he has dared to be critical of Communism," and "Alexander Solzhenitsyn has repeatedly made precisely the same point that Ambassador Funderburk made in this book." The vote was 75 to 19, with liberal Democrats in opposition: Baucus, Biden, Bumpers, Byrd (Robert C.), Cranston, Dodd, Eagleton, Hart, Inouye, Kennedy, Leahy, Levin, Matsunaga, Metzenbaum, Mitchell, Riegle, Sarbanes, Tsongas, and Zorinsky. Cannon, Moynihan, and Randolph did not vote.

The ambassadorial appointment letter was dated October 2nd. I was sworn in by "Judge" William Clark at the State Department with my family present. We arrived in Romania on October 10th.

An American ambassador is one appointed by the President and confirmed by the Senate to represent the United States to another country. He or she is the personal representative of the President who received "policy guidance and instructions from the Secretary of State . . . or from the President directly." The duties are embodied in a presidential letter to the newly appointed ambassador.*

---

* See the Presidential Letter of Ambassadorial duties in Appendix I.

As the representative of the President and the American people to Romania in commercial, political, cultural, and other concerns, the U.S. ambassador cannot only base recommendations on preferences or on knowledge of the actual situation, but on a careful mix of various influences. For example, the principal government agencies or departments interested in Romania are the departments of State, Commerce, Agriculture, and Defense, the National Security Council, and intelligence agencies. Congress has constituent concerns regarding Romania. The major non-governmental groups interested are: commercial and business companies;[1] agricultural researchers and exporters; human rights and religious organizations; and ethnic Romanian-American associations. Individual Americans interested include tourists, travelers, students, professors, filmmakers, sports enthusiasts, health buffs, and senior citizens looking for age-delaying processes. All of these and other interests have to be taken into consideration, with the result being that agreements are made that often water down U.S. principles. Back in Washington the government departments, Congress, the White House, group, and individual influences can weigh heavily on decision-making. This means, in effect, that the embassy in the field (American embassy, Bucharest, for example) has some influence and input but usually not decisive impact on policy. There are occasional rewards when your letter or cable recommendation is used to advance or block certain policy decisions. Usually there are no immediate indications of the effectiveness of the day to day efforts of an ambassador.*

CHART 1:
A Day in the Life of a U.S. Ambassador in Bucharest, Romania, with a sample schedule of activities.

8:30 a.m. arrival in the embassy chancery office at downtown Tudor Arghezi Street, after a ten minute drive in a semi-armored (Buick Park Avenue) limousine from the ambassador's residence at 21 Kisselef Boulevard in northern Bucharest;

8:30-
10:00 a.m. review of the day's newspapers and the latest cable traffic from Washington or other points around the world regarding international developments, especially events in Romania and Eastern Europe;

* See Chart 1: A day in the life of a U.S. ambassador in Bucharest, with a schedule of activities.

10:00-
11:00 a.m.   staff meeting with a small core of principal officers includ-
              ing the Deputy Chief of Mission (DCM), chief of the po-
              litical section (POL), chief economic officer (ECON), pub-
              lic affairs officer and head of USIA (PAO), agriculture
              officer (AGR), administrative chief (ADM), consular chief
              (CON), general services officer (GSO), chief defense at-
              tache (DATT), and others. Once a month the meetings in-
              clude all interested U.S. employees (of 58).

12:30 p.m.   lunch either at the residence or with other ambassadors or
              local officials, or a national day reception on the occasion
              of some country's independence day (with over 60 nations
              represented in Bucharest, it happens often);
2:00-
5:00 p.m.   work in the office including drafting cables or policy dis-
              cussions with officers, telephone calls to or from Washing-
              ton, opening exhibits or attending Romanian Foreign Minis-
              try meetings (at the call of the Romanian officials), or
              discussion of embassy related problems such as personnel,
              security, mail, food, the American School, Fulbright gran-
              tees, vehicles, weather related crises, air flights, etc. (with
              individual American officers);
6:00-
8:00 p.m.   receptions or national day occasions hosted by the diplo-
              matic corps and Romanian officials;
8:00-
10:00 p.m.   formal dinners hosted at the residence, or by other ambas-
              sadors, or Romanian officials (at a hotel/restaurant).

Other days included a full schedule of activities when traveling to
provincial centers in the country, to American government instal-
lations in Western Europe, or to Washington for consultations.

As a political or non-career appointee to a country usually re-
served for career ambassadors, my appointment went against the
grain of the Foreign Service elite. While not welcoming any non-
career ambassadorial appointments, the State Department has come
to expect presidential selection of some friends and political supporters to two or three dozen more desirable posts, like London,
Luxembourg, or Canberra. But typically posts in Third World and
Communist countries, with few exceptions, have gone to the career ambassador. Thus my appointment to a relatively important

and sensitive post in Communist Eastern Europe was not welcomed by the rank and file diplomats, regardless of my background and experience in the area. Of those who have held the title of ambassador, i.e. since 1964 as opposed to the earlier and lower designation of minister, I was one of two non-career ambassadors to Romania out of seven.

Another factor was political ideology or philosophy. In their political philosophy and party affiliation, Foreign Service officers are considered to be more liberal than the population as a whole. The case of Lawrence Eagleburger is instructive.

Lawrence Eagleburger served as an ambassador, the head of European affairs and as the Under Secretary of State for Political Affairs (the third ranking position in the State Department). As the highest ranking career officer and as a protégé of former Secretary of State and NSC Advisor Henry Kissinger, Eagleburger virtually ran the State Department. It is noteworthy that Eagleburger made the maximum financial contribution to the 1986 primary campaign of liberal Democrat Terry Sanford for the U.S. Senate from North Carolina. Eagleburger became president of Kissinger Associates after retirement from the State Department in 1984. He had been considered a moderate to liberal Republican who gained rapid promotions during the Nixon, Ford, Carter, and Reagan presidencies. Like Kissinger before him, and his own protege—Robie Mark Palmer,* Eagleburger opposed conservatives at every turn. He led the fight for careerist appointments, including liberal and non-ideological technocrats in opposition to conservative political appointees. From his perspective the Foreign Service was the sole province of the career elite.

Thus, Eagleburger's utter horror at David Funderburk being named ambassador to Communist Romania, after being promoted by Senator Jesse Helms. Helms, after all, had held up Eagleburger's own appointment as Under Secretary. I only later learned that from the outset Eagleburger considered me as one planted by Helms to carry out a separate, parallel foreign policy *vis-à-vis* Romania and Eastern Europe. I therefore had to be circumvented, discredited, and frozen out of the decision-making process. As a former colleague of mine put it in an interview with *The Charlotte Observer* of March 16, 1986: "He [Funderburk] was cursed before he ever

---

* Mark Palmer served as Deputy Assistant Secretary for European Affairs before becoming ambassador to Hungary in 1986.

got there because Jesse Helms was his patron. . . . There was nothing he could do, right from the beginning, that could have made them happy."[2]

Despite a good inspection report and complimentary letters from the President regarding my job performance in Bucharest, State Department officials leaked a steady stream of critical comments to newspapers and magazines.[3] The following items are typical examples. In a piece critical of political ambassadors, the author writes that "equally troubling to the Foreign Service establishment are some of Mr. Reagan's appointments of ideologically conservative academics. . . . David Funderburk of Campbell University, an ally of Senator Jesse Helms, Republican of North Carolina, is Ambassador to Romania. Mr. Funderburk wrote a 1978 book on the 'misteaching of communism' in U.S. universities."[4] Another item appeared under the heading "Whither Funderburk?" in *The New York Times* "Washington Talk" column which stated:

> The Foreign Service experts at the State Department currently regard Eastern Europe as a very sensitive area, one that should be served by experienced professional diplomats rather than the political appointees. . . . As a result, these professionals were encouraged to hear that a new ambassador was going to Romania, to replace David B. Funderburk, who has served in Bucharest since 1981. Before he became a diplomat, Mr. Funderburk had been a history professor at Campbell University in Buies Creek, N.C. His application for the ambassadorship was forwarded to the White House by Senator Jesse Helms, Republican of North Carolina.[5]

Another factor, however minor it may have been, was the resentment or rather envy on the part of some Foreign Service employees at having a political appointee who had experience in the area to which he was posted. One might think the idea of having a non-career envoy who knew the language and history of the country would be welcomed. *The Washington Post* and *The New York Times* delighted in joining the State Department careerists in attacking some of President Reagan's political ambassadors by saying their only qualifications for the job were knowledge of the English language (in the case of London), and contributions to President Reagan's election campaigns. But having studied the Romanian language at U.C.L.A. and the University of Washington, worked in Romania as a U.S.I.A. (United States Information Agency) officer, lived in Romania on three other occasions with research grants, and written a Ph.D. dissertation on Romania, they had to shift the criticism to my being an "ideological conservative."

Having someone who was familiar with the country to which he was posted also undermined the flawed tradition of the State Department rotation of assignments. Instead of terms of three or four years in one place which the U.S.I.A. and some other departments/agencies have, the State Department usually sends diplomats for a stay of about two years. It is obvious that with a Romania Desk chief at State who may know nothing firsthand about Romania, combined with Deputy Assistant Secretaries of European Affairs, and others in the department who may have little if any experience, diplomats in the field who can stay only two years in on-the-job training are severely handicapped. The institutional experience of an embassy or of the State Department regarding any given country is appallingly low.

American foreign policy toward Romania or almost any other country is thus carried out by persons whose knowledge is greatly limited. On the other hand, Romania's foreign policy *vis-à-vis* the United States is carried out by officials who have spent years studying about America. This gives Communists a real advantage in dealing with the West. Although there are some changes at the top every election year in our system, there is a real need for long-term experts or specialists on Romania and other parts of the world who actually weigh in on U.S. policy decisions. The State Department rationalization for this dearth of specific expertise is that by frequent rotation of officers at various levels, each diplomat gets a broad experience of different world regions and of the department's bureaucratic requirements in Washington offices.

What in fact develops, is a superficial generalized expertise, rather than a real in-depth knowledge of any given country or region. Just when a diplomat has learned the language of a country so that he can get around, and some knowledge and familiarity with the country and its officials, he is sent to another part of the world—in effect losing that experience. At some times because of rotation convergences, the embassy in Bucharest would only have a handful of people who had lived there for an extended period of time i.e. a year or more. The Communist officials or those of any other nation can thus watch with glee as the inexperienced Americans regularly rotate, and go through the process of learning the ropes without much benefit from their predecessors' experience. It is no wonder that there was not enough firsthand awareness of the reality of Romania's foreign policy to advise against continuation of a misguided "differentiation" policy that rewards Nicolae Ceausescu.

The following chapter on the State Department problem focuses on the situation I observed firsthand regarding Eastern Europe in general and Romania in particular. At the same time, much of what is said regarding that region is applicable for State Department policies worldwide.

CHAPTER ONE:

The State Department Problem

Policy as implemented by the State Department is flawed because of the individuals who make up the leadership elite.* It is the career Foreign Service's elite which has run U.S. foreign policy for decades. It has found a virtual "convergence of interests" with some Communist regimes like the one in Bucharest. It has carried out a policy frustrating and unrepresentative to many Americans—almost unchallenged by democratic elections and different administrations. In this regard the Reagan Administration has disappointingly changed little.

Conservatives consider that Reagan has brought a greater sense of realism to U.S. policy toward the Soviets. He has tried to return the U.S. to the higher moral ground in the eyes of our own people. We are dealing not with Sunday School teachers but the "evil empire," he has pointed out. The Soviets cannot be trusted. They have violated agreements like SALT even though they were more in Moscow's interest. They do not place the same value on individual human life that we do. This has been shown by the downing of KAL 007, the saturation bombings of whole communities in Afghanistan, the vast gulag of political and religious dissidents, and the refusal to allow but a trickle of Jews and others to emigrate. They operate the world's last giant empire. And their system's survival seems to be based on militaristic expansion and aggression. The slaughter of women, children, and the elderly, wherever nec-

---

*Beyond the personnel problem at State there are structural deficiencies. Perhaps chief among them is the regional affairs bureau set-up that includes all of Europe, the Soviet Union, and Canada together in one bureau. For starters, State must separate the U.S.S.R. and Eastern Europe from the rest of Europe and Canada in distinct bureaus.

essary, is acceptable to Moscow to bring about ultimate Soviet objectives.

Reagan has considered that exposure of the real Soviet practices would help put the world's struggle for freedom under U.S. leadership in the proper perspective. And even the major media and centers of "learning" in the U.S. which have long virtually ignored greater Soviet sins while dramatizing U.S. mistakes, have been welcomed to review their one-sided accounts. After all it is difficult for a conservative member of the Reagan Administration to speak or be honored on some campuses in America but not for avowed Marxist-Leninists. Similarly the major television networks show Soviet commentators skilled in the English language, propaganda, and disinformation on American TV programs alongside U.S. Government officials—giving them equal stature. But American officials do not appear on Soviet television beside Russian ones. Reagan appreciates the values of ideas and images.

In keeping with President Reagan's attempts to restore sanity and realism to the U.S.-Soviet relationship, he has worked to rebuild America's defenses. He knows intuitively that the Soviets best understand strength and seldom deal from a position of weakness. It is also important that America be perceived as strong, determined and willing to fight for freedom. Reagan is aware that the perception can be as important as the reality. Thus symbolically and psychologically he has endeavored to restore America's confidence and belief in itself as well as the actual military strength. And to conservatives he has boosted the inner strength of the U.S. by his domestic efforts to reset priorities. He has appointed strict constructionists of the Constitution as judges who look out for the interests of the civilized community and its hard working law abiding members instead of obsessive concern over the "technicality" rights of the criminal. He has tried to show that the interests of the 95% or so of Americans who believe in God are as important as the 4% or so who do not. He has spearheaded a tax reform which incorporates the view that the family unit should not be penalized by the tax laws of the country but encouraged. And perhaps above all he has reminded us that America is great because America is good. It is our values and sense of decency which have propelled us to this point in history. Our true strength is in our belief in God, the worth and dignity of the individual soul and spirit, and freedom for all people. We are stronger when we restore our traditional faith and when we proudly proclaim our distinctive principles.

In addition to President Reagan's general defense and political policy toward the Soviets, I considered his statements on Eastern Europe to reflect his preferences regarding the region. His annual Captive Nations Week statements were consistent with his campaign speeches through the years. On the 25th annual observance of Captive Nations Week, Reagan said that he was speaking to "all in Eastern Europe who are separated from neighbors and loved ones by an ugly Iron Curtain" and "to every person trapped in tyranny . . . we send our love and support and tell them they are not alone. Our message must be: your struggle is our struggle. Your dream is our dream. And someday you, too will be free." Reagan went on to say that "as we mark this 25th observance of Captive Nations Week, I have one question for those rulers: If communism is the wave of the future, why do you still need walls to keep people in, and armies of secret police to keep them quiet? Democracy may not be perfect, but the brave people who risk death for freedom are not fleeing from democracy. They're fleeing to democracy from communism." Finally Reagan stated that "once a communist revolution occurs, citizens are not permitted free elections, a free press, free trade, free unions, free speech, freedom to worship, or property, or freedom to travel as we please," and quoted Alexander Herzen who warned: "To shrink from saying a word in defense of the oppressed is as bad as any crime." It is because of that duty that we seek to strengthen the Voice of America, Radio Free Europe and Radio Liberty, Reagan pointed out. In his proclamation number 5223 of July 16, 1984, on Captive Nations Week, 1984, Reagan said in part (from the White House press release):

> We must draw strength from the actions of the millions of freedom fighters in Communist-occupied countries, such as the signers of petitions for religious rights in Lithuania, or the members of Solidarity, whose public protests require personal risk and sacrifice that is almost incomprehensible to the average citizen in the Free World. It is in their struggle for freedom that we can find the true path to genuine and lasting peace.
>
> For those denied the benefits of liberty we shall continue to speak out for their freedom. On behalf of the unjustly persecuted and falsely imprisoned, we shall continue to call for their speedy release and offer our prayers during their suffering. On behalf of the brave men and women who suffer persecution because of national origin, religious beliefs, and the desire for liberty, it is the duty and privilege of the United States of America to demand that the signatories of the United Nations Charter and the Helsinki Accord live

up to their pledges and obligations and respect the principles and spirit of those international agreements and understanding.

During Captive Nations Week, we renew our efforts to encourage freedom, independence, and national self-determination for those countries struggling to free themselves from Communist ideology and totalitarian oppression, and to support those countries which today are standing face-to-face against Soviet expansionism.[1]

In the 1985 Captive Nations Week Proclamation Reagan again said: "Those nations of Eastern Europe that have known conquest and captivity for decades . . . our nation will continue to speak out for the freedom of those denied the benefits of liberty."

These statements by the President are my sentiments and those of most people living in Eastern Europe. I certainly heard these views expressed frequently in Communist Eastern Europe. And I told President Reagan in August of 1983 that his Captive Nations addresses meant a lot to the people behind the Iron Curtain.

To change U.S. foreign policy *vis-à-vis* Eastern Europe into a pro-freedom, anti-Communist posture requires more than encouraging rhetoric. And it requires more than spreading such rhetoric via souped up Voice of America and Radio Free Europe/Radio Liberty broadcasts. For starters it calls for numbers of individuals in top policy-making positions at the State Department who believe such rhetoric and actively work to assist the oppressed. It means a revolutionary change in the way policy-making goes on at State. A giant shift in attitudes is needed. It is difficult to see how a pro-freedom policy which more realistically views the true nature of the regimes in Eastern Europe can be carried out by those who specialize in maintenance of the status quo and business as usual.

The President can appoint hundreds in a shop run by thousands of careerist diplomats. If the Secretary, Deputy Secretary, Under Secretary, Assistant Secretaries, Deputy Assistant Secretaries, key ambassadors, and others are appointed by the President to carry out a tougher policy which defends U.S. national security interests while supporting the aspirations and rights of oppressed people instead of oppressive regimes, policy could change. But to date, instead of hundreds of such appointments the President has made dozens. More importantly, he has kept the leadership elite in effective charge of foreign policy by appointing Secretaries of State who have left the institution intact. Both Al Haig and George Shultz, who had worked with bureaucracies before arriving at State, were satisfied to let the elite implement day to day policy.

Secretary of State Shultz has turned out to be a major disappointment for conservatives. He has not really interfered with the department's previous status quo-oriented policy. He has led the fight for the department's bureaucratic interests with the zeal of a recent convert. And in his advocacy role he has gone beyond previous Secretaries in defending State's turf and privileges. He has, for example, pushed for increased spending by the State Department bureaucracy when other government departments have been encouraged to limit expenditures. And he has helped the State Department restrict the Presidential prerogative of appointing who he wants as ambassador.

Shultz—no doubt at State's urging—placed limits, beginning in 1985, on the terms of non-career ambassadors to a couple of years instead of at the pleasure of the President. But career ambassadors have no such limits. This was surely intended to both reduce the influence of political appointees and to give the State leaders more opportunity to have Foreign Service diplomats put in Chief of Mission (COM) positions. Even without this new State tool, Shultz had systematically reduced the number of non-career appointments in the State Department including ambassadors by attrition, firings, and replacements. Under Shultz, the percentage of political appointees as ambassadors has dropped with COM slots in such places as the Vatican, South Africa, Hungary, Romania, Brazil, Canada, and Korea, moving from the political to career category.

In explaining how the State Department hierarchy undermines the President's foreign policy, it may be instructive to use the words of an experienced career Foreign Service officer:

> In those areas of the Department of State hierarchy that deal with Eastern Europe, as well as in other agencies, are several influential career officers who apparently hold firmly to views of Romania and East Europe fashionable during the Nixon years and to a policy toward Romania shaped in that period. As these officers have a large hand in choosing and assigning officers to key positions in the region and some hand in selecting their own on-going assignments and their successors, there has been a pronounced tendency to select personnel who share establishment views—and thus, to perpetuate them in the Department of State EEY/Romanian policy management. These views of a bell-weather thinking in higher policy levels of government, force a re-thinking of conventional wisdom. In many cases these career officers' views of Romania were not gained first-hand, but rather from Washington and in nearby capitals. Many of these views stem from the halcyon years of U.S.-

Romanian relations of the early-to-mid 1970's. There seems to be
a persistent vein of wishful thinking in the way our government
regards Romania and how our policy toward it is shaped. Wanting
independent Romanian behavior, we tend to focus on appearances
of such behavior and not on continuing, inevitable cooperation. As
independence of behavior of a Soviet satrapy is highly desirable,
there has been a tendency to look for it, concentrate on it, and
downplay the oppressiveness of the Soviet-imposed government and
system of rule. Evidence developed in the field that challenges
prevailing views is interpreted in the framework of conventional wisdom or in some noteworthy cases apparently simply ignored. As
relatively few people in the U.S. Government pay any attention to
Eastern Europe, and fewer to Romania, those career officers involved on a day-to-day basis with the region and Romania to a significant degree make our policy regarding them. Presidents under-
standably concern themselves with Romania on the occasions of
visits and noteworthy developments—and then are dependent upon
material and suggestions presented to them by subordinates in the
Department of State career bureaucracy. The power of these career
officers stems from the fact that they have the field largely to themselves. This group of individuals are men and women who have
worked together and for each other, a regional bureau team resem-
bling others in the Department of State. The men who have had such
a large influence on U.S. regional policy are Foreign Service
officers who spent much of their careers working on European affairs, particularly in Eastern Europe and the Soviet Union and in
Washington covering these areas. They are a typical Department
of State regional bureau grouping in many respects, but because language requirements are more demanding and the posts by and large
not widely sought after it is a more tightly woven clique. Most of
the older Eastern European hands have worked with each other at
least once. Recently, close FSO associate of Henry Kissinger,
Lawrence Eagleburger, has been the dominant figure in the group.
His associates and protégés have retained great influence over the
day-to-day conduct of our policy toward the region.[2]

Toward the end of my term as ambassador, in the wake of our
strong position papers which challenged the State Department elite's
wisdom, departmental pressure was put on us [the iconoclasts].
Knowing that there were others at the Embassy in Bucharest who
saw what I saw and wanted a more realistic, pro-America foreign
policy *vis-à-vis* Romania, the elite flexed its muscles. During the
time of normal rotation, for many of my key officers who had
helped immensely in sending evidence which ran counter to State's
differentiation policy toward Romania, ominous signals were sent.

That is, the key officers who had been my allies were either put on hold in terms of career advancement, transferred to less desirable posts (not requested and not constituting career advances), or put in comparatively minor positions where they could do no more damage to the system's sacred policy. While the officers eventually got assignments of some kind and were not dismissed from the Foreign Service, most were not given assignments befitting their levels of experience, rank, and quality. Two were not promoted to the senior Foreign Service, thus effectively ending any advancement hopes and limiting their terms at State to only a few more years in effect being forced into early retirement. A few were given Washington "paper positions" where they would be outside the policy/decision-making process. So much for rewarding the hardest-working, most inquisitive officers looking out for the best interests of the United States government.

Other Foreign Service officers with more conservative views than the average State Department employee did not have the brightest prospects for advancement—particularly if their real views became known. Loyalty and obedience were more important than expertise and knowledge. Many of those who backed my efforts in Bucharest had previously been stymied due to their views. One bright young officer quit the Foreign Service some months after my departure. He wrote to me that one reason he was leaving the Foreign Service was philosophical and that he generally agrees with Reagan's foreign policy. But with his views he felt constrained in the Foreign Service.

During the Reagan Administration, U.S. policy toward Eastern Europe was determined largely by a small coterie of Kissinger/Eagleburger clones who focused on it on a day to day basis. The Secretary of State, Under Secretary of State for Political Affairs (after Eagleburger), and Assistant Secretary of State for European Affairs were too preoccupied with world-wide events to devote time to Romania. Secretary Shultz's comment to me that he thought Eagleburger was taking care of things regarding Romania and Eastern Europe reflected the fact that the Secretary has little if any time for Romania. Prior to his departure, Under Secretary Eagleburger stayed involved because of his personal interest dating back to his days as Ambassador to Yugoslavia. This however was hardly necessary because cronies such as Deputy Assistant Secretary Mark Palmer, who had worked for him in Belgrade, marched to his drum beat on policy. Following Eagleburger's departure, his network proved that it was perfectly able to implement the Kissinger-Eagleburger policy without Kissinger and Eagleburger.

One character in U.S. policy toward Eastern Europe who was not part of the careerist elite by training was Richard Burt, a former *New York Times* correspondent. He was appointed first to Political-Military affairs at State and later as Assistant Secretary of State for European Affairs.* During half of the time of my tenure he headed the European Affairs Bureau. But Burt's chief interests seemed to be the political and military issues in East-West relations. He did not have the same interest in Eastern Europe and generally let Eagleburger and his deputy Mark Palmer run that show. Nevertheless, he displayed some resentment at being left out of the picture in terms of day to day U.S. policy toward Eastern Europe. For example, in 1983, he told me that he had not even received the final drafts of papers and talking points for an upcoming meeting between the Secretary of State and the Romanian Foreign Minister until minutes before the session. The preliminary session before the Secretary's meeting involved Palmer and Romanian Ambassador Mircea Malitza, but not Burt. He also noted that Eagleburger and Palmer had to be restrained from giving away too much in negotiations, because they had a soft spot for Yugoslavia (and Romania). Once I asked Burt about visiting Bucharest in view of the fact that almost everyone else in a high position at State had done so. He said in effect that he considered Bulgaria and Romania to be the pits of Eastern Europe and he had no desire to visit them.

In response to a request by Senator Helms (after my return to North Carolina from Romania), I testified against Burt's nomination as ambassador to the Federal Republic of Germany. In view of his low profile role in terms of Eastern Europe, there was precious little to say about him in specific terms other than his nominal implementation of misguided policy. Burt's sins were more those of omission. He left Eastern European affairs in the hands of the elite and did not weigh-in with efforts to change policy for the better. To preserve his credentials as a would-be insider Burt made an inaccurate criticism in a newspaper interview. He erroneously claimed that I did not send cables or reports that were critical of U.S. policy toward Eastern Europe.

In the specific case of Romania, the State Department process worked something like the following. The Deputy Assistant Sec-

---

*Burt is currently serving as U.S. Ambassador to West Germany.

retary for European Affairs who handled Eastern Europe assigned tasks to the Director of the Office of East European/Yugoslav Affairs and his deputy. At the bottom was the Romania Desk officer who did much of the spade work. Daily meetings of these officers ensured a coordinated front against the American Embassy employees in Bucharest who had different views.*

What motivated each of the players was the desire to succeed in the Foreign Service. James T. Hackett of the Heritage Foundation has spelled this out in some detail, showing that in order to get ahead the Foreign Service masses must do the bidding of the leaders of the good ole boy network.[3] A State-USIA response to Hackett's reports reflected the same arrogance in saying that they did not really think anyone would take Hackett's suggestions seriously. One gets rewards and promotions by loyalty to the elite. Some of the required elements of fealty include: (1) rather liberal or at worst non-political technocratic views politically; (2) antipathy toward conservatives and political appointees; (3) pro-internationalism and detentism; (4) activistic clientitis; and of course (5) total unquestioning loyalty to the leadership elite. The leadership elite is made up of those who get the principal ambassadorial posts, the largest monetary awards (they give these to themselves) and recognitions, and the top career positions in the department. One has only to look at the recipients list in the *State* magazine to know who is running the show. For example, the Senior Foreign Service Performance Pay Awards for outstanding performance between April 1983 and April 1984, awarded 262 payments ranging from $4,500 to $9,000. Many of the recipients who had made their marks in European affairs constituted a Who's Who of the elite in the *State* magazine.[4] A partial list includes the following:

Armacost, Michael H.	Kirk, Roger
Barnes, Harry G.	Kuchel, Roland K.
Barry, Robert L.	Ledsky, Nelson C.
Bergold Jr., Harry E.	Matlock Jr., Jack F.
Bridges, Peter S.	Palmer, Robie M. H. (Mark)
Combs Jr., Richard E.	Ridgway, Rozanne L.
Davis Jr., John R.	Simons Jr., Thomas W.
Eagleburger, Lawrence	Spiers, Ronald I.
Farrand, Robert William	

*See charts following page.

Chart 2:
Principal State Policy-Makers For Romania

THE PRESIDENT

VICE PRESIDENT

SECRETARY OF STATE

NATIONAL SECURITY
ADVISOR (NSC)

DEPUTY SECRETARY OF STATE

** *UNDER SECRETARY FOR POLITICAL AFFAIRS*

UNDER SECRETARY
FOR ECONOMIC
AFFAIRS

* ASSISTANT SECRETARY FOR EUROPEAN AFFAIRS

COUNSELOR

** *DEPUTY ASSISTANT SECRETARY FOR EUROPEAN AFFAIRS*

POLICY
PLANNING
STAFF

** *DIRECTOR, EAST EUROPEAN AFFAIRS OFFICE (EE/Y)*

** *HEAD, ROMANIA DESK*

AMBASSADOR

U.S. EMBASSY, BUCHAREST, ROMANIA

---

*Ordinarily the Assistant Secretary of State for European Affairs would take a
direct supervisory role over policy toward Eastern Europe, but during most of
my tenure this position was often by-passed.
**The underlined officers were in actual practice most actively involved in the
formulation of U.S. policy toward Eastern Europe including Romania.

Chart 3:
Department of State Policy Positions in Eastern European Affairs, 1981-1985

SECRETARY OF STATE	Al Haig / George Shultz
DEPUTY SECRETARY OF STATE	William Clark / Kenneth Dam
UNDER SECRETARY OF STATE FOR POLITICAL AFFAIRS	Lawrence Eagleburger
ASSISTANT SECRETARY OF STATE FOR EUROPEAN AFFAIRS	Lawrence Eagleburger / Richard Burt
DEPUTY ASSISTANT OF STATE FOR EUROPEAN AFFAIRS (DAS)	John Scanlan / Mark Palmer
DIRECTOR, OFFICE OF EAST EUROPEAN AFFAIRS (EUR/EEY)	Peter Bridges / John Davis
DEPUTY DIRECTOR, OFFICE OF EAST EUROPEAN AFFAIRS (EUR/EEY)	William Farrand / Richard Combs
ROMANIA DESK HEAD	Todd Becker / Jonathan Rickert / Thomas Lynch

United States Embassy, Bucharest, Romania

AMBASSADOR	David Funderburk
DEPUTY CHIEF OF MISSION (DCM)	Samuel Fry / Francis Corry

A word of elaboration is in order for number 4: activistic clientitis. It goes without question in the Foreign Service that one's all out effort to favor and bestow largesse on the area or country of specialty, is the expected and preferred policy. For instance, all of the State officials from the embassy in the field to the desk officer to the bureau chief to the Deputy Assistant Secretaries and Assistant Secretary, try to outdo one another in "improving" bilateral relations with any given country by dreaming up things to do for the other government. There is a clear distinction between the unpopular and repressive regime in Bucharest and the majority of people in the country. Unfortunately the games played in Washington to reward various countries usually result in helping government officials—chiefly Communist Party members in Romania—but not the average person or even the country as a whole. In my particular area at State, the Deputy Assistant Secretary (DAS) and his underlings felt it necessary for their individual advancement to propose roughly a gift a month to the Romanian government. Their preoccupation was with what the U.S. could do for the Romanian regime to shore up bilateral relations, to reward Romania's so-called independent foreign policy, and to constantly show the validity of U.S. policy toward Romania and Eastern Europe.

Consistent with the steady stream of gifts was the understanding that the boat should not be rocked, and that a close relationship should be maintained with the Romanian government and with the Romanian Embassy in Washington.

A foreign policy tragedy of the Reagan Administration is that the State elite has had a virtual free hand to implement policy as usual on a day to day basis. This has led to a policy carried out which is not consistent with President Reagan's stated objectives or principles. Those who correctly figure that they will be there [in the State bureaucracy] after Reagan is long gone, do not worry much about outlasting him. They may mouth Reagan's foreign policy aims in public, with anti-Soviet language, but work at the same time with the department to undermine his real policies.

Leaders at State even overlook violations of human rights by repressive internal regimes in Eastern Europe. They sometimes pressure or even threaten those who show concern for human rights. They oppose efforts to stop the transfer of high technology to Warsaw Pact regimes like Romania. They do not require real *quid pro quos* in exchange for assistance or favored treatment to Communist regimes, or insist that promises made need to be kept.

More importantly, perhaps, they play the game of the crafty Communist leadership, but ignore the wishes and concerns of the masses in the Communist countries. Their actions help perpetuate the Communist leadership in power, but help make the U.S. "resented" by the masses who see us capitulating to the tyrants. The people do not see America caring about freedom, democracy, and Western values, which we profess to believe in. The elite at Foggy Bottom tends to satiate the appetites of the suppressors, but does not play "futures" as far as the masses are concerned. State policymakers seem too eager to maintain good relations with other countries, and too sympathetic with the needs of foreign leaders (especially in countries where they serve). It often appears that Foreign Service officers think that because of winks from Communist rulers they can be trusted personally, despite evidence to the contrary from intelligence sources.

New information of Romanian duplicity toward Washington and close collaboration with Moscow periodically reached the U.S. from the American Embassy in Bucharest, from high level defectors like Ion Pacepa, and from elsewhere. All of this had to be downplayed or dismissed outright. New ideas and information that went contrary to policy, or different points of view, were not welcomed. The time and energies of the elite were devoted to the preservation of a flawed and failed policy known as *differentiation*.

CHAPTER TWO:

U.S. Policy Toward Romania and Eastern Europe

The United States policy of differentiation in Eastern Europe dates back to the late 1960's strategy developed by Nixon and Kissinger. It has continued to be American policy through Republican and Democrat administrations, in large part because the elite in the State Department has made it a litmus test for any who would advance in the European affairs area. Differentiation means that the U.S. treats Eastern European Communist nations differently, not as a solid monolithic bloc. Thus Washington distinguishes between the Warsaw Pact allies of Moscow, rewarding some—the "good" Communists—and withholding rewards from others—the "bad" Communists.

The elite tries to brand opponents of differentiation as cold warriors who lump all Communists together in a monolithic bloc. They have taken this so far that they have lost sight of the predominant monolithic elements of Warsaw Pact membership. The U.S. treats some bloc countries favorably to supposedly create problems for the Soviets in their backyard. Another thesis of the State policymakers is that the U.S. presence facilitates disintegration in Eastern Europe. As Richard Burt—would-be State elitist—explained it to me in London in December 1982, "over a period of time disintegration is occurring and the U.S. should stay in Eastern Europe and encourage the process." Their admonition at the 1982 London Chiefs of Mission Conference was "to not say screw them, lump them together or write them off."

Under the aegis of former Ambassador to Yugoslavia, Lawrence Eagleburger, the State Department removed Yugoslavia from the differentiation equation as a special case, i.e. beyond the differences of Communist countries within the Soviet Bloc. Thus the designation was even changed in the department from EE (Eastern Europe) to EE/Y (Eastern Europe/Yugoslavia) to satisfy Yugoslav concerns that it not be grouped together with the likes of Romania or Hungary in the minds of American policymakers. So Yugoslavia is not to be treated as part of Eastern Europe, which implies the Warsaw Pact countries of the Moscow-dominated bloc. In line with this, efforts are made to ensure that the trips of high level American officials to Yugoslavia are not always in conjunction with visits to Romania and Hungary. In other words Yugoslavia, according to Eagleburger *et al*, would alone prefer to be the object of American affections, not via the three B's lineup of U.S. visits. When Vice President Bush traveled in September 1983 to the good guys of Eastern Europe, the three B's of Budapest, Belgrade, and Bucharest, he did not make Yugoslavia happy. State hands have also succeeded in getting more technology and military-related shipments approved for Yugoslavia than for Romania, Hungary, or Poland, arguing that being outside the Warsaw Pact, Yugoslavia would not need to transfer the technology to Moscow even if she wanted to. They forget the same argument when Romania is involved. Romania is inside the Warsaw Pact, but State somehow argues that Bucharest is a better bet than Budapest (for example) in not transferring technology to Moscow.

For the six Warsaw Pact members, differentiation results in rewards for some and no rewards for the others. In the eyes of the State Department/U.S. government, differentiation means rewarding the so-called good Communist regimes while not rewarding the so-called bad Communist regimes in Eastern Europe. Currently Romania and Hungary have Most-Favored-Nation treaty status (MFN), while Czechoslovakia, East Germany, and Bulgaria do not.* Those rewarded as good Communists with MFN and the other related benefits, were those which: (1) showed evidence of internal reform, human rights and emigration improvements, and/or liberalization domestically in terms of free enterprise and capitalistic incentives-initiatives; or which (2) took positions in foreign policy that differed from those of Moscow.

These previously classified policy objectives of the U.S. were put in Vice President Bush's speech in Vienna on September 21, 1983, by Eagleburger protégé Mark Palmer (then DAS, now Ambassador to Hungary). That is, U.S. policy objectives and goals included en-

---

*MFN was restored to Poland in 1987.

couraging Eastern European countries to make internal improvements or foreign policy positions of "independence"*vis-à-vis* the
Soviets. Bush stated it in public this way:

> . . . some have shown a greater measure of independence in the
> conduct of their foreign policy. Some have introduced greater open-
> ness in their societies, lowered barriers to human contacts, and en-
> gaged in market-oriented economic reforms. Others, unfortunately,
> continue to toe the Soviet line. Their foreign policy is determined
> in Moscow, and their domestic policies still flagrantly violate the
> most fundamental Human Rights. In our relations with the coun-
> tries of Eastern Europe, we take these differences into account, our
> policy is one of differentiation—that is, we look to what degree
> countries pursue autonomous foreign policies, independent of
> Moscow's direction; and to what degree they foster domestic
> liberalization—politically, economically and in their respect for Hu-
> man Rights. The United States will engage in closer political, eco-
> nomic and cultural relations with those countries such as Hungary
> and Romania which assert greater openness or independence.[1]

Bush went on to say that: "we will not, however, reward closed societies and belligerent foreign policies—countries such as Bulgaria
and Czechoslovakia, which continue to flagrantly violate the most
fundamental Human Rights; and countries such as East Germany
and again, Bulgaria, which act as proxies to the Soviets in the training, funding, and arming of terrorists, and which supply advisors
and military and technical assistance to armed movements seeking to destabilize governments in the developing world."[2]

The idealistic goals of the State Department are not as bad—
even if largely unrealistic—as is their implementation. The lines
of distinction drawn in differentiating are perhaps not as great as
they might appear, and thus should not be frozen in concrete. The
elite goes to considerable lengths to protect the MFN status of the
good Communists, to the point of almost sounding like spokesmen
for the regimes. When Poland lost MFN status due to the imposition of martial law, the crushing of Solidarity, and the resultant out-
cry in the U.S., it was a moment of great wailing in the State
Department.

The push in the department—also sought by Moscow—is to get
good guy MFN status for all of the Eastern European countries.
Only East Germany, Bulgaria, and Czechoslovakia have not at one
time had MFN, but some at State were even making a desperate
effort to have the U.S. Government view the worst of the "bad"

Communists in a more favorable light. I "learned" that East Germany was liberalizing and Honecker was getting ready to cozy up to the West, and that Bulgaria, with no involvement in the assassination attempt on the Pope, had indicated readiness to help us in our efforts to fight drug trafficking and terrorism. Ambassadors Rozanne Ridgway and Robert Barry wanted some gestures of appreciation to East Berlin and Sofia, respectively, where, they worked.* The sending of middle level officials from Washington was among the ideas suggested.

MFN status and related benefits are highly significant to the Communist nations involved and to the Soviets, even though State spokesmen downplay them in Congressional hearings on MFN. The rewards are many for being classified as a good Communist country. The three main benefits to the Communists are (1) credits and tariff reductions, (2) greater access to American technology, and (3) high level visits.

The specific economic and commercial advantages to an MFN country involve first and foremost, credits and tariff reductions. In fact, MFN means the granting of non-discriminatory tariff status for a non-market economy such as Romania's. Through this status the favored country becomes eligible for certain credits such as Commodity Credit Corporation (C.C.C.-agricultural), Eximbank reduced interest loans, and G.S.P. (Generalized System of Preferences).[3] MFN enables countries like Romania to export goods to the United States which it could not otherwise do, since the goods would not be competitive because of poor quality and marketing techniques. Since 1975 when Romania was first granted MFN, for example, Bucharest has used over one billion dollars in C.C.C. credits and Eximbank loans—U.S. backed credits. It has also sent about six hundred million dollars in goods to the United States under the G.S.P. In recent years (1984-86), Romania's exports to the United States totaled three quarters of a billion dollars annually with about half a billion dollars directly due to MFN status. Without MFN most of Romania's exports to the U.S. would become much less competitive due to higher tariffs, and more than one-third of Romania's most important exports would be forced out of the market. Romania's largest exports are rolled steel plate, gas and oil products, textiles, and food. Romania's biggest imports from the

---

*Subsequently Ridgway became Assistant Secretary of State for European Affairs, and Barry headed the U.S. delegation to the Stockholm "Conference on Confidence and Security Building Measures and Disarmament."

U.S. include corn, soybeans, wheat, coal, cattle hides, and cigarettes.

In addition to the MFN benefits of credits and lower tariffs, State representatives, in conjunction with Commerce Department officials, help Romania get out of anti-dumping suits (regarding steel) and go over quotas (textile products). Because of MFN status, Eximbank, the World Bank and individual American banks such as Manufacturer's Hanover Trust help Romania in various ways beyond reduced rate loans. In such a non-market economy with a scarcity of hard currency, the MFN trade related benefits are very important and would be difficult to replace.[4]

According to State Department arguments the benefits to the U.S. from the MFN relationship are chiefly trade and emigration.* In trade the U.S. has maintained that the market for export of agricultural products to Romania was a major boon for American farmers. But what has been happening instead is that Romania has boosted its food exports to the U.S. while reducing its agricultural imports from the U.S. Ironically this has taken place when the sanitary/health condition of Romanian products has been increasingly questioned. Meat inspectors who visited Romania periodically told me that the sanitary conditions in the beef producing industry for export were deplorable. Similarly a visiting official of the American Meat Institute who visited some pork producing plants in Romania with me found similar results. He observed as we visited the pig plant near Alexandria, that the conditions were terrible in terms of protective devices for workers, and cleanliness.

On a regular basis Romanian food exports failed to meet inspection standards. Canned hams, canned picnic products, and chopped pork in cans were refused entry into the U.S. due to container defects, composition standard and residue violations (high levels of oenzene hexachloride BHC). Most of these products were destined for Celebrity Foods. The general feeling behind the scenes was that many more such products were making it into the United

*Currently State argues that "leverage" is the main benefit to the U.S. MFN is supposed to give the U.S. leverage in human rights and emigration cases. MFN was intended for countries to improve human rights and allow freer emigration, not those that decide on gestures just prior to annual MFN renewal. State *post facto* puts the cart before the horse. If Romania lost MFN, it would be hard to imagine treatment of political and religious dissidents getting worse. For one thing, conditions are presently deplorable. Also it is probable that Romania would make some improvements in order to win back the MFN it so desperately needs.

States despite inferior standards and specifications. More disturbing were the U.S. Agriculture Department and Romanian government efforts to let Romania serve as a supplier of meat products (turkeys, beef and pork) to U.S. military bases in West Germany and to the U.S. embassy in Bucharest itself.

After 1981 Romania's exports to the U.S outstripped imports from the U.S. by annual margins of two to one, three to one and nearly four to one. Ceausescu, using draconian measures, virtually stopped importing needed items from the U.S. and the West where hard currency was required. All-out efforts were made to export everything the government could get its hands on. By 1984 Romania was sending more to the U.S. in dollar values than any other Eastern European country including the Soviet Union. By contrast the two countries which got more imports from the U.S. than Romania (i.e. Poland and the U.S.S.R.) had unfavorable trade balances with the U.S.*

Secondly the MFN relationship enables a Communist Bloc country to get a more receptive hearing in Washington in terms of technology sales from the U.S. Despite evidence that Romania had transferred American and other Western technology to the Soviets—as indeed Bucharest is required to do by Warsaw Pact agreement—State and Commerce pushed vigorously for trade of questionable items to Romania. During my tenure, the items Romania tried to get up front—i.e. separate from what they were trying to get illegally through third countries—were a Landsat satellite ground station and airport computers. I refused to sign on with State in support of the Landsat satellite sale to Romania. Along with the Defense Department we managed to hold up the sale. The Defense Department agreed with those of us at the embassy who felt that Romania would transfer the technology to Moscow and that it was too advanced to safely let them have. It was one of the few victories over the elite at State in concrete terms.** Not surprisingly State, Commerce, and NASA officials gave me briefings which invariably compared the technology of the items to 20 year old black and white television. They claimed the Romanians and Soviets already had technology at that level and that the benefit would be to

*Bulgaria's export-import figures which were so small comparatively are not factored in this 1984 assessment.

**Romanian transfer of technology is mentioned in greater detail in the next chapter in this book.

American companies who needed to sell their products. The Romanian government sought a NOVA 3D computer to go with NOVA 3D and NOVA 3-12 computers from Data General Company (via Thomson CSF in France) which required export and/or reexport licenses from the U.S. During my tenure, Romania was not given the Landsat but did receive computers for the airport terminal.

Thirdly, MFN means a better political relationship than non-MFN and thus makes the recipient country eligible for high level visitors from the United States. Similarly the MFN country can send its officials to Washington to be received by U.S. leaders. Despite warnings that such visits dissipated the prestige of the United States and its President and boosted the stock of the resented Communist bosses, such visits promoted by the group at State occurred with unfailing regularity. Visitors to Romania—many coming despite my misgivings—between the fall of 1981 and the summer of 1985, included Secretary of State Al Haig, Vice President George Bush, Deputy Defense Secretary Frank Carlucci, Under Secretary of State Lawrence Eagleburger, Arms Control and Disarmament Agency head Kenneth Adelman, Assistant Secretary for Human Rights and Humanitarian Affairs Elliott Abrams, Ambassador to the C.S.C.E. Max Kampelman (personal visit), United States Information Agency Director Charles Wick, Secretary of Commerce Malcolm Baldrige, Chairman of the Joint Chiefs of Staff John Vessey Jr., various Congressmen and former Cabinet secretaries.* Many other visitors interested more in emigration or business, included leaders of Jewish organizations and presidents of banks and companies.

Romanian President Ceausescu wants the big visit by President Reagan to Romania most of all. Ceausescu has made four trips to the U.S. during the Nixon, Ford, and Carter presidencies, and Ford and Nixon visited Romania. With Ceausescu's desire to continue recent tradition, pressure was put on willing State officials who regularly considered it. To date, the visit has not been approved due to the opposition of a handful of NSC and Defense officials along with some concerned Congressmen and religious leaders in the U.S. While I was at the embassy in Bucharest, we consistently recommended against such a visit—either by Reagan to Bucharest or Ceausescu to Washington—because of the wrong signals it would send regarding what Ceausescu represents.

---

*See chapters on high level visitors to Romania.

During most of the visits, Romania's rulers gained and the U.S. lost. With the exception of a few quiet expressions of concern for individual human rights cases or the emigration situation, U.S. officials were in the position of thanking Ceausescu for his supposed "courageous defiance of the Soviets"—the mistaken differentiation formulation. In fact, briefing papers prepared for all high level American officials visiting Romania included praise for Ceausescu's "courage" and so-called independent foreign policy. Constant reassurance had to be given that the U.S. appreciated Romania's policies.

Romania was repeatedly thanked for attending the 1984 Summer Olympic games at Los Angeles, even when such attendance threatened no vital Soviet interests. Additionally, a Romanian official told me in private that Romanian and Soviet leaders jointly decided several months before that it would be in the best interests of Romania to go. Anatoliy Golitsyn's belief in *New Lies For Old* that Romanian disinformation helped project the idea of Romanian independence when in reality it was largely the product of Soviet-Romanian collaboration, was consistent with this. Romania had to go to the Olympics in order to maintain its credibility as a maverick in the Warsaw Treaty Organization and thus be eligible for MFN, credits, technology, and high level visits. All of these things also benefit the Soviets who cannot provide the technology and assistance needed by every ally. Furthermore, if needed by the Soviets any high technology gained by a Warsaw Pact member would have to be transferred to the U.S.S.R., according to an agreement made by the pact members in force by the 1970's.

Romania's leadership gained prestige, support, and credibility with the Third World and non-aligned countries by having a steady stream of U.S. visitors in Bucharest. Ceausescu's harsh domestic policies were in effect given a stamp of approval by such visits. On the other hand, America's position as the symbol of freedom, democracy, and human rights was eroded by its visits with Ceausescu, which appeared to most Romanians as support for his regime and policies. Following each visit, spot checks (by visiting Voice of America and Radio Free Europe correspondents and others) indicated that most Romanians could not understand why the U.S. wasted its reputation on this hated tyrant. Romanians whispered this to me often. It was especially resented that little was done to expose or call to task Nicolae Ceausescu's total lack of concern for the economic, social, and religious rights of the average

Romanian. The miserable condition of the populace was reflected in Romania having Europe's lowest standard of living, with the possible exception of Albania.

Little was ever said publicly to criticize Ceausescu for his evil policies, because this was not the diplomatic way to deal with sensitive "friends." One U.S. official from the State Department blatantly showed this groveling attitude in a January 1985 visit. In a meeting with the President's brother General Ilie Ceausescu (Deputy Defense Minister) and A.C.D.A. Director Ken Adelman, State official Tom Simons told Ilie Ceausescu that it was great to be among friends.* He went on to explain that all of the Americans present were interested in very good relations and were appreciative of the courageous independent foreign policies of President Ceausescu. Not a word was said about Ceausescu's repressive policies or human rights abuses.

Romanian officials travel to Washington and weasle their way into the offices of the Secretary of State, Vice President and President, always with a "dramatic" letter containing new initiatives on INF, disarmament, and the like. The arrangements for such meetings usually came via then Ambassador Mircea Malitza of Romania's embassy in Washington. The State group led by the DAS had a very cozy relationship with Malitza, right hand man and henchman of Ceausescu. The cozy relationship involved U.S. officials accepting at face value the word of Communist officials. Malitza's charm and accessibility easily won over the State group. He used the ploy of confidentially whispering the real situation as opposed to the official communications. I was in many sessions with Romanian Ambassador Malitza who made one statement after another which he knew were totally untrue but which fooled the State network.

Foreign Minister Stefan Andrei, Foreign Trade Minister Vasile Pungan, Vice President Manea Manescu, and many other lesser lights visited Washington during the 1981-1985 years. Each visitor carried an urgent letter or message to U.S. leaders and made an effort to see the highest ranking U.S. officials as a way of pleasing the boss in Bucharest and boosting his own stock. The State Department tried to accommodate them.

When Washington planners got together to set up places for the Vice President or Secretary of State to send signals of American

---

*Simons who was traveling as part of the Adelman delegation, later became Deputy Assistant Secretary of State and elite leader in Soviet/EE affairs.

policy, Budapest, Belgrade, and Bucharest were always at the top of the list while Sofia, Prague, East Berlin, until recently, Warsaw, were at the bottom. The Vice President visited Belgrade, Bucharest, Budapest, and Vienna (non-Eastern Europe) on his September 1983 trip. A similar trek was taken by Secretary of State George Shultz in December 1985. Washington, in like manner, received comparable level officials of those favored Eastern European nations, but did not undertake exchanges at high levels with Bulgaria and Czechoslovakia, for examples. Such visits help prop up the regimes and enable them to better use their repressive organs of control to increasingly persecute the people who do not play their game.

The State Department is always ready to send whoever can be most effective to Capitol Hill to defend the differentiation policy of MFN for the good Communists. Those State representatives will apparently slant anything to make regimes like Ceausescu's look good. Before the House of Representatives Foreign Affairs Committee's Human Rights and International Organizations subcommittee, May 14, 1985, Deputy Assistant Secretary Gary Matthews* said: "Good relations have enabled us to make a difference in the Romanian internal scene," and "the Government of Romania remains relatively tolerant of the 14 major recognized religious groups and there have been no signs in recent years of a serious countrywide attempt to suppress religion or any individual religious group. The Government of Romania has not undertaken a wholesale program of religious persecution."[5] But no matter how the State Department experts "craft" a paper, the documented murder of a Roman Catholic priest, the disappearance of several Baptist pastors, the demolition of scores of churches, and the regular publication of anti-Semitic tracts, must constitute suppression of religion. Also Gary Matthews said "Romania's relatively independent foreign policy [is] a significant factor in the evaluation of Eastern European relations with the Soviets." In other words, the Romanian government's documented transfer of technology from the U.S. and West to the Soviets; Romania's allowing Soviet troops transit through its territory; Romania's export of military arms to radical Arab countries and Marxist-Leninist forces for the Warsaw Pact; Romania's consistent votes with the Soviets at the U.N.; Romania's

---

*Gary Matthews subsequently became ambassador to Malta (1985-1987), and Special Coordinator for Management issues at the American Embassy in Moscow (mid 1987).

involvement in international terrorism and close military collaboration with the Soviets; and the shared objectives of the Communist Parties of both countries apparently have no bearing on the State Department's classification of Romania's foreign policy as independent or relatively independent.

In the final analysis, a generation of Foreign Service officers have earned their stars by loyalty to the U.S. policy of differentiation, the brainchild of Nixon and Kissinger. It is one thing for Eagleburger to say: "up to the decision, fight; after, salute and march."[6] The only problem with that noble sounding statement is that few were allowed to fight or participate "up to the decision." Their minds were already made up and there was no room for new ideas or new intelligence information.

The elite considers something like a gift a month to be necessary for the orthodox Stalinist leader of Communist Romania. I heard it said in other words that a particular Eastern European country was up for its gift or reward. One month the State chiefs said Romania at the crisis time must be dealt with first. The next month—crisis free—a sop to a country theretofore ignored (i.e. Bulgaria or East Germany) would be suggested. Apparently this was done so the State elitist-aspirants could stay active, keep the pot boiling and gain recognition and awards.

One month the gift might be a license granted for a high technology shipment to the country. Another time it might be an extra quota of sweaters/suits dumped on the U.S. market for hard currency. In the past some of the major gifts were C.C.C. credits, I.M.F. reduced rate loans, G.S.P. and other related benefits. Cooperative endeavors usually meant U.S. funding and information for the other side's participation, ranging the gamut from joint economic and agricultural ventures to workshops on biochemistry, trade and tourist promotion. Another favorite gift or reward is the high level visit.

Essentially the gifts which go in many forms but in one direction, represent a mistaken U.S. policy toward Romania and Eastern Europe. Rewards should not be given to regimes which carry out harsh reigns of repression against their own people. It is recognized that Romanians even if Communists are not Russians. Americans should not accept any permanent Soviet domination of Eastern Europe or abandonment of the people there, but must share the aspirations of the people for national sovereignty and assist the internal elements struggling for rights and freedom. Washington should be concerned with those indigenous forces striving for change. Instead the official U.S. policy of rewards for Bucharest is based on the false premise of "Romanian foreign policy independence."

CHAPTER THREE:

Romanian Foreign Policy: The Myth of Independence

Romanians yearn to be free and independent, in keeping with a few brief moments in their history and with the feelings of the people. Romanians have traditionally both looked to the West and have had no love lost for their Slavic neighbors to the East. In other words, Romanians consider that they are an island of Latins in a sea of Slavs, even though they are surrounded by Slavs (Russians, Bulgarians, and Yugoslavs) and Hungarians. Much of Romania's language and ethnic background derive from Western (i.e. Roman, Latin) sources, dating back to the Roman Empire's settlement of Dacia by Latin-speaking colonists during the second century A.D. Culturally and intellectually during the past few centuries, Romanians looked to Paris, Rome, and Vienna. French became the second language of the Bucharest-based *Regat* (Old Kingdom) area, only being challenged by English during the last two decades.

On the other hand, Romanians have not looked to the East despite significant Slavic influences. With the exception of Hungarians to the West, Romanians are surrounded by Slavs—most menacingly the Russians to the East (and more recently to the North also). There is a minority Slavic element in the Romanian language, and the dominant Romanian Orthodox Church is kin to the Russian Orthodox Church as an autonomous branch of the Byzantine-Eastern (Greek) Orthodox Church derived from Constantinople. Romanians have nevertheless looked on the Russian neighbors more with fear and resentment than with admiration. While Transylvania is no doubt Romania's most prized disputed possession, Hungary has not been singly feared by the Romanians—only when it was in alliance with more powerful friends such as Germany or more recently the Soviet Union. But the Soviet Union is resented by most Romanians as the source of an alien Marxist-Leninist system imposed by the Russian Slavs from the more uncivilized East. And beyond that Moscow represents a territorial expansionist power which annexed Romanians lands from time to time. Since World War II the Soviets have absorbed the formerly Romanian territories of Bessarabia and northern Bucovina which include some three million Romanians. Those Romanians from Bessarabia are referred to by the Soviets as ethnic "Moldavians" in the Moldavian S.S.R. Today the Romanians may resent the uncertainty and threat the Soviets hold over their heads regarding Transylvania. Whether real or only perceived many Romanians feel that Moscow uses Transylvania—the home of perhaps two million Hungarians, as a means to further intimidate Romania by appearing to give Hungary the green light to play the Transylvania Card. That is, the concern that the Soviets with Hungary could transfer Transylvania to Hungary if Romania does not play her cards right.

Romanians prefer the West and resent the Russians. But reality also tells them that they are stuck with a Soviet-imposed Communist system and stuck in the Moscow centered Warsaw Pact, at least for the time being. Geography and fate have determined that. Thus while Romanians almost to a person would opt for independence with sympathy for the Western world, they are in fact trapped under the world's leading imperialist power which has part of their territory and people and which dominates the rest via its local Communist Party. There is no doubt that Romanians would prefer to be independent than to be Soviet-dominated. A distinction, however, has to be made between Romanians as a whole and Romania's current leaders.

The Romanian Communist Party which runs the country was put in power after the Second World War by the Soviet Communists. In fact, the early Romanian Communist Party was so subservient to Moscow that it was considered un-Romanian. Most of the early members—perhaps 1,000 in number before World War II—were not ethnic Romanians but Jews, Hungarians, Germans, and Russians. The average Romanian looked on the Romanian Communist Party as something alien to Romanian traditions with foreigners at the helm. The Romanian Communist Party was less an indigenous one than the others in Eastern Europe, and has had great trouble gaining credibility and legitimacy in the eyes of the people. Thus to this day there is basically an insecure Communist Party defending alliance with a traditional adversary of the Romanians and operating contrary to Romanian aspirations. It is also a Communist Party which needs the Soviets to maintain itself in power. Its chief mission has been to find a way to gain support in the eyes of the people, requiring a delicate balancing act in Romanian tradition. That is, it was necessary to try to show the Romanian people that the regime is somehow "Romanian" and anti-Russian, while at the same time doing Moscow's bidding and staying in the Soviets' good graces.

One solution to the Romanian Communist Party dilemma is for the regime to appear to act independently on the world stage, and thus appeal to the true independent aspirations of the Romanian people and gain credibility from acting in their interests. At the same time, the Romanian Communist Party, having been established by the Soviet Communist Party and in effect dependent on it, can not do anything antithetical to Soviet interests. Thus the near contradiction fooled much of the world. If it is in the Romanian Communist Party's interest to appear to be "relatively" independent from Moscow while at the same time doing nothing to threaten Moscow's fundamental interests, the needs of both parties can be served. In fact, Moscow gains by having its neighboring ally strengthened by assistance, prestige, and trade from the West and the Third World by posing as a Communist country inside the Warsaw Pact which acts more as a Yugoslavia—separate from Moscow. The Soviets would not have to spend as much money and resources propping up its ally. It would be especially important, though, not to let the illusion develop any substance.

Behind the scenes it was particularly necessary for the Romanian Communist Party to confirm and reaffirm its total loyalty to the Soviet alliance, with every "empty" gesture for the world to see. But if both Bucharest and Moscow viewed such an arrangement as in their best interests (i.e. strengthening the Romanian Communist Party's hold on the Romanian people and saving Soviet resources), it was something which could be done jointly. There are other benefits for Moscow in terms of potential technology acquisitions which Bucharest can obtain that the Soviets can not. Also Romania serves as a go-between in dealings with certain countries more difficult for Moscow to deal with directly such as Israel, West Germany (in the past), and several neutral Third World and Arab nations. There is enough evidence to indicate that a mutually satis-

factory arrangement was reached between the Soviet and Romanian regimes to perpetuate the Romanian projection of independence.

The chief flaws in the argument that Romania has any real independence in its foreign policy are: (1) the behind the scenes close
relationship between the two parties in policy (with Ceausescu's
past in the U.S.S.R. being a considerable factor); (2) the Romanian record of technology transfer from the West to the Soviets; and
(3) the extent of military, intelligence, and economic collaboration
with the Soviets and the Soviet presence in Romania.

The prevailing point of view in the State Department and in academic circles in the United States is that Romania's government pur-
sues a foreign policy independent of Moscow, a move that was initiated by Romanian leader Gheorghe Gheorghiu-Dej and further
developed by Nicolae Ceausescu. The evidence we observed at the
American Embassy in Bucharest indicates that this conventional
wisdom is way off base. With considerable insight, intuition, and
factual observation, several brave souls have questioned the popular
view in the West through the years. These objectors include Ion
Ratiu, Vladimir Socor, Paul Shapiro, Anatoliy Golitsyn, and to
some extent Ion Pacepa and Robert Kaplan. While each one has
a different emphasis, elements of their analysis add up to a realistic assessment consistent with what we saw in Romania.

One must start with the obvious political and geographical facts
of life as Ratiu and Kaplan have. Romania has no direct frontier
with a Western country and is surrounded by Communist countries,
with only Yugoslavia not being a Warsaw Pact member. Nearly half
of Romania's land border is with the Soviet Union. Thus, in large
part due to fate and geography, Romania is trapped between the
Soviets, Hungarians, and Bulgarians. Romania represents no threat
to the U.S.S.R., and it "is not going to 'get away' " as Kaplan puts
it.[1] Ratiu accurately says that Romania is a vassal state which cannot really be independent of Moscow, and can only act in an " 'independent fashion' . . . to the extent that Moscow tolerates it."
Ratiu, in pointing out that Romania cannot carry out her own foreign policy free of subservience to the Soviets, refers to the Treaty
of Friendship and Collaboration between the U.S.S.R. and Romania. The treaty stresses the necessity of mutual consultations on
all international positions; the obligation to collaborate with the
other socialist states, and the agreement to take such measures " 'as
are judged necessary' by the Warsaw Pact powers in the event of

aggression from whatever forces of imperialism."[2] Both the Warsaw Treaty Organization (W.T.O.) and COMECON (CEMA)agreements bind Romania to the Soviet empire.*

A special relationship has existed between the Soviet and Romanian Communist parties and leaders. While we may never have all of the evidence on this aspect of Soviet-Romanian relations, there are much closer ties behind the scenes than meet the eye. Romania's political relationship with the Soviet Union is that of a satellite having a Communist party monopoly of power derivative from Romania's political, military, and economic alignment with the U.S.S.R.[3] An official of the Romanian Institute of Historical and Social-Political Studies of the Communist Party confirmed that the Soviet Ambassador to Bucharest meets with the Romanian President on a very regular basis. The official said that between 1981 and 1985 the Soviet Ambassador met with Ceausescu at the Presidential Palace and in other places frequently, that is up to several times a week.[4] The American ambassador, by contrast, meets with Ceausescu several times a year, usually on special occasions like national holidays or in conjunction with high level visits to Bucharest by the Vice President or Secretary of State. Furthermore, meetings between the Soviet and Romanian leaders take place more often than are reported in the press for public consumption. We noticed—as Socor reported—that on periodic Romanian trips to Peking since 1964, unreported stop-overs in Moscow going or coming between Bucharest and Peking involved meetings between the highest level officials in both countries.[5] Gheorghiu-Dej and Ceausescu maintained close ties with their Soviet counterparts.

Gheorghiu-Dej worked closely with Nikita Khrushchev between the 1950s and 1964. Golitsyn says that Gheorghiu-Dej was "an agent of Soviet intelligence" who carried out, under the direction of Soviet intelligence, elimination of Social Democrat leaders in the 1940s and purges of leading Communists in 1951-52.[6] But Ratiu believes there was no collusion between Gheorghiu-Dej and Khrushchev in the initial projection of an independent Romanian foreign policy. In any event, his actions proved his loyalty to Moscow. He knew very well that the Romanian Communist Party's survival was dependent on Moscow, saying that "the close friendship and fraternal collaboration with the great Soviet Union . . . are the measure of our national independence and our state security."[7]

*COMECON (CEMA) is the Soviet Bloc's Council of Mutual Economic Assistance.

Ceausescu has maintained a close collaborative relationship with Soviet rulers. Perhaps he has played more of the nationalist theme than his predecessor and perhaps it even had some limited meaning for him personally. And his relationship with the Soviet rulers included some small differences based in part on personality. But in the final analysis, Ceausescu also views the Soviet Union as the mother center of Communism. He knows he is inextricably bound with the Soviet Communists.

Among the many conversations I had with Romanians was the instructive one of April 22, 1983, with a well-educated, middle-aged Romanian who had been well-placed in military circles. The fiercely patriotic and nationalistic Romanian told me: Ceausescu is the Russian's man; the Ceausescus run the country through the Securitate (secret police, KGB equivalent); Romanian spies in France send information directly to Moscow through Aeroflot; all those who studied in the U.S.S.R. are in great positions; Ceausescu is "very well viewed by the Russians"; and he was chosen after the death of Gheorghiu-Dej at the order of Moscow. Beyond that, the Romanian gave a view that reflects the thoughts of many Romanians about Ceausescu. He said that Ceausescu is crazy and is carrying out the destruction of Romania. The country is in need of fresh blood, he noted. But there are children who are giving their blood: "he (Ceausescu) sells children in foreign lands. He destroys the biology of the country, as now the culture is going down with the dogs in the rear, with tiny cars; such has not been seen in Romania."*

Frank Corry, former Deputy Chief of Mission (DCM) at the American Embassy in Bucharest, who has done in-depth research on the subject, found that Ceausescu likely spent at least two years in the Soviet Union. Ceausescu was in training at Moscow and Leningrad working with the Soviet KGB, something he has subsequently tried to hide from his official record. Corry also points out that Soviet confidence in Ceausescu derived from his "reported" Soviet training, the support of older Romanian Communist leaders, and the ruthlessness and loyalty he displayed in early party jobs.[8] This is not inconsistent with Golitsyn's argument that there are even fewer grounds for thinking that Ceausescu as Gheorghiu-Dej's right hand man would lead a Soviet-Romanian

---

*The exposure of this Romanian's name could result in his imprisonment or death.

break.⁹ In a conversation with Romanian Foreign Minister Stefan
Andrei, he confirmed that Ceausescu speaks Russian. It should be
noted that most nationalistic Romanians today would not admit to
speaking Russian.

Ceausescu has stayed in close touch with the Soviet ambassador
in Bucharest and with other Soviet leaders, in part through intelligence collaboration. The former Deputy Director of the Romanian Intelligence Service (Securitate), Ion Pacepa, has documented
in detail KGB-Securitate cooperation and joint activities.¹⁰ I can say
firsthand that the United States has much information which sub-
stantiates many of the reports of Pacepa. Pacepa lists many cases
involving Ceausescu working closely with Brezhnev in the acquisition and transfer of sensitive Western technology for ultimate
Soviet use.

U.S. policy differentiates toward Romania in terms of technology because it argues that Romania, as a less reliable ally of
Moscow, is less likely to transfer high technology to the U.S.S.R.
A National Security (Decision) Directive—the executive basis for
foreign and defense policy differentiation, treats Romania as a better
risk or bet than the other Warsaw Pact countries as far as access
to technology and military contacts are concerned. The Nixon-
Kissinger differentiation policy advocated by the State Department
incredibly bases part of its pro-Romania argument on the Romanian *promises* that Bucharest does not transfer U.S.-Western technology to Moscow. The evidence shows that Romania's pledges are
not kept. The U.S. government, led by the State Department,
chooses *either* to ignore the facts of Romanian technology transfer to the Soviets, or to claim that the level of technology is not high
enough to be damaging. If State policy is based on the latter, it is
admitting Romanian deceit and duplicity after promising "no transfer." If State policy is the former, it is in effect covering up a critical element in the determination of U.S. foreign policy. The State
case has been based on the National Security Directive and MFN
for Romania.

The State Department, along with its allies at the Commerce
Department, invariably pushed for the sale of certain sensitive technology items to Romania during my tenure as ambassador between
1981 and 1985. I was asked periodically by State to give my approval
or recommendation for the sale of advanced computers and a Landsat satellite ground station to Romania. During annual consultations
in Washington NASA and State officials would lobby me to get my

concurrence. Typically I was told that the items promoted for sale to Romania were of no real value to the Soviets but were potential benefits for the U.S economy and trade. Rationalizations or justifications were galore and one official said that the computer and Landsat sales should proceed because their technology level was relatively primitive (i.e. equivalent to 20 year old black and white television). The Defense Department did not agree. I did not give my okay to these few items of sensitive technology. During my stay the satellite sale was held up, but one advanced airport computer was sold to Romania.

I wrote several letters expressing my opposition to the sale of high or sensitive technology to Romania. In addition to the letters to President Reagan, Frank Carlucci and others, I wrote Senator Paul Laxalt and "Judge" William Clark. I explained my concerns of Romania's Warsaw Pact membership and transfer of high technology to the Soviets. Laxalt transmitted gratitude for the information and assessment, but was somewhat equivocal in his observation. By contrast Clark was very supportive, as Defense Secretary Caspar Weinberger and other high Pentagon officials were in conversation. In responding for the President, National Security Advisor Robert C. McFarlane expressed the President's appreciation in a letter of November 21, 1983.[11] Also the President personally showed recognition of support for American national security interests in Europe.*

The government of Romania has transferred technology from the West including the U.S., to CEMA countries including the U.S.S.R. Evidence of such transfers taking place covers the mid-1960s through the 1970s, concomitant with Romania's increased ties with the West. While I am not at liberty to present the intelligence information which documents case after case, I can say that Pacepa has publicly reported on many of them. Also I was told at a CIA briefing during the summer of 1984 that Pacepa was never asked questions about tech transfer by U.S. intelligence when he came out in 1978. This seems like a strange omission. Subsequently Pacepa has said that the government of Romania had an agreement with Moscow on the transfer of Landsat technology. The State Department can continue using minute discrepancies to discredit all of Pacepa's revelations, but it will not erase reports he has made which ditto other evidence U.S. intelligence already has.

As Pacepa has reported, Romania under Ceausescu has actively

*See Presidential Letter of April 29, 1985, in Appendix II.

stolen and transferred technology from the West to the Soviets. The Romanian intelligence stole everything from the technology for metallurgical rolling mills and steel mills, to silicon semiconductors and integrated circuits, to projects for nuclear power reactors and heavy water installation for a nuclear power plant. The Romanians illegally acquired everything from American hybrid corn to Leopard II (West German) tank engines which they then transferred to the Soviets. Romania at the behest of the Soviets either purchased or stole American and Western technology in the steel, aluminum, and silicon industries for transfer to the U.S.S.R. Highly advanced computers were and are much sought after by both the Soviets and Romanians. In addition to Romania's official efforts—largely successful—to get Data General Corporation (French Thomson subsidiary) NOVA 3D and other computers, COMECON's joint computer network program of the late 1960s included Romania. The unified computer system joined by Romania and the other bloc countries was copied from the IBM 360 series, which was stolen.[12]

It should come as no surprise that Romania transfers technology to the Soviets. After all, Romania is obligated by the COMECON conventions of 1956 and 1965 to transfer technology if required by Moscow or other COMECON countries. CEMA members are required to share any technology they get from the West under the terms of a technical trade (technology) agreement between the Soviet Union and the other bloc members of 1965. This accord was broadcast at one time on Bucharest Radio and is thus not unknown to the Western World. Pacepa reports that the Soviet KGB chief Lavrenti Beria instructed the Romanian Securitate in 1952 to begin industrial espionage to benefit the Soviets and other W.T.O. allies. Interestingly, one top Soviet official told the Romanian security that Rosenberg's achievements in the United States were as important as the defeat of Nazi Germany.[13] Ceausescu himself, very much aware of the value of Rosenberg to the Soviet Bloc Communists, said to Pacepa in 1977 in reference to a secret nuclear power intelligence deal with an agent of Pakistan's President: "You must be terribly careful! We badly need to keep our Rosenberg."[14] Even the Yugoslav Ambassador to Romania (Milos Melovski) told me in September 1982 that he does not doubt Romania transfers technology to the Soviets.

Romania's strenuous efforts to acquire Western technology partly reflect Bucharest's need for advanced technology for its own industry, military, and trade. Additionally, Romania's regime wants to be valuable to the Soviets and finds that this is one area in which Bucharest can pay Moscow what they "owe." It is also important symbolically for the government of Romania to officially purchase significant technology items like the airport computers from the United States. Such technology trade establishes precedents the Romanians can refer to later in getting other things of ever greater value. The precedents help distinguish Romania as different from other bloc countries. This is just another reason I thought such trade would not be wise.

The Communist regime in Bucharest and the State Department both agreed on the desirability of technology trade and worked together to put the squeeze on anyone who dared to raise the flag of caution and concern for U.S. national security interests. I was from time to time pressed to sign off on the computer and Landsat items for sale to Romania by officials at the State Department. State tried to make me feel isolated and unreasonable by opposing such sales. Romanian Communist officials kept the pressure on U.S. officials of all stripes to concur with the requests in order to "confirm" differentiation and satisfy or pacify Ceausescu. It greatly concerned me that State played the game with the Romanians. In October of 1984, Major General William Cooper, Deputy Defense Intelligence Agency (DIA) Director said he was told by Romanian officials that State informed him that the Department of Defense (DOD) and DIA were the main obstacles in the way of Romania getting high tech from the U.S. Such a coziness with Communist representatives, allowing them to play one U.S. agency off against the other, is inexcusable. I asked United States Information Agency (USIA) Director Charles Wick, during his visit to Romania in October of 1984, to pass along this message and my concern to Secretary of State Shultz. No response to this was forthcoming.

Beyond Gheorghiu-Dej's and Ceausescu's close connections with Moscow and Romania's record of technology transfers to the Soviets, is the considerable extent of Soviet-Romanian military and economic collaboration. As is the case with technology transfers, many of the Soviet-Romanian military connections contradict Romanian claims and State Department reports. Romania maintains that it does not allow Soviet troop transit across Romania, that it does not export military arms, and that it does not aid radical Arab terrorists. The State Department supports the Romanian claims as part of its case for differentiation. Thus evidence to the contrary lessens Romania's credibility and the State Department's pro-MFN for Romania arguments.

As difficult as it is to get while dealing with a closed society, there is credible evidence of close Romanian military cooperation with the Soviets.

The Romanian government has allowed Soviet troops to move through Romania; it has been engaging in a giant arms sale effort; and it has worked cooperatively with the Russians in other activities such as aid to Marxist-Leninist governments and guerrillas, terrorist endeavors, and stalking for the Soviets in nuclear disarmament-type initiatives. During my stay in Bucharest one American official accidentally stumbled on a large Soviet convoy crossing Romanian territory. He fell in line and observed at length the Soviet troop transit. Confronted with this news and other reports of Soviet troops traveling through Romania—usually between Soviet Moldavia and Bulgaria—Ceausescu himself admitted in a July 1984 interview with John Wallach, that Warsaw Pact troops on their way to exercises in Bulgaria have passed through Romania. He further admitted that Romania had taken part in a series of joint exercises with Warsaw Pact countries.[15]

Little Romania which says it wants good relations with all countries, world peace, dissolution of rival armed pacts, and disarmament, is one of the world's leading military arms exporters. In fact U.S. Arms Control and Disarmament Agency (A.C.D.A.) figures printed in *Business Week* showed Romania in fifth place in 1982 behind only the U.S.S.R., the U.S., France and Great Britain. The report showed that Romania had well over one billion dollars worth of arms deliveries in that year alone.[16] On top of this, one must consider the significant arms exports transhipped via third countries that Romania attempts to conceal from public view.

Romania makes virtually all types of military arms and equipment, and exports them to gain hard currency and to help further world Communist aims in conjunction with the Soviets. Romania's arms exports include tanks, jeeps, trucks, armored carriers, guns, explosives, mines, artillery shells, aircraft (fighter planes and helicopters), and spare parts.[17] In addition, Romania sends military uniforms, boots, food, and other equipment items to combatant countries. Most of the arms go to Third World countries, or to Communist countries. Much of it goes to places like Libya, Angola, Mozambique, Nicaragua, Egypt, and Middle East countries.

It goes for political, economic, military, and ideological reasons. When not sending assistance to Marxist-Leninist guerrilla movements in Africa, to the Sandinistas of Nicaragua, or to radical Arab states like Libya, it sends aid to help Soviet Communist aims in other ways. For example, if the Soviets are forced out of a country after leaving massive amounts of weapons, the Romanians may be called in to replace out-of-commission Soviet arms systems and to provide spare parts.

Despite all of the evidence of military arms exports, Romanian officials tell American officials they do not export arms. The State Department, instead of factoring Romanian arms exports into U.S. policy in the name of national security concerns, works to help Romania in denials of such reports. During a January 18, 1985, meeting in Bucharest involving a brother of the President-General Ilie Ceausescu and U.S. A.C.D.A. Director Ken Adelman, Ceausescu said Romania exported no military arms but only bicycles and clothes (non-military items). Ceausescu incredibly said that, after being shown A.C.D.A. figures listing Romania as the fifth largest military arms exporter in 1982. It was in the same meeting that State Department official Tom Simons felt compelled to say assuringly that Ceausescu should know that all of the Americans present considered the Romanian leaders our friends. In a meeting between the U.S. Chairman of the Joint Chiefs of Staff, General John Vessey, and the Romanian Defense Minister Constantin Olteanu, on March 27, 1985, Olteanu also said that Romania does not export military arms.

The extent of Romanian collaboration with the Soviets in economic, energy, intelligence, and propaganda matters calls into serious question any Romanian foreign policy "independence." While I was at the U.S. Embassy in Bucharest, we counted well over a thousand Russians attached to the Soviet Embassy. By contrast, the American officials numbered about 58, while the largest other embassies totaled under 100. Also at least several hundred "advisors" from the Soviet Union manned key Romanian industrial complexes and factories. These "strategic" advisors differ from the more recently announced factory-to-factory direct links. The direct links announced in 1984 intended to more closely coordinate complementary production between the Soviets and their allies. One result of both "strategic" and direct links is to give the Soviets closer supervision over military and other industrial production in the bloc.[18]

Romania's commercial and energy ties with the U.S.S.R. are extensive. In the 1960s and 1970s, Romania's trade increased with the West and Third World countries while it decreased precentage-wise with the Soviets and CEMA members. Of the bloc countries, Romania's percentage of trade with both the Soviets and other member states was lower than that of any other COMECON country. This two decades old trend has changed since 1981. Two facts remain clear throughout, however. The Soviet Union is by far Romania's largest trading partner with over 20% of the total (and a new five year trade protocol calls for bilateral exchanges to virtually double). Also, nearly half of Romania's trade is with Communist countries, including almost 20% with COMECON countries other than the U.S.S.R.[19] And as Pacepa and others have pointed out, there is doubtless much more trade under the table in trans-shipments than has been reported.[20]

Romanian-Soviet commercial exchanges cover the gamut of industrial and agricultural goods, but perhaps in no area are they more valuable and extensive than in energy. Romanian participation in joint energy projects with the Soviets and other COMECON members has been significant for decades.[21] More recently the Romanians and Soviets signed a comprehensive long-term energy agreement that will send natural gas from the U.S.S.R. to Romania via a new pipeline built across Romania. Part of the Romanian contribution is in assistance in the building of the gas pipeline and in skilled and unskilled laborers from Romania working in the U.S.S.R. in the development of energy—chiefly gas—resources.[22]

Romania and the Soviet Union work together in assisting terrorists, drug dealing, intelligence, and propaganda. Romania serves as a safe haven for well-known international terrorists and as a training ground for radical Arab terrorists. Some 20,000 so-called students from radical countries such as Libya, Syria, Iran, and Iraq, in addition to the PLO, "study" in Romania. Included are terrorists who reportedly train with weapons and explosives not far outside Bucharest. It should have come as no surprise, even in a police state like Romania, when a radical Palestinian murdered the Jordanian *Chargé d'Affaires* in downtown Bucharest in early December 1984.[23]

There is much evidence of Romania's involvement in international terrorism. Bombs and poison were sent to assassinate leading Romanian émigrés in Paris and Cologne in 1981 and 1982. Radio Free Europe was bombed and several of its Romanian born employees were severely beaten or stabbed by Romanian-hired hit men. Pacepa also has revealed massive evidence of collaboration between the PLO and Romanian intelligence and between Libya and Romania in the military arms trade.[24] Ceausescu's close personal ties with Yassir Arafat, Muammar Khaddafy, and Hafez Assad of Syria are well documented. Romania carries out extensive trade, military, and terrorist connections with the most extremist of the Arab states. This includes Romania's shipment of military arms and export of workers to places like Libya (joint energy projects), frequent high level visits both of a political and military nature, and the use of Romania as a conduit for drugs and terrorist planning.

Information abounds which links Romania with drug shipments and dealings in the Middle East and South America and other places around the world.[25] When the Romanian government was confronted with evidence of its drug activities (by the U.S. government) it of course denied having anything to do with them. Needless to say, Romania's activities with terrorists and drugs helps further the objectives of the Soviet empire in terms of destabilizing the West, appealing to the Third World, and especially radical Arabs, and gaining needed hard currency.

Romania works closely with the Soviets in propaganda endeavors such as world peace movements, nuclear free area proposals, nuclear disarmament demonstrations, and rival pact dissolution propositions. Much of this cooperation is done by the intelligence agencies of the two countries. Virtually every "new" move by the Romanians in the matters of non-intervention in internal affairs of nations, equality of all states, dissolution of military blocs such as NATO and the Warsaw Pact, nuclear free zones and nuclear disarmament in Europe, is coordinated with Moscow. In fact, Romania acts as a stalking horse for the Soviets in many of these areas.

Those in the West "looking for Romanian independence" are lulled into ignoring the tight bonds and collaboration between the Soviets and Romanians while falling head over heels for the well-publicized but superficial differences. The Romanian "differences" with the Soviets are first and foremost advertised by the Romanians through leaks, whispers, and confidential rumors out of every Western capital.[26] In 1984-85, when Romania quietly signed on again with the Warsaw Pact renewal on Moscow's terms, the great Balkan intrigue in the diplomatic circle was Romania's loud and overt disagreements with Moscow—which were to change the terms of the W.T.O. renewal. Romania would spread its so-called differences with Moscow to Western diplomats who were all too eager to listen and believe. Thus Romanian officials in Washington, London,

Bonn, Vienna, and other capitals would tell the Western officials—obviously well-known to the Soviets—of Romania's behind the scenes battles against Soviet aims and interests. A minute, nuanced divergence blown way out of proportion would be projected by the Romanians to "confidants" on the questions of missile deployment in Europe and nuclear free zones.

Considering the extent to which Western officials believe the "whispered differences" regularly disseminated by the Romanians, Bucharest has few rivals in the art of disinformation.

Romanians were also highly successful in terms of convincing Western representatives that they needed to give concessions to Bucharest in order to confirm differentiation and in order to pacify Ceausescu. After all, they said endlessly, Ceausescu needed to be constantly bolstered for his courageous defiance of the Soviets. Washington has chosen to believe this elaborately orchestrated sham. Bucharest and Moscow are laughing all the way to the bank.

In the two to three decades of Romania's so-called independent foreign policy, Romania has proved to be a very loyal ally of Moscow. In international fora, Romania's positions have been overwhelmingly in line with those of Moscow and other Warsaw Pact members. On the occasions of Warsaw Pact intervention in Czechoslovakia in 1968, and Soviet action in Poland and Afghanistan more recently, Romania has closely toed the Soviet line. For a country that is supposedly carrying out an independent foreign policy, it is odd that only a couple of percentage points separates Romania's votes in the U.N. from those of her other bloc allies. Similarly, Romania voted in opposition to American interests some 85% of the time, as did the other bloc countries. In 1985, Romania voted with the U.S. only 14.6% of the time, worse than Poland and only barely better than the Soviet Union. When Romania voted 19.4% with the U.S. in 1982, only Poland in the W.T.O. voted fewer times. The U.S.S.R., Hungary, Bulgaria, East Germany, and Czechoslovakia voted more times with the U.S. than did Romania. But the difference between Romania and the Soviet Union was 1%. And in 1984 Romania voted only 10.1% of the time with the U.S. compared with 13.2% for the U.S.S.R.![27]

Based on the available evidence, Romania's efforts at projecting occasional differences with Moscow are acceptable to the Soviets. Under present circumstances there is not and cannot be any real independence from the Soviets. And the Soviets have accepted the original "Romanian game plan" of getting valuable aid from the

U.S. and the West to benefit not only Romania but the whole Warsaw Pact. As Pacepa puts it: "within the limits of Marxist-Leninist principles and Warsaw Pact obligations," Bucharest makes occasional gestures of divergence from Moscow with the sole purpose of acquiring Western technology and money to help build Communism. In so doing, Ceausescu seduces Western leaders by winking and expressing "discreet anti-Soviet allusions."[28] Tremendous resources have gone into getting financial assistance and Most Favored Nation treaty status—annually renewed since 1975—without giving up anything substantial in return. According to Pacepa, Ceausescu's plan called "Horizon" was directed at gaining financial asistance, technology, and political support from the U.S.—most notably via MFN—while keeping Romania's orthodox Communist rule intact. In fact, the improved relations between Western countries and Romania over the past decade and a half have not led correspondingly to a better standard of living or an improved human rights situation for the Romanian people. And the evidence is clear regarding Romania's transfer of technology from the West to the Soviets.[29]

A telling conversation took place some years ago in the wake of the defection of a foreign trade minister from Romania. When Americans asked the Romanian defector if it was not a U.S.-Western plan to lend money to Romania to make Bucharest more dependent on and tied to the West (thus helping separate the Romanian Communists from Moscow), the answer was not publicized. It did not fit U.S. policy theories. In the conversation the Romanian said matter of factly that he spent considerable time each week coordinating with the Soviets plans to get more money in the form of loans, credits, grants, and even technology from the U.S. and the West.[30] The record speaks for itself in terms of how successful they have been and continue to be in accomplishing their objectives and fooling American officials.

It is curious that the State Department's differentiation policy and Romania's projected "independent foreign policy" dovetail. There is a strange convergence of interests between the U.S. Foreign Service elite and the Romanian Communists. In view of this, Washington is not without some responsibility for the Communist-imposed tragedy that has befallen Romania.

Chancery Building, American Embassy, Bucharest, Romania

Romanian Foreign Ministry Building, Bucharest

Soviet Embassy, Bucharest

Romanian President Nicolae Ceausescu (foreground)
Romanian Foreign Minister Stefan Andrei (far left)

Funderburk with Romanian President Ceausescu

Food lines at store in Bucharest

"Long Live Communism: the Bright Future of Mankind,"
slogan on factory near Risnov, Romania

Elderly lady in Transylvania

Apartment Blocks in Bucharest

*In a Baptist church in Bucharest (words: We Preach
Christ the Crucified)*

*Banners in Bucharest
The (Communist) Party
Ceausescu
Romania*

*Funderburk with his wife and Baptist
pastors Gheorghita (l) & Talos (r)*

*Greeting Chief Rabbi Moses Rosen at residence reception. To the
right of Funderburk facing camera, Mrs. Funderburk, DCM Corry &
DATT Col. Mastro*

CHAPTER FOUR:

The Communist Imposed Tragedy in Romania and The State Department

There are fast becoming two Romanias. There is no question that Nicolae Ceausescu and his Communist predecessors have succeeded—where many centuries of past invaders and occupiers had failed—in creating a new Romanian for the new society. In Ceausescu's words, the new society is *Romania on the Road of the Multilaterally Developed Socialist Society*, the theme title of Ceausescu's policy and "white book" collection of speeches. The new socialist man is dependent upon the state, as he owes everything to the Communist Party leader Ceausescu. Everything from his apartment flat to his meager food distributions to public transport to whatever heat, electricity, and hot water he may have. Having been taken from the land, food supplies, and private dwellings, to the urban/town apartment blocks reliant upon food supplied from the farm cooperatives, the new person is almost totally dependent on the regime for livelihood.

To create a new man totally reliant on the state and a new, controlled society, Ceausescu personally initiated sweeping changes. The heavy industrialization and the showcase projects—absurd for a small country and extremely uneconomical—proceeded unabated. The Danube-Black Sea Canal was completed in 1984, and proclaimed a tribute to Ceausescu's genius, foresight, and wisdom. It took decades of work to build using slave labor from Romania's vast gulag, and claimed the lives of countless thousands of workers. Nevertheless it hardly carries any cargo. Perhaps as tragic as the canal and scores of giant petro-chemical, nuclear power, and military armaments plants, are the targeting for destruction of peasant dwellings, individual houses, and historical monuments and churches. In a classic Stalinist effort to destroy any vestiges of an independent-minded peasantry, Ceausescu embarked on a massive program of demolition.

Nothing less is happening than the destruction of Romania's past heritage and culture. De-privatization and de-individualism have to be completed. Ceausescu seeks to put all Romanians, except of course the Communist Party elite and its other allied new class members, in apartment flats that are crowded, shabby, and shoddily built. The ugly, monotonous-looking blocks are sprouting up in every town and city of any size.* The old, individual houses and peasant dwellings are fast disappearing—being torn down—even before the replacement blocks are built. It is these new blocks in the cities that are left without hot water, heat, and cooking gas in the winter, whereas at least in the village dwelling, wood and coal were usually available for heat and cooking purposes. In the city and town, people are often living with less food because of dependency on government-controlled supplies, distribution, rationing, etc. The people in the blocks have become more dependent on the government for survival. And as one Romanian dissident put it, to survive physically means to die morally.

The new person is also subservient, submissive, easily intimidated, and destroyed mentally and spiritually. This is not the time or place to argue the merits of *Miorita*, the national epic poem of the peasant past. In the land of *Miorita* there was not a national tradition of betrayal of relatives and friends, along with bribery, corruption, duplicity, and submission to authority. Today, in the new society, the land of *Miorita* is fading into the land of Ceausescu. It is accurate to say that Romanians do not have the same history or political-spiritual development as other peoples in East-Central Europe. But the Poles and Hungarians shared with the peoples of Eastern and Central Europe—including the Romanians—successive waves of invaders, plunderers, and rulers at the crossroads of several civilizations and empires.

There are several reasons why Romania is different from other countries in the area. In the southeastern part of Europe, the Romanians constituted an eastern line of defense for Western civilization in the face of Asiatic tribes and other non-Western invaders. In virtual isolation as the only Latin-based language-speakers in

---

*See illustrations on page 59.

Eastern Europe surrounded by Slavs and Hungarians, the Romanians expended much energy trying to survive. Romania's national religious heritage was Eastern (Greek) Orthodox from Byzantium, with its tradition of state control over the church. Romania did not have the more Western, Catholic or Protestant traditions and influences, which influenced Poland and Hungary. Having thus been more isolated—excepting principally Transylvania—from the main currents of the Renaissance, Reformation, and Enlightenment, Romania's religious and, to some extent, political inheritance resembled that of Western Europe perhaps less than Hungary and Poland did. It is true that Romania looked more to the West than the other Balkan states, principally to Rome and Paris, to rediscover its linguistic and ethnic roots. Romania and the Romanians derived from the Romanized-Latinized colonists of the second and third centuries A.D. But isolation through the centuries of occupation and domination by the Russian and Turkish empires, to some extent cut off the Romanians from the central currents of Western historical development.

Romanians as a whole have responded to alien governments and systems differently than the Hungarians and Poles. It was the tragic fate of Romania to be a front line defense protecting Western civilization. Virtually isolated and under constant pressure, the Romanian had to learn to survive against all odds. An old proverb from the region says that "the bent head escapes the sword." This means that the Romanians learned to bend when necessary in order to survive. It is the clear objective of the orthodox Communist rulers of Romania to crush courage and ensure the victory of fear, intimidation, and brute secret-police power over the populace. With the total power of the Communists and the lack of outside—Western and other—support for the almost forgotten repressed people, Romania's "alien-to-tradition" rulers have had much success.

Much of the success of the rulers and what is now missing most in Romania and other Communist countries goes beyond the dearth of creature comforts and material wealth—nice clothes, apartments, cars and available nourishing food. The lack of freedom, human dignity, and basic rights are reflected in a beaten spirit, sense of depression, and lost hope. In 1982, I was told by one of the leading intellectuals of Romania that "it is over for our generation—we wait for it all to be played out. But for the children the only choice is a new world i.e. the United States. There are only two kinds of people: those who care about their jobs (read means of

physical subsistence) and those who care about something else beyond that." During the following years I heard similar stories
repeated over and over. Many people appear not to care about anything from the doctor in a hospital to the pedestrian oblivious to
vehicle traffic. One need only look at the facial expressions of the
people, the condition of public toilets, restaurant service, food store
lines, and degradation required to survive via bribery, corruption,
and dishonesty. But despite the depressing atmosphere in Bucharest,
the system has not had complete success because of the heroic resistance of countless individual Romanians.

That is where the other Romania comes in. However fragile and
minuscule it may be in the overall picture, the existence of courageous individual opposition to the regime has significant meaning.
It proves that an element of the true traditional Romania survives
as a fine thread alongside the new Romanian man. As long as this
occurs, Romania's meaningful religious and cultural heritage will
not perish. Mention must be made of the hundreds of thousands
of the brightest and most courageous people of Romanian-descent
living today outside Romania from France and West Germany to
Canada and the United States. From Nobel Prize winner Dr. George Palade to Nobel Peace Prize winner Elie Wiesel to Paul Goma
and Father Gheorghe Calciu-Dumitreasa as well as the late Mircea Eliade and Georges Enescu, there are numerous overseas
Romanians who have made outstanding contributions to human-
ity. They have also helped maintain and preserve the best elements
of traditional Romanian heritage and culture. In the United States
one Harvard University Press study in 1975, entitled *Peasants and
Strangers* by Josef J. Barton, documents the success and contributions of Romanians in an American city. It shows that Romanian
immigrants, chiefly from pre-World War I rural Transylvania in the
Sibiu-Fagaras area, fared better than some other ethnic groups in
Cleveland, Ohio during the first half of this century.

Needless to say, the odds have never been more stacked against
a collection of noble individual characters than in the case of the
true-to-history Romanians. They may even be more oppressed than
the spiritual voices of Russia's heart and soul. It is time that they
are supported and recognized. Who are they? Obviously, to mention most would merely draw more repressive attention to them,
while the West is hardly aware of their existence. But their significance should be magnified because of the disadvantages they

have had to face. They have lacked a real forum, such as a national church, through which they could articulate their protest. And with Ceausescu's omnipresent security forces their colleagues and would-be allies have been forced to give up a lot morally and spiritually in order to survive physically and protect their families.

In part because of their unique circumstances in Romania, politically and religiously the opposition to the imposition of an alien "new socialist man" has been more individual than organized.

From the beginnings of Soviet-imposed Communism in Romania four decades ago, there was significant opposition to the drastic, nontraditional, transformation of society by the atheistic and materialistic Marxist-Leninists. Some of the strongest resistance came from the peasants who resolutely fought against the collectivization of agriculture. Massive killings and arrests resulted from peasant opposition. It was not some minority of *chiaburi* (so-called Romanian kulaks or better-off peasants) but the masses of middle peasantry who strenuously objected to the loss of land and the takeover of farms by the state. I met a few descendants of such peasant fighters high up in the mountains of Romania near Paltinis in May 1982. These nearest-thing-to-free-peasants who roam the mountain peaks as shepherds, issued a plea for help. They told me about the poor conditions throughout the country for the members of the former peasantry, the resentment the people felt for Ceausescu, and the struggle still going on by individuals in the mountains to survive with dignity. Their plea was for Americans not to forget Romania's loss of freedom, and the fact that there are still freedom-loving individuals in the country.

Other opposition has come from the factory workers and intellectuals. Workers in factories and mines have periodically resisted the strict dictates of Communist rule. Many have protested in various ways the low wages, long working hours, unsafe working conditions, and lack of worker input in factory management and operation. Sabotage and strikes have occurred more frequently than has been reported in the outside world. Most such actions have only led to greater repression by the security forces and to the arrests and jailing of the most active resistance leaders. One of the cases in point is the crushing of SLOMR, the trade union of coal miners in the Jiu Valley area, that struck for better conditions beginning in the late 1970s. I have heard many Romanians say that a deliberate practice exists in many factories of "making things not work" as a form of protest against the hated system. There is no question of the extraordinary loss of productivity in factories being at least partially due to the dissatisfaction felt by workers.

With the Ceausescu clan having little appreciation for academic learning or intellectual endeavors, they early decided to crush intellectual opposition and forcibly bring intellectuals into line with Communist aims. Among the intellectuals there have been varying degrees of compromise. Many try to keep their integrity and dignity in day to day life while "capitulating" only by writing something like a tribute or homage to Ceausescu in the foreword or introduction to a published work when "required" to do so.

But some individuals have continued to protest without compromise of any kind. They have refused to join the Communist Party even though under constant and severe pressure to do so. Some have written and distributed dissident materials in opposition to the regime. Poems, written by Ana Blandiana for publication in *Amfiteatru* in December 1984, were quickly withdrawn, having attracted the ire of the authorities. As these poems reflect the crying out of many others, they merit inclusion here. In one poem "Eu Cred" ("I Think"), Blandiana expresses frustration at the apparent lack of revolutionary (opposition) fervor, saying:

> I think we are a vegetal people.
> From where, otherwise, the calm
> In which we await our leaflessness?
> From where the courage
> To leave ourselves on the slide into sleep
> Almost up to death
> With an assurance
> That we will be in a state
> To be born again?
> I think we are a vegetal people.
> Whoever saw
> A tree in revolt?

In a second poem "Limitings" Blandiana describes the poor conditions of life and the absence of free emigration in stating:

> We, the plants,
> We aren't protected from illnesses
> Nor from madness
> (Have you ever seen a plant

Losing its wits
And reentering the earth with its buds?)
Nor from hunger
Nor from terror
Nor from prison
(Have you ever seen a stalk
Yellow, hanging on the bars?)
The only thing we are protected from
(or perhaps deprived)
Is flight.

Another poem "The Children's Crusade" refers to the President's wife Elena Ceausescu's program for increasing the population of Romania, by ending abortions and penalizing mothers who do not have four children or more in the following graphic language:

A whole people
Still unknown
But condemned at birth,
Lined up even before birth
Foetus alongside foetus
A whole people
Which doesn't see, doesn't hear, doesn't understand,
But moves forward
Through writhing troops of women,
Through the blood
Of unasked mothers.

Finally Blandiana presents a visual montage of some of the basic aspects of everyday life in Bucharest and all Romania through a poem called "All" or "Everything." To the side in brackets I have noted by explanation a few of the more notable but painful happenings. While Blandiana's "All" does not depict everything, it does pinpoint many of the highlights as follows:

. . . . leaves, words, tears
canned goods, cats,
occasionally trams, lines for flour   [long lines for hard-to-
weevils, empty bottles, speeches,   find food items are a way of life]
prolonged fantasies on television,   [Communist propaganda]
red beetles, gas,

pennants, the European Championship cup,
busses with gas cylinders, well-known portraits,   [Ceausescu]
apples refused for export,
newspapers, sentences,
mixed oils, carnations, welcomes at the airport,
cico-cola, breadsticks, Bucharest salami, dietetic yoghurt,
Gypsies with Kents, eggs from Crevedia,   [Kent cigarettes are
rumors,   black market currency]
Saturday serials, coffee substitutes,
the fight of the people for peace, choruses,
production by the hectare,
Gerovital, the boys on Victoria Street (Calea),
The Song of Romania, tennis shoes (Adidas),
Bulgarian compote, jokes, ocean fish,
All.[1]

The noted dissident Mihai Botez, mathematician and futurologist, asked what have the Americans gained after 20 years of close co-operation with the Romanian government.* Botez said: "Instead of promoting an economy which works or socialism with a human face, you have helped legitimize a corrupt communist regime which has ruined our country."[2]

Probably the most dedicated and unbending opposition has come from religious dissidents. The underground Lord's Army—the conscience of the dominant Romanian Orthodox Church whose official leaders were co-opted by the Communist state—has helped keep the traditional faith alive. And most symbolically religious Alexander Solzhenitsyns (like the Orthodox priest Father Gheorghe Calciu-Dumitreasa) have kept alive the unbreakable and indomitable spirit of the true believers.[3] The cultural figure Dorel Catarama, an Adventist, languished in jail for years for his outspoken beliefs. And deceased pastors Father Geza Palfi (Roman Catholic) and Sabin Teodosiu (Baptist) along with many others, paid the highest price with their young lives to preserve a measure of dignity in spirit for the whole nation. While Ceausescu faces no united "Polish Catholic Church" and keeps very tight control over religious groups, his fear of these believers who cannot be so easily crushed

---

*In March 1987, it was reported in *Lupta* (March 15, 1987, nr. 75, p. 1) that he was beaten by the local secret police (Securitate), hospitalized, and subsequently held incommunicado. He had criticized the regime.

was made evident in many conversations I heard between him and U.S. leaders.

There is an unmistakable revival of religious fervor spreading throughout Romania particularly among the so-called neo-Protestants (Baptists, Pentecostals, Adventists, Brethren, and others). This growth has continued despite heightened repression by the government in terms of churches demolished, pastors jailed, and leading laymen persecuted. The largest Baptist church in Southeastern Europe, the Second Baptist Church of Oradea, has been blessed with a recent history of courageous pastors like the present Dr. Nic Gheorghita and the Rev. Paul Negrut. According to an American embassy officer who worked with religious and political dissidents for several years, perhaps the main, courageous opponents of the regime are the Baptists, Pentecostals, and other neo-Protestants actively challenging the state at every turn.* Some of them belong to official and others to unofficial churches. In any event every religious group has its active dissenters. There are many other individuals who have not surfaced who continue the opposition in their own ways.

Examples of attempts by religious figures at organized protest include the ALRC (Christian Committee to Defend Freedoms of Religion and Conscience) activities and the pastors petition of 1982. ALRC was formed in 1978 as an independent religious rights committee which endeavored to monitor religious persecution. It also appealed to the state to guarantee religious rights. The group was crushed with its leaders either jailed, expelled (in the case of Pastor Pavel Nicolescu who continues to head the group in exile from New York City), or killed (examples: Sabin Teodosiu, Traian Bogdan, and Daniel Pausan) between 1981 and 1983. Sixty six Baptist pastors petitioned President Ceausescu for religious rights, such as Bibles made available, training of pastors, and some control over their own church funds. The government did not reply to what it considered anti-state activity, but subsequently made life more difficult for the signers of the petition.

The Communist government of Romania has one of the worst records in human rights. Political, cultural, and religious repression are widespread and prevalent. First of all, it is extremely dif-

---

*Interestingly the Consortium for the Study of Intelligence advised U.S. intelligence analysts that closer attention would have to be paid to Baptists in Romania in the 1990s as key players in potential upheavals (see *U.S. News & World Report,* April 20, 1987, p. 25).

ficult to find out all that is going on beneath the surface in a Communist country. Most information is a state secret off-limits not only to foreigners but also to the natives. Access by Westerners to the inner workings of the system: the Communist Party operations, the military apparatus, the omnipresent security police, the courts and prisons, the factories and companies, is virtually impossible. Thus perhaps it is natural that most U.S. embassy officials and the infrequent visitors (journalists, tourists, businessmen, etc.) do not often make the effort. It is in large measure the nature of the job and environment to deal with what is made available by the regime: dinner, luncheon, and reception sessions with high Romanian Communist Party officials and the ancillary cultural and intellectual elite (of those who cooperate with the state and receive its perks and rewards).

Most American officials and many non-officials are surveilled wherever they are in the country. Telephones are tapped, and electronic listening devices are widely used in houses, cars, hotels, and restaurants, in addition to government buildings. Lengthy, meaningful, and candid conversations with "ordinary" locals are hard to come by and can of course result in problems for them.

Having established a climate of fear and intimidation through government murders, gulag imprisonments, slave labor, and purges during the worst Stalinist days of the late 1940s and 1950s, the regime has been able to maintain the intimidation/fear atmosphere right to the present. Of course maintaining a *Securitate* (secret police force), which the people feel involves one of every three persons, effectively keeps the people in line. While slightly more subtle and perhaps less overt, the state tools of control continue to maintain near total subservience and control without the frequency and use of all of the earlier methods. People were so beaten into submission that the lessons learned are remembered today. Unlike in Poland there is no national church rival to the state in authority or influence.

A giant security force would seem to be needed because the government has not addressed most basic needs and aspirations of the people. Unlike in Hungary there is no economic liberalization or government effort to begin to address consumer needs. There are no publications which express non-state points of view. Western publications are not made available to the public. Television, radio, newspapers, books, and magazines reflect the government's anti-capitalist, anti-religious, anti-free enterprise, anti-NATO, and anti-U.S. policy. Students are taught that those in the West—especially the U.S.—are the enemy. There are no worker's unions since an earlier attempt was crushed and disbanded. Cultural expression reflects government-directed and imposed lines. The arts, theater, film, and music world all do the bidding of the state. Private enterprise is almost nonexistent, as the state owns the property, land and means of production.

Those perceived as threats to the regime have been handled accordingly by the government. There is still a large prison gulag and slave labor force. Additionally, soldiers and even students do road and field work periodically. There are still hospitals where dissidents are given "psychiatric treatment." The main political and religious threats to the regime are either imprisoned, isolated and persecuted, exiled (in a few cases), or killed. Peasants are sometimes executed for stealing pigs or grain from farm cooperatives. And examples of state-sponsored murders include the deaths of Roman Catholic priest Geza Palfi and Baptist pastor Sabin Teodosiu.

The human cost of communism in Romania has been enormous. The focus of this work is not to chronicle in voluminous fashion the human cost, as Robert Conquest and Alexander Solzhenitsyn have done with Soviet Communist history. A high price in human lives was paid during the imposition and complete establishment of the Soviet-style Communist system in Romania. Countless thousands of peasants—many of them Romania's so-called kulaks, bourgeoisie members, workers, and others were put to death by the new Moscow-directed regime. And from the post-World War II period to the present people have been put to death by the state either instantly or via disappearance into the vast prison network. From the beginnings such killings and imprisonments have served the dual purpose of ridding the regime of opponents and providing a symbolic lesson to all others of the fate of opposition. This atmosphere of terror and fear has served its purpose well. It is important to understand that while some of the repression of the state may be more subtle and less obvious today, there is little qualitative difference in the actions of present day rulers against enemies compared with their Communist predecessors.

While persons from all walks of life can still disappear from the face of the earth in Romania, the current regime seems to specialize in religious and to a lesser extent political or cultural nonconformists. Dissident Orthodox priest, Father Calciu, was released from jail after years of imprisonment and allowed to go to the U.S. in

1985. Calciu subsequently catalogued for us some of the leading religious figures who paid for their beliefs with their lives.

According to Father Calciu, more than two million people have been imprisoned and over 200,000 executed since Communism arrived. Calciu also states that several hundred thousand believers were charged and convicted in courts for their religious beliefs, including over 4,000 priests and pastors (Orthodox, Catholic, Uniate [Greek Catholic] and Protestant). Of these, at least 63 were beaten to death including 17 bishops and metropolitans. Roman Catholic bishops who died in jail or under arrest include Augustin Pacha (died in prison in 1950), Anton Durcovici (died in prison in 1951), and Aron Marton (imprisoned for nine years and held under house arrest until his death in 1979). Ion Ratiu has pointed out that all Uniate bishops died a martyr's death.[4] Iuliu Hossu, made a Cardinal "in pectore," died in exile in 1970 after many years in prison. Bishops Vasile Aftenie, Alexandru Rusu, Ioan Balan, Ioan Suciu, and Valeriu Traian Frentiu, all died between 1950 and 1953.*

The deaths of leaders of various Protestant churches have also been catalogued. For example, Dr. Alexander Havadtöy, has described the state murders of such Reformed pastors as Kalman Sasz, Bela Bonczy, Gyorgy Fabian, Istvan Kali, Janos Baranyi, Sandor Major, Peter Andras, and Kalman Szilagyi.[5] Christian Response International (Christian Solidarity International in Europe) and other groups with ties to Christians behind the Iron Curtain, have publicized the persecution and slayings of Protestant pastors and lay leaders in Romania.[6]

Almost as tragic and depressing as the murders themselves is the record of Western collaboration with the perpetrators of such crimes. There is often silence by groups and governments in the West in the wake of such murderous deeds, while simultaneously working with them as if nothing out of the ordinary has happened. Calciu aptly describes one example: "Under Communist rule, churches are destroyed, believers and clergy persecuted, thrown in jails, tortured and killed . . . Meanwhile the World Council of Churches holds festive receptions where church leaders embrace atheistic Communist ministers expressing brotherly love while millions of people die of famine in Communist camps. These 'missionaries' and collaborators have to ask themselves if they are drink-

---

*Calciu also includes Liviu Titu Chinezu as another Uniate Bishop who died in prison (in 1953).

ing wine, or the blood of martyrs whom they are sacrificing for an illusory peace with Communism."[7]

The most glaring and deplorable example of a *convergence of interests* between the State Department and the Romanian Communist Government followed the tragic death of Roman Catholic priest Geza Palfi. The information available to Washington is as close to a smoking-gun linking the Romanian government to the murder of Father Palfi, as can be found in a tightly controlled Communist state. But as in other instances, it seemed as if the State Department elite was more interested in downplaying any information or intelligence reflecting negatively on Romania, than getting the truth out and calling Bucharest to task. To protect the special Bucharest-Washington relationship, the State Department acted defensively about the Palfi reports and tried to discredit them. Concurrently, the Romanian government was also denigrating the reports and elaborately covering up the actual developments of the Palfi case. Again, there was a convergence of interests.

A letter sent by Calvinist (Presbyterian) minister Bela Szigethy of Bainbridge Island, Washington, to Congressman Joel Pritchard on May 24, 1984, probably comes as close as anything to what really happened to Palfi. Szigethy said that Palfi mentioned at an evening Christmas service in 1983, that Christmas should be a national holiday in Romania, as in neighboring Hungary, instead of a nationwide work day. The next morning, the Odorhei security police took Palfi away and "beat him within an inch of his life. They directed their hits with particular accuracy at his liver resulting in the splitting of his liver. Then they took him to the hospital in Tirgu Mures . . . where after a two-month 'unsuccessful treatment' eventually he died of his injuries." He further noted that the autopsy and records were kept secret, while the death certificate claimed Palfi died of liver cancer.[8]

First hand information gotten by Americans included eyewitness accounts. One witness was a close relative of Palfi and others were parishioners of the church. This and other evidence regarding the death of Geza Palfi, beaten by the Romanian authorities and left to die in the hospital without proper medical care, is solid.

But despite our efforts from the embassy in Bucharest to get the State Department to publicize the facts, very little was ever done with the information. And then only vaguely worded mentions of the case were made in official reports which cast no blame on the Romanian government, and in remarks to Romanian officials that amounted to nothing. No mention at all would have been made of the murder if it had not been for the uproar made by religious groups, Hungarian groups, and some members of Congress. The dissembling by the State Department paralleled the Romanian cover-up, and was later joined by similar disinterest on the part of other Americans in high places. When I testified before the Senate Finance Committee's International Trade Subcommittee on July 23, 1985, mentioning this and other similar cases the chairman, Senator John Danforth, seemed singularly uninterested.[9]

Meanwhile the Romanian Communists were actively engaged in their own cover-up lest the Palfi case mushroom into something big that would jeopardize their prized MFN. Romania's Ambassador to the United States led the repression of the truth of Palfi's death. In a letter Ambassador Mircea Malitza sent on July 20, 1984, to a Mrs. Newberry, the envoy claimed that Palfi "was well known as a man who suffered of kidney and liver diseases and in the later period of his life his complaint became very serious, for which reason he was in the hospital in Odorheiu Secuiesc, between October and the end of December 1983." Malitza went on to allege that "at the beginning of January 1984, he was transferred to the Clinical Hospital in Tirgu Mures where he died in March 13, 1984. During all the period of his hospitalization, GEZA PALFI had a very good medical treatment . . . His diagnosis, confirmed by the necropsy made after his demise was, 'generally ganglionar cancer metastasis of his liver, kidney and lungs.' " Malitza also wrote that the "vulgar sensationalisms and untruths like that of GEZA PALFI's death" were the result of ethnic Hungarian extremists and irredentists.[10] The State Department is hypersensitive on the score of the Romanian-Hungarian argument over Transylvania. Nevertheless attributing the death of Palfi (Romanian-Hungarian origin) to the historical conflict and exaggerations by the Hungarians outside Romania was not the major factor in State's decision to downplay it.

The Romanian officials made sure that the new death certificate was signed by a cooperative physician of ethnic Hungarian origin, presumably so they could not be charged with ethnic repression. Similarly from Malitza's claim to those printed in newspapers in Romania, the government's standard line was that Palfi died of liver cancer. Stories were fabricated saying (as Malitza did) that Palfi was not even in church that day—even though hundreds of worshippers are testimony to the reality that he was—but was in the hospital the last few months of the year. Neither the October-December hospitalization nor the cancer diagnosis were factual. Palfi was a young man in good health with no liver problem or history of alcohol use, according to eyewitnesses, parishioners, and relatives. Thus the government assertions that Palfi was never even arrested or beaten and that he made no Christmas sermon, were part of a concocted story Bucharest thought Washington would buy. By constant and consistent repetition of this story, the Romanian officials believed the State Department could be dissuaded from pursuing the truth. They were right. A Romanian official told me in July 1984, that Palfi was in fact killed as we at the embassy maintained, not as was reported by the Romanian government. Other evidence confirmed our account.

The lack of concern shown by the State Department over the Palfi case prompted me to send another cable to Washington and a letter to Senator Jesse Helms on July 20, 1984. On August 10th, Senator Helms entered into the Congressional Record a "Voice of America Transcript: Romanian Priest." Helms added that

> there are hundreds of cases similar to Father Geza Palfi . . . who are persecuted, denied jobs, beaten and imprisoned for long periods of time for 'crimes' such as Bible smuggling and exercising their rights of freedom of speech. In this Senator's opinion trade must be tied to the improvement of political circumstances, particularly those bearing on human rights . . . we can demand that Romania take steps that will lead to an improvement of the system . . . Therefore, this Senator remains opposed to granting most-favored-nation trade status to Romania and will continue to oppose such concessions until Romania joins the civilized nations of the world with respect to human rights and free emigration.[11]

But MFN continued for Romania. The general attitude of State was echoed by the liberal Democrat attorney Alfred Moses, who visited Romania in August and spread the word there and in Washington that I was not interested in listening to Romania's side of the story regarding Geza Palfi. That was correct, when I had the facts of the Palfi case and knew the Romanian story was a lie. It is sad that the U.S. still favors and rewards the Romanian regime. But Palfi and other martyrs of Romania will not be forgotten.

There can be no other gods. Absolute power attained by a ruler and his elite demands the total submission of the citizens. Marxist-Leninist slogans and Communist rhetoric are used to maintain power. In Romania's case the Communist Party and its leader serve as the god, to which all else has to be made subservient. The people are held in check by intimidation, fear, and insecurity. Radical punitive measures also play their role in eliciting near total fealty. Orwell's totalitarian state has been extended and refined by the highest of all Communist gods in Eastern Europe.

There appears to be no limit to the extreme punitive measures taken by Ceausescu. They range from a scientific diet to a typewriter decree to banning of automobiles on the roads and highways to a four or more children policy to a destruction of historical and religious monuments strategy. The people—not the leaders—must do without hot water, heat, and electricity, periodically during the winter months. Daily homage must be given Ceausescu by the people via television, radio, newspapers, magazines, and books.

He decreed a scientific diet with little or no meat to be followed by Romanians. The scientific diet was one of the sickest jokes played on the Romanian people. When the average Romanian was doing without meat, standing in long lines day after day, and scrambling around for scarce rationed items such as cooking oil, coffee, milk, eggs, cheese products, and other foods, as well as shampoo and soap, Ceausescu warned the people of the dangers of overeating. Claiming falsely that Romania was among the world's leaders in per capita calorie consumption, Romanians were advised to eat less meat.

A U.S. Department of Agriculture study in 1982 showed Romania's per capita meat consumption among the lowest in the Western world. The study showed that East Germany, Czechoslovakia, and Hungary, had over three times Romania's consumption. Poland, Bulgaria, Yugoslavia, and the Soviet Union had roughly three times Romania's per capita meat consumption.[12]

Romanians were assured by their government that special programs would provide varied solutions for the improvement in the quality of food articles. This Orwellian rationalization for the diminution of food supplies in Romania—even as massive amounts were being produced and exported abroad for hard currency to finance uneconomical pet projects—was designed to cover up for the actual scarcity and rationing. The populace was told that food shortages if they existed, were due to greedy speculators and other criminals of society. Such statements also helped pave the way for the drastic reductions in supplies which were yet to come. Massive reductions occurred in meat, milk, oils and fats, vegetable products, fruit products, and even potatoes, averaging over 50% cuts in deliveries in late 1984 and early 1985.

As an example of how other persons or other things are always scapegoated for mismanagement from the top, three workers were sentenced to death for stealing meat from their packing plant in Tirgoviste in December 1983. In addition peasants were sentenced to death for stealing grains of wheat and livestock animals from farm cooperatives. Citizens were urged at cooperatives to eat more rabbit and less beef, pork, and chicken, as an important element of the so-called scientific diet. It was not mentioned that even rabbit is not widely available across Romania but only at a few rabbit farms and in the wild in a few places.

In late March and early April 1983, the Romanian government declared that all typewriters owned by Romanians had to be registered at police/security headquarters. If the government considered that an individual should not have a typewriter, it would be confiscated, as would all unregistered typewriters. Owners were subject to arrest and imprisonment. To buy a new typewriter one must wait until all files have been thoroughly checked out and the authorities have cleared the individual as reliable. Duplicators or copy machines cannot be owned by individuals, but only by government officials. The decree ensures government control and discretion in saying that "Persons whose behavior poses a threat to public order or state security will not be authorized to own a typewriter."

Even foreigners are subject to the law. When *Washington Times* correspondent, Andrew Borowiec, came to Romania on October 17, 1984, he was given the typewriter decree form—a copy of which he passed on to me. It reads as follows: "Customs Declaration for Travelers: *1 masina de scris marca Brother folosita in interes serviciu*" (1 typewriter "Brother" type used in the occupation). The typewriter decree was no doubt declared to ensure that the state has a monopoly on the printed word. The great fear of the regime is that the handful of religious and other dissidents would print and reprint typed copies of scriptural passages and other revolutionary, anti-socialist, and anti-state propaganda which might inflame the masses. Anyone considered a "danger to the public order" is not allowed to have a typewriter. Practicing Christians fit this category. The decree shows the lengths to which the government will go to stop the spread of what it considers ideas harmful or threatening to the Communist Party's control over the population.

Beginning in December 1984, following several heavy snows and very cold weather, the government announced that private cars would be banned from the nation's roads and highways until further notice. The state action remained in effect until April 1985, even though virtually all the snow and cold weather had disappeared by early March. It was another drastic measure to solve a problem created largely by blatant mismanagement at the top. There is no doubt that the winter of 1984-85 was one of the most severe in Romania in decades, in terms of both cold temperatures and snowfall. But even before the snow and cold arrived in late December, an energy crisis had developed in the country. Every recent winter had seen power shortages, heat, electricity, and hot water cutoffs with gasoline at the pump rationed.

But even before the severity of the winter of 1984-85 became apparent, it was obvious that no adequate preparations had been made for energy supplies in the country. Because of mismanagement, reduced imports of all kinds, and increased exports of gas and oil products, among other things, Romania was left without enough power. The country's power grid actually came perilously close to breaking. Ceausescu looked around in desperation to find radical Arab friends willing to send emergency supplies on credit or for barter. The small amount of energy saved by banning private cars and drastically cutting back electricity, hot water, and heat in apartments, factories, and buildings in general was not in any way worth the illnesses and deaths caused by the draconian measures. Reports indicated that one of every three babies born in hospitals in Romania during the winter of 1984-85 either died or was born severely ill and deformed. Many babies died in hospitals when the incubators' electricity plugs were pulled to save energy! Scattered reports confirmed that unusually large numbers of both old and very young people died due to lack of heat and food.

Another almost incredible measure taken by the government was the campaign to increase the population and stop abortions. In March 1984, the Political Executive Committee of the Communist Party announced that a resolution had established measures for boosting the population. In its efforts to get the people to have at least four children or face penalties, the government said that it would begin checking women every month to see if they were pregnant. If the doctors found them pregnant, they would be required to follow through the full term and have the child.

Abortions were already illegal, but even the state admitted that over half of all pregnancies were aborted, contributing to a stagnating birth rate in the country over the past few years. The real reason for the decline in birth rates, as everyone in Romania knows, is that few women want to bring children into the world of present-day Romania. With food supplies unpredictable, but usually scarce, and with apartments difficult to acquire for young couples, parents were putting off having babies. But because of faulty planning, low productivity, too much heavy industrialization, and inadequate agricultural production and deliveries, more bodies were needed to fill the factories and fields.

Sad aspects of the measure to increase population have come to light. Women in their late thirties and early forties who were bent and broken from heavy duty work throughout their lives and often plagued by illnesses and diseases, were encouraged under threat of penalty to join the campaign and have more children for the good of the country, party, and its leader. Reports persisted of many cases of women becoming seriously sick, but not being allowed to have an abortion or proper medical care, and subsequently dying. On the other hand, teenage girls in the high schools were encouraged to have babies out of wedlock to get medals from the state for contributing to socialist construction! After all, what do families count for when compared with the higher needs and position of the always right government?

The heart of Ceausescu's policy of creating a new man and a new society called for the destruction of individual dwellings. On the ring road outside Bucharest, and throughout the countryside, one can see the razing of peasant houses. In their place, at the state's pace usually well behind the destruction of the single family dwellings, are town/city apartment blocks which all look alike and which are shoddily constructed and usually inadequate in terms of room. The main point, though, is that the blocks herd the human cattle together under the watchful eye and total control of the state commissar. Dependency is being accomplished step by step. But one of the chief problems is that when winter comes the town peasant can no longer get a piece of wood for heat or cooking but is dependent on state supplies of gas and electricity.

It has long been Communist Romania's policy to destroy church buildings, something they have steadily done during the past few decades. On occasion the state does allow the renovation of select churches and even the construction of a few showcase churches for the purposes of showing the world Romania's religious freedom and tolerance, and giving compliant priests and congregations a sop as a lesson to the others. But overall, the number of church buildings has declined significantly for all denominations since the Communist takeover. The fourteen religious denominations—called cults by the government—"officially recognized" are the Armenian, Baptist, Catholic, Evangelical Christian, Lutheran (German), Reformed (Hungarian), Islamic, Jewish, Old Rite Christian, Pentecostal Evangelical, Presbyterian Evangelical, Seventh Day Adventist, Romanian Orthodox, and Unitarian.

The dominant Romanian Orthodox Church, which has been declining in dedicated believers, has lost numerous historic churches, even though it is the most favored of churches in Romania. Catholics (both Latin and Byzantine rites) have had a harder time of it. In the case of Catholics who are mainly ethnic minorities, they are strictly controlled and restricted. Similarly neo-Protestants who are ethnic Romanian for the most part, are persecuted harshly because of their success. While many of their churches have been destroyed, permits for new buildings and renovations have been incredibly slow in coming. In the cases of some Pentecostal and Baptist church congregations, ten to twenty years have passed without permits being granted.

Beyond the traditional government policies, the new practice is to destroy some of the greatest *historical monuments* of Romania's past. This is not inconsistent with the ultimate goals of the state leaders, since creation of a new man and new society necessitate a new history. A central aspect of this policy is the demolition of ancient buildings in downtown Bucharest to make way for the new victory of socialism and realm of Ceausescu complex. An irreplaceable and priceless element of Romania's heritage in the capital city is being erased to make way for one of Ceausescu's most extravagant and self-serving schemes. With no consideration for the historical value of the buildings in the quaint, old Rahova-Antim-Uranus area of Bucharest, the government planners blasted away a vast neighborhood of houses, churches, and other buildings. Way had to be made for a new civic center, known to Bucharesters as "Ceaushima," in order to bring about, in Ceausescu's words, "the passage from the bourgeois-landlord society to the multilaterally developed Socialist society."[13]

The latest buildings to go down were the Spanish Synagogue, and a Protestant church. The last Sephardic synagogue in Bucharest, the Spanish Synagogue, was destroyed in late July 1986, while the country's largest Seventh Day Adventist church was demolished in early August. The cynical timing—in the wake of President Reagan's recommendation to Congress and U.S. approval of MFN status for Romania for another year—was typical of Ceausescu. Just after presenting the best possible face to the U.S. government during the late spring of each year to win continued MFN status, the Ceausescu regime mocks the gullibility of the American lawmakers by undertaking blatant violations of human rights and increasing the repression of religious groups. Even though all of this is meticulously documented before the Congress each year, until 1987, few Congressmen had bothered enough to change things.

The plan of destruction of many great historical monuments, ostensibly to make way for Ceausescu's gawdy new civic center, aroused some of the leading cultural figures of Bucharest. Some of the leading Romanian historians, architects, and archeologists stuck their necks out by protesting the government's demolition plans. Dr. Dinu Giurescu,* perhaps Romania's leading historian, was joined by others in sending a memorandum to the top government officials calling for measures to stop the demolition of the Vacaresti Monastery and the Mihai Voda Church.[14] Giurescu, in his capacity as a member of the Central Commission for the National Cultural Patrimony, sent copies of the document to President Ceausescu, the Romanian Orthodox Church Patriarch Iustin Moisescu, Madame Suzana Gadea—President of the Education and Cultural Ministry, and Mr. Petru Enache—Secretary of the Central Committee of the Communist Party. The memorandum also described in some detail reasons of history, culture and harmonious construction-development for preserving the main elements of Romania's cultural heritage. Citing examples of other Communist countries' urban development, the unique value in Romanian history of the old city centers, and the historical importance of Romania's architectural patrimony, Giurescu and others made an eloquent appeal for the preservation of the irreplaceable monuments of Romania's past. It was stressed that the Mihai Voda Church dated back 400 years symbolizing the richest aspirations of Romania's past, and was a symbol of Bucharest itself. And the Vacaresti Monastery was described as having supreme architectural significance for all Romanian and Southeastern art, representing the creative strength of the Romanian people.

Romanian intellectuals were joined by American Embassy officials—principally Kiki Munshi and Ernest Latham—in trying to publicize the situation in hopes of reversing government demo-

---

*Giurescu applied for emigration in early 1987.

lition plans. Romanian émigrés around the world showed concern, and Radio Free Europe broadcast the appeals. But with Ceausescu hell-bent on rebuilding Romania in his own Balkan, Stalinist image, it was to no avail. The world was made aware of the destruction of Romania's cultural and historical treasures carried out by an anti-intellectual cult leader with hardly a cultural veneer. And perhaps too the world will recognize Ceausescu's real purpose in destroying the heritage of a whole people, including distinctive historical monuments, great churches, and other valuable works of architecture.

Religious persecution is widespread. Even though some small denominations are actually gaining in membership, the general situation is bleak. The overall number of churches is declining and the dominant Romanian Orthodox Church—long ago captive to the state—is losing members and influence. The Roman Catholic Church which lacks a favored position and involves mainly ethnic Hungarian and German minorities, is losing members through emigration, as are the Lutheran, Calvinist (Reformed), and Unitarian churches. The Jewish community has dwindled to fewer than 25,000 members and three rabbis—due to emigration, and still faces periodic anti-Semitic publications and attitudes of the government. Several seminaries are severely restricted in entrants; church building permits are not usually granted—more churches are being demolished than are being built; and many pastors are not given licenses to preach by the state. Churches are controlled by the government's Department of Cults, whose director is an avowed atheist and Communist Party member with no sympathy for religion. The state does not allow believers in most cases to be members of the Communist Party or its allied new class of key cultural and scientific figures. Children of Christian believers find life at school more difficult and most avenues for advancement closed.

Active church members are discriminated against in significant ways. They are not allowed to hold certain jobs of importance such as factory foremen, teachers, or cooperative managers. This is made quite clear in Resolution Number 2508 of the Research Institute of Rubber and Plastic in Bucharest, dated February 15, 1982; and in Resolution Number 588 of the Inspectorate of Schools in Bucharest, dated November 24, 1980. According to Resolution 2508 Ilie Dumitru was found "guilty of serious misconduct of the socialist ethics and of the political and moral behavior he had to show as a foreman" (Article 64, paragraph 1, letter "t" of Law 5/1978).

Further because of Article 17 from law 6/1977 regarding the fore-man's duties and role, Ilie Dumitru "as a foreman had to prove his political and moral authority in the midst of the co-workers and his activity within the Baptist cult is inconsistent with his position." For the above reasons the resolution stated that his contract as fore-man at the prototype workshop was cancelled.[15] Similarly Reso-lution 588 said that Daniel Stauceanu, according to Order 4198/1980 of Articles 11 and 37 of the Law 6/1969, was dismissed from his position as teacher of music in the Department of Teaching and Education at General School Number 180 (section 1, Bucharest) because "applying for definite leaving (sic) the country he became inadequate for training and education of the pupils."[16] Four years later Stauceanu was still without a job before finally getting per-mission to leave the country.

One glaring example of Romania's contempt for both religion and adherence to agreements and the State Department's naïveté, con-cerns Bibles. Religious publications, including Bibles, are in short supply. This is a problem for all religious groups in Romania, but a bigger plight for Protestant denominations, because they lack the publishing houses the official Orthodox Church has. And Protes-tants, with their evangelistic bent and daily religious activities that revolve more around the Bible, have a greater need for them. Af-ter repeated requests and continual Western pressure the Romanian government "agreed" to let the World Reformed Alliance send some twenty thousand Bibles to the Reformed Church (predominately eth-nic Hungarian, centered in Transylvania). This agreement was an element in the preliminary discussions which ultimately led to MFN for Romania. Romanian officials sometimes referred to their Bi-ble import agreement as proof of their "good faith" toward reli-gious groups and minorities.

As part of the agreement, two roughly equal shipments of Bi-bles were sent in 1972 and 1981. But fewer than two hundred out of the promised twenty thousand were actually delivered to the churches. Instead, pieces of the Bibles appeared in toilet paper made at a factory in Braila. The Rev. Dr. Alexander Havadtöy of Yale University has meticulously documented this blasphemy.[17] In-terspersed throughout strips of toilet paper which made their way to the West were letters and words from the Bibles of the type sent to Romania. The toilet paper samples and a scholarly examination of the words and letters on the paper were unveiled at press con-ferences in the United States, including one I attended at the U.S.

House of Representatives in the summer of 1985. Dr. Havadtöy and I were joined by several Congressmen and Senators as well as leaders of human rights and religious groups.

Concern on the part of the World Alliance of Reformed Churches was expressed to me in a letter written by an official of the Alliance's Executive Committee and of the Presbyterian Church U.S.A. The American church official told me that "the World Alliance of Reformed Churches was the coordinator of the effort to place these twenty thousand Bibles in the hands of the Reformed people in Romania. . . . I hope that we can secure an action of formal protest, not only to the government of Romania, but also to the government of the United States for a continued failure to consider such actions as this in the establishment of its policies towards Romania." I could not agree with him more. He added that he was most disturbed by the violation of trust: "The Bibles can be replaced, and God cannot be damaged by such human desecration. But I serve an honorable organization that negotiated in good faith, and pledges made to that organization were broken."[18]

As with many other such incidents, the State Department has floundered around in its maze of indecision and conciliation. On the one hand, it initially did not react because it could not believe the Romanians would do such a thing. On the other hand, lacking the expertise and will to undertake its own investigation it no doubt let the affair slide into the inaction file. On this matter of both significance and symbolism barely a peep has been heard from the State Department.

During my tenure in Bucharest, I personally made an effort to address the Bible-religious publications shortage. It all began when I received a letter from Mrs. Ted Warren of Jackson, Mississippi. Mrs. Warren had read in the Mississippi Baptist paper that the newly appointed ambassador to Romania belonged to a Baptist church in North Carolina. She sent to me in Bucharest hundreds of small Bibles—both New Testaments and complete Bibles—printed in the Romanian language. In one letter she wrote: "I know of the conditions in Romania, I know you love the Lord after reading your letter, and I would appreciate it very much if you would accept these Bibles as a gift from a fellow Baptist and Christian who has a desire as you have to help the people of Romania to come to know Jesus Christ as their Lord and Savior."[19]

Some other Bibles and religious literature were sent by the Eastern European Bible Mission, directed by Ruud van Dijk and headquartered at Roosendaal, the Netherlands. I opened the boxes behind the desk in my chancery office, took out the Bibles and other publications, and placed them in several large envelopes. Several interested embassy officers were subsequently given the envelopes for distribution among believers in the country as they saw fit.

Additionally, my wife Betty took the lead in visiting Romanian families in Bucharest. Some were friends of ours from earlier days and others were visited upon request by Americans. Trying to help alleviate the misery, which was especially marked for the elderly, Betty distributed meat, milk, coffee, and fruits, as well as vitamins and aspirin. She also passed letters from American friends or relatives. On occasion, embassy officials also helped in the effort to deliver medicines to desperate Romanians either under house arrest or pressure of other kinds. DCM Frank Corry, for example, delivered needed medicine, sent in late 1984 from Christian Response International, to Romanian dissident Traian Dorz in Sibiu, Romania.

The degree to which religious groups in the West are used by Communist regimes for their own purposes is appalling. Father Calciu and others have documented ways in which the Romanian Orthodox Church advances the cause of the Bucharest regime through the World Council of Churches.[20] And despite the extensive evidence available on the death of Father Geza Palfi, much of which was in the hands of the Roman Catholic Church in Rome, the Vatican chose to overlook Romanian government complicity in the priest's death. Apparently the Vatican considered the possibility of negotiation to improve the position of the Catholic Church in Romania more important than causing problems over Palfi's death. With the official Orthodox Church in Romania an active agent of the Bucharest regime and the Catholic Church officially quiet, there are of course individual priests and laymen of both churches who fought against the government and paid the price. Neo-Protestant groups like the Baptists, Pentecostals and Adventists were typically the most outspoken foes of Communism. But even those churches are divided into official and unofficial—often underground—groups. It was painful to find that even representatives of my own "conservative" denomination, the Southern Baptist Convention (SBC), played into the hands of Ceausescu.

At a meeting in my office on January 10, 1985, I learned about *de facto* SBC assistance to Bucharest. Paul Thibodeaux, SBC Foreign Mission Board Representative stationed in Vienna, told me that the SBC had deposited $21,000 a year and one half earlier for a church in Baia Mare and had an additional $30,000 for a Hungarian-language church in Tirgu Mures. Also there was $50,000 for renovation of the Baptist Seminary in Bucharest. The $21,000 deposited in 1983 in a government of Romania bank was not distributed. Thibodeaux was given the typical Romanian run-around being told that previous bank managers who agreed to terms of $1 to 18 lei (Romanian currency unit) were no longer there. Despite that experience and without our advice from the embassy he had deposited the $30,000, getting no promises from the Romanians on distribution of the funds. This came after the earlier deposit was frozen with the Romanian government making interest.

Unwisely the SBC representative had chosen to deal with the Romanian Communist officials without any legal protection. I noted in my diary and wrote to U.S. Baptist officials that "the true believers who have sacrificed most and chosen not to compromise their consciences and beliefs by dealing with the state and in fact being used by the Communist party/Securitate, deserve our support and not to be forgotten or ignored." I concluded by noting that "to only deal with collaborator/officials is misappropriated priorities." Even though the amount of money was minuscule compared with U.S. government subsidies to Bucharest via MFN, a principle was involved. In my expressed view the trust of millions of Southern Baptists, who had given money to foreign missions e.g. Lottie Moon and other such designated collections in SBC churches, had been violated. I made this case known to the SBC through Baptist officials. In addition I shared material on religious persecution with SBC officials. The North Carolina Baptist State Convention of the SBC had adopted a 1985 resolution on religious liberty in places like Romania which said in part: "Be it further resolved that we encourage our people to pray for those throughout the world who are suffering persecution for their religious beliefs and practices."[21]

Also especially disappointing was the manner in which the Rev. Billy Graham's representative for Eastern Europe, Dr. Alexander S. Haraszti, set up Graham's visit to Romania. During the three years leading up to the Graham crusade in Romania, Haraszti visited Bucharest several times usually including stops at the American Embassy. Haraszti impressed those of us at the embassy who met him as a wheeler-dealer interested in setting up a grandstanding ego trip. In fact he tried to outdo the worst of the concessionary diplomats in giving away even more than was necessary to ingratiate himself to the Communists. On April 18, 1983, I wrote that Haraszti was still showing desperation in order to get the Communist invitations. On August 2, 1982, I had recorded in my diary that Dr. Haraszti seemed unconscionable, slick, and a disgrace to Billy Graham.

Some of the most incredible things he said had to do with the religious situation in Romania and Billy Graham's attitude toward Communist states, their churches, and religious dissidents. According to Haraszti, Baptists in Romania were free to practice their religion. Since Billy Graham considered the Orthodox Church as the true church in Romania, his policy was to support the national church. Graham's main objectives, said Haraszti, were to preach the gospel and bolster the relations between Bucharest and Washington. He did not want to support dissidents or minority churches. The most telling claim was that Graham was not interested in (and did not meet) radicals (read dissidents) like Alexander Solzhenitsyn, Aurel Popescu, or Joseph Ton, but only works with the Communist government's officially appointed "cult" leaders. I expressed my disappointment at what Haraszti was saying and made clear my own views on the general religious situation in Romania. It is probably no coincidence that the Billy Graham trip to Romania did not take place until some months after my departure as ambassador.

Prior to his visit to Romania, Billy Graham telephoned me for a half hour conversation on August 13, 1985. In a friendly discussion, I told Graham that his visit could be meaningful if he met with religious dissidents and "unofficial," dissident churches and did not follow the staged route of the Romanian Communist government. Bucharest, of course, wanted to use the Graham visit to show the world it has religious freedom, and had every intention of controlling the trip by limiting it to stops at selected official churches. Graham said that he understood the Bucharest regime's intentions, and what signals could be sent by the visit. He had had discussions with some neo-Protestant leaders who had recently emigrated from Romania and thus understood the overall picture. He also expressed his intention to talk with me again before his departure, but that was our last conversation to date. Based on various reports I have seen regarding his actual visit in Romania, the trip had both good and bad results. The best printed account is probably the *samizdat* open letter from a Romanian Baptist to Billy Graham which was published in *Religion in Communist Lands*. The Romanian writer said that the fact of Graham's visit was a blessing and: "the greatest public miracle I have experienced in the conditions of social and political dictatorship of Romania's Communist government." At the same time, the writer said that Graham had unfortunately contributed to the maintenance of MFN for Romania, and that much of the financial cost of the tour was being imposed on religious groups in Romania, even though Graham had already paid for it. The writer concluded by pointing out that Graham had gratuitously paid political homage to the Romanian regime by prefacing his messages with social and political points which praised the leaders, and the religiousness of the people, but advised all Romanians to stay in their place in Romania and not try to emigrate to the U.S.[22]

The situation of the Jews in Romania is virtually unique in the Communist world, because Ceausescu made a deal with Israel to allow the Jews to emigrate to Israel in return for payments per head. Israel was also permitted to have an embassy in Bucharest, which served in fact as a benefit for Moscow which did not have one. Before World War II, there were nearly one million Jews in Greater Romania, but this number was cut in half by the war and the postwar territorial losses. In any event, Jews played a significant role in Romanian history in the nineteenth and twentieth centuries. By 1987, there were only some 25,000 Jews left, and most of them were elderly. Most of those remaining are better off economically than average Romanians because of assistance from groups in the U.S. and Israel. Despite declining numbers, there were periodic reports of anti-Semitic publications in Romania. Many of these printed attacks on Jews were brought to my attention by the Chief Rabbi of Romania, Moses Rosen. Similarly, there were reports of desecration of Jewish cemeteries and more recently the destruction of synagogues. Some individual emigrant cases involving Jews were difficult.

Traditionally the number two ranking diplomat at the U.S. Embassy had worked as a liaison with the Jewish community in Bucharest as part of his duties. All of us at the embassy stayed in close touch with both the Jewish community and the Israeli Embassy. Personally I met often with the Israeli Ambassador and Rabbi Rosen, and attended special functions of the Jewish community. While I participated in several ceremonies at the main synagogue in Bucharest, one such occasion stands out. On June 15, 1984, I filled in for 1986 Nobel Peace Prize winner Elie Wiesel at the main synagogue on the occasion of the Holocaust Commemoration.

Wiesel arrived in Bucharest late, but asked me to deliver part of his address. I read for Wiesel: "I do so wish I could be with you today to commemorate together the death of thousands. . . . I have known those Jews of Transylvania; I was one of them. . . . I so wish I could, together with you, include their lives and their songs and their deaths in our memory today—not because we wish to weep for them; it is too late for weeping. It is because we must remember lest we ourselves be forgotten."[23]

Most people are not allowed to travel freely, certainly not out of the country, for fear of defections. The government has an official anti-emigration policy. Bucharest permits the annual emigration of about 11,000 ethnic Germans and 1,000 Jews largely because they are paid for in hard currency by the governments of West Germany and Israel, respectively. Some 2,500 to 3,000 Romanians are permitted to annually emigrate to the U.S. as part of the U.S.-Romanian Trade Agreement of 1975, which is affected by the Jackson-Vanik Amendment. In effect, some Romanians are allowed to emigrate in exchange for MFN status, which results also in substantial financial and economic benefits for Bucharest's government.

But the overwhelming majority of Romanians cannot emigrate. And most of those who attempt to emigrate pay a very heavy price. I received thousands of letters from Romanians, Romanian-Americans, and interested Americans describing the difficulties for those who applied for emigration.* A typical letter is the following one to Senator Howard Baker from an American who married a Romanian and attempted to get his brother and wife to the U.S. between 1980 and 1983. The writer of the letter said that after application for emigration:

> They had lived in intimidation and insecurity. Sandra has been demoted from program analyst in systems engineering to file clerk as punishment for wanting to leave. Gheorghe has been periodically threatened and harassed at work. They have four times been denied emigration with no reasons given. They can no longer cover maintenance cost of their home, yet because of their pending petition to leave Romania, they cannot sell their apartment or exchange it for a smaller dwelling. They have been repeatedly interrogated and intimidated to renounce their petition. Their sons, aged nine and eleven, are growing up in an atmosphere of confusion and uncertainty.[24]

*Two years after my departure from Bucharest, I was still getting several letters and telephone calls each week for emigration help.

Other cases were more tragic. In March 1985, the embassy was notified that an applicant for immigration had committed suicide. Mrs. Georgeta Rugan informed the embassy that her husband Ioan had killed himself because of despair over being unable to leave the country sooner. The Rugans had applied through the U.S. Embassy as early as February 1983, and had been put on a waiting list for immigrant visas. They were the beneficiaries of fifth preference category approvals and were consequently alerted that the wait would be a long one. Thousands of Romanians emigrate illegally each year and many are shot trying to cross the border into Yugoslavia for points west.

University students are instructed to stay away from the tiny American Embassy (USIS) library, to avoid and ignore exchange professors and students, and not to study English. French has been replaced by English as the most popular foreign language of students. But the government has severely restricted the study of English. Unauthorized Romanians are told not to fraternize with Westerners. The government's greatest fear is what the Romanians might tell the foreigners about the reality of life. Thus there is the need to watch every move they make. Of course the accurate perception by Romanians that the moves of foreigners are being monitored by the state acts as an additional intimidating factor. Romanians assume, with good reason, that the houses or apartments where foreigners stay are bugged, along with hotel rooms, restaurant tables, and automobiles. Romanians would point to the flower on the table in a restaurant and say that behind every flower is a Philips, i.e. Philips listening device. Beyond that they consider that Americans are tailed and that telephones are tapped. After all, it has been confirmed in several publications, e.g. John Barron's *KGB*, that a top American diplomat in Bucharest had his shoes wired with an electronic listening device by the Romanian employees of his residence. Consequently there was a lot of looking over one's shoulders and whispering outdoors in Romania when Romanians and foreigners got together.

When a visiting American or Westerner got too close to the people he could be warned to stop fraternization or be kicked out of the country. During my first year as ambassador, one of the embassy employees was warned to back off or be kicked out of the country. Donald Kyer, a Baptist pastor from the U.S., was in fact declared *persona non grata* in December 1984, presumably for the extensive contacts he had with local Christians.[26]

This is the Romania of Nicolae Ceausescu. Who then is this man that for two decades has accelerated the destruction of the past in Romania, and who runs the whole show personally along with other family members?

CHAPTER FIVE:

Nicolae Ceausescu—The Mad Man Favored by Washington

Nicolae Ceausescu has been ruler of Romania for more than twenty years, making him one of the longest tenured Communist leaders in the world. Ceausescu, like Joseph Stalin, Kim Il Sung, or Mao Tse-Tung, is not an abberation but rather the logical result of a system which concentrates its power in the hands of a few party leaders. The principal assets required of a Communist leader are the ability to out-wit, survive and crush one's opponents. It is necessary to ruthlessly seek and control all avenues of power possible, because the main Communist requirement is the maintenance of power. Obviously Ceausescu has all of those attributes. In addition, he has increasingly created a god out of himself in his own mind and through the exactions demanded of his subjects. And subjects, not citizens, is the proper word because his people must be dominated and dependent. They cannot be members of a nation with privileges, rights and legal protections. Ceausescu demands near absolute fealty. The deification of his family cult is only rivaled today by his good friend in North Korea. Ceausescu required it be shown that all of the 73,027 so-called voters in his district in the March 1985 "sham" elections voted for him. It was so reported. Similarly the March 1985 unanimous reelection of Ceausescu at the Grand National Assembly—Ceausescu's rubber stamp parliament—took place with him decked out in regal splendor, i.e. scepter and sash.

Giant portraits of him, usually showing a man ten to twenty years younger with black not gray hair, are put up on all special occasions. Other portraits of him are displayed in every government building as well as in many shops and stores. Every word that he utters, his red books (some of which are red but typically, white-covered) can be found in every book store in the country. Signs, posters and banners saying "Long Live Ceausescu" and poems lauding him as the greatest son of the country ranked among the gods, are omnipresent. At government and Communist Party meetings, prolonged chants venerate Ceausescu. Most frightening is the fact that he believes the applause he gets is real. Every time he gets it he revels in it, first waving with one hand back and forth and smiling sheepishly. If he starts a marathon speech with strained smiles and waves, it grows to a determined smile with both hands clasped over his head—Nixon style. Little effort is made to stop the orchestrated applause, and of course it would not go on at all if his henchmen did not think it was his wish. Homage to him and his family are required nonstop throughout the country in television and radio broadcasts, publications of all types, during visits at the airport and in the city by foreign dignitaries, and in each *vizita de lucru* (work visit) at provincial seats and at urban markets which seem to go on endlessly in political campaign fashion.

Ceausescu looks quite ordinary. He is short and has dark hair (i.e. before it greyed), dark eyes and rather unattractive facial features. He stands erect despite his age and ailments. Perhaps he has a Napoleonic complex of insecurity because of lack of height which he must make up for in other ways. He certainly projects two persons almost at the same time. On the one hand he appears at first glance as the simple peasant-origined shoemaker with only a limited grammar school education that has been so often reported. His unusual table manners may tell more about his origin than his character. Like his former Foreign Minister Stefan Andrei he slurps soup, but beyond that he has used the table cloth for a napkin. He gobbles food instantly. Obsessive attention is paid to covering the hands of waiters, checking food, and spraying plants for germs or poison. On the other hand, at closer and deeper observational range his talents become obvious. His shrewd, demanding characteristics become apparent in the course of a long discussion.

Perhaps Ceausescu and former President Richard Nixon are admiring friends because they have such a fixation on power—its acquisition and retention. Nixon had much to do with the establishment of MFN treatment for Romania and special consideration of Ceausescu. A lot of this evidently began when Ceausescu—ever the globetrotter and inviter of dignitaries to Bucharest—hosted Nixon in Romania in 1967, before Nixon was elected President and when he seemed to be politically down. Nixon remembered the invitation and the red carpet treatment in Bucharest. And when Nixon became the first U.S. President to visit Communist Romania, he was given a virtual hero's welcome, stage-managed by Ceausescu. Of course the Romanians rejoiced in sincerely welcoming the one who symbolized America to them. Nixon and Kissinger apparently became convinced that Ceausescu could be trusted and was a *bona fide* maverick. Thus they could use him. In reality he has used them. Nixon has stayed in touch with Ceausescu through the years and even traveled to Romania in 1982. I was in Washington at the time of his visit so I did not personally witness it.

Nixon has expressed the esteem in which he holds Ceausescu, in statements, books, and in correspondence. For example, in January 1983, Nixon sent a congratulatory letter to Ceausescu on the occasion of his 65th birthday. In the letter, a copy of which was passed to me along with the original for delivery, Nixon referred to Ceausescu as one of the greatest leaders of the world who valiantly carries out an independent foreign policy. When I saw Nixon's letter to Ceausescu, I noted that anyone who could say such things: 1. does not know Ceausescu; 2. must be especially grateful for getting the welcome treatment in Bucharest which is not available to him everywhere; and 3. must share the conviction that the accumulation, misuse, and imposition of unchecked power equals greatness. In any case, Nixon's stock went down in my book after that.

Beyond a love for power, Ceausescu intimidates those coming in contact with him. It is easy to see why he is increasingly hated by the people and resented by officials around him. He trusts no one and makes all the decisions himself. This is taken to such extremes that he makes decisions covering all facets of life in Romania.

Ceausescu is known to have a personal hand in virtually every decision right down to the peasant-village level, and this is in a country the size of Oregon with a population of 23 million. For examples, he has ordered the execution of workers and peasants for stealing meat from packing plants and grains of wheat from local cooperative farms, the pulling of plugs in hospitals killing babies in incubators ostensibly for energy-saving reasons, and the crackdown on religious figures that led to the deaths of several Baptist, Catholic, and Pentecostal pastors.[1]

But perhaps his obsession with keeping tabs on everything and dispensing superior wisdom for all kinds of problems best expresses his madness. He has been known to fly around the country in a helicopter and drop down on a farm cooperative to tell peasants how to farm. What does it say about a leader who feels compelled to tell farmers how far apart they must plant the corn rows, reportedly telling some that the corn rows should be planted about 1½ feet apart instead of the 3-4 feet he observed in order to double the yields? The end result was the disastrous failure of the corn crop that year with production far less than previously.

Ceausescu has a talent, as Pacepa has put it, for subtly telling his counterpart what he wants to hear. At the same time Ceausescu does his homework in learning extensive background information about the individuals with whom he meets. He tries to stay one step ahead of his discussion partner and to impress him with his wide range of facts and details spanning world events. This knowledge is embellished and made more impressive by his ability to quote the latest stances of key world leaders. Few heads of state travel as extensively as Ceausescu or receive as many visitors as he does, which are all part of his fathomed role as special world leader along the lines of Tito. Thus he can sprinkle his conversations with current words from Arafat, Khaddafy, or Mubarak, for examples. He is without question intelligent in the sense that he has a capacity for facts and details, a good memory, and an ability for expressing ambiguous nuances. In this way he can keep people guessing as to what he really means. But watching him deliver the same general themes over and over to U.S. officials, who in most cases were hearing it for the first time and thus duly impressed, led to a diminishing respect for his creativity or in-depth knowledge.

Part of Ceausescu's success with Westerners no doubt has come because he has studied the psychology of his adversaries and has appeared to them to be different from other Communist leaders. That has been part of Ceausescu's game plan from the beginning. Some Western observers have referred to a wit and charm that has enabled him to score points with his American discussants. Evidently this refers to the periodic quips he makes to contradict his counterpart during the conversation or to interjected retorts which he obviously considers humorous. When Al Haig told Ceausescu that Reagan did not intend to punish the Polish regime of Jaruzelski, Ceausescu wagged his fingers and said: in that case help him, don't punish him. Similarly Ceausescu responded to Haig's comment that the U.S. was a nation borne out of revolution by saying: Marx said Lincoln was a President from the workers. Ceausescu laughed as he said: Romania favors religious freedom, and has 14 cults with 6 cult representatives in parliament, making Romania more advanced than the U.S. Yet it is apparent that he is dead serious about it in his own mind. Compared with stone faced chiefs of some other Communist countries, however, Ceausescu may appear to have wit and humor.

One characteristic, however, gives Ceausescu away during his conversations. He has the habit of stuttering, especially when he seems under pressure or has to listen to something critical. In response to tough words from a U.S. official—admittedly not often—his voice will begin clicking, and his mouth will move without the words coming out. Invariably it comes when he is irritated and made uncomfortable. Then he might go into antics of waving his arms and lecturing, as if in retaliation. Also, he so obviously soaks up praise and compliments that his ego can be seen ballooning before your eyes.

In my view, it is important to keep in mind when dealing with Ceausescu (or a similar Communist boss), that his single-minded objective is to further the aims of Communist power and rule. Thus any agreement he signs is going to be in his best interest. Equally important in talking with Ceausescu is remembering what he has done. It should be sobering to keep in mind that the one you are talking to has ordered the assassination of his enemies. Whether it was the Radio Free Europe broadcaster, the cultural émigrés in Paris, the religious and political dissidents, or the *chiaburi* during collectivization in Romania, Ceausescu has shown he does not value human life in the same way that we do. To use President Reagan's terminology, he does not abide by the same rules of civilized behavior we expect in the Western world.

Ceausescu must see himself as the "benevolent ruler-father" of modern Romania. He equates himself with the country. He is convinced that he is indispensable to the Romanians and uniquely great in the history of the nation. I think he truly feels that he has created a new Romania of greater wealth, with cars, apartments, and factories that have brought Romania out of the dark ages. Whatever has happened during his rule he considers to be progress for which he alone is responsible. Ceausescu believes the people do not realize what he has done for them and what they owe him. Because the people have not advanced to proper levels in their thinking—as regards religion, the class struggle, and material wealth—he must nurse them along.

Ceausescu obviously thinks that he has created modern-day, industrialized Romania, transforming the country from a land of peasant farmers to a semi-developed country of factories. It is not really relevant to him that neighboring countries and other ones in Europe more backward industrially and more agricultural in the pre-World War II period have made greater strides and progress, materially speaking. And in most cases they have done it without the same human cost and destruction of the culture and heritage of the past. But Ceausescu has probably achieved just what he intended, by trying to erase the past and construct a new man and society dependent upon the Communist Party and its organs of terror and intimidation. Thus it is easier to understand why he fully expects, if not absolutely requires, the unbelievable adulation for a leader in the twentieth century and in Europe at that.

Ceausescu is the *Conducator* (all encompassing leader). In 1984, he was described in Biblical terms as "the creator of thought," "the giver of strength," "the giver of meaning to our thoughts and meditations," and as the one (who): "Thou hast shown us the way."[2] The West German Ambassador in Bucharest, Harmut Wolfgang Schulze-Boysen, sent me a copy of the ethnic German newspaper *Neue Banater Zeitung* of July 19, 1984, with an article by Franz Johannes Bulhardt entitled "Sie Sprechen Deinen Namen Aus" ("They Pronounce Thy Name") which describes Ceausescu in the above mentioned ways. Schulze-Boysen said that Hitler and Goebbels must be turning over in their graves because not even Hitler was prayerfully referred to by the capitalized (family-familiar) terms meaning Thou and Thy.

He has been compared with Alexander the Great and Julius Caesar, and grouped in portraits of homage with Romania's past historical heroes: Michael the Brave and Stephen the Great. He has also been classed with another Romanian hero—Vlad Tepes who was known as Dracula. Vlad Tepes, alias Dracula (literally the son of the devil, his father being called Vlad Dracul or Vlad the Devil), means Vlad the Impaler. Although he is considered a hero in the sense that he fought against the Turkish enemy in the 1460s, he is well known for his sick methods of killing domestic enemies by impalement along the border regions of Transylvania and Wallachia.[3] In that way he disposed of thousands of Germans and Hungarians as well as ethnic Romanians he considered dishonest or lazy. To be classed with even the historical Dracula—as opposed to the Hollywood bloodsucking version hyped from Bram Stoker—

is a dubious distinction for Ceausescu. But then in view of Ceausescu's penchant for getting rid of enemies—through beating, incarceration and execution, the resemblance to Vlad Tepes (Dracula), is perhaps not so far fetched after all.

Ceausescu is classed as the fount of all wisdom and knowledge. Perhaps some of the more telling descriptions are the following: "Nicolae Ceausescu, the revolutionist . . ., the undaunted patriot . . ., the builder of new Romania, the man who gave his name to a whole era in the history of the Romanian people," and:

> the thinker who has enriched the theory of the socialist revolution and construction with tenets and concepts of an inestimable theoretical and practical value, nationally and internationally, who has imprinted his own genius, his farsighted mind and daring spirit on all the Party and State fundamental documents, the initiator of the Programme of the Romanian Communist Party of Building the Multilaterally Developed Socialist Society and Romania's Advance towards Communism.[4]

His years have been called the years of light and he has been equated with the country and the country with him. Examples include, "when we say Ceausescu, we say Romania, when we say Ceausescu, we say the flag (tricolor), and these heroic years of the Ceausescu era are years toward the golden future, toward communism." From all parts of the country "we honor the most beloved hero of Romania; we climb toward communism, creating a new history of Romania." He has been represented as the embodiment of the nation in sculptures, portraits, wooden icons, paintings, cloth art works, statues, and in poems and other literary forms.[5]

Every year from 1981 to 1985, as conditions of life worsened, required devotion to Ceausescu increased. It reached a crescendo of fervor each January during his birthday celebration. During the 65th birthday celebration on January 26, 1983, an official portrait showed him in regal garb. At the National Museum of History in Bucharest Ceausescu is pictured in sovereign pose alongside the ancient kings of Romania. Nearby are the various decorations, titles, orders, and special tributes to Ceausescu, including a certificate designating him an honorary citizen of Disneyworld.[6]

In recent years it has become a practice to pay similar—though not as great—homage to Elena Ceausescu. "Dr." Elena Ceausescu, wife of the President, who ranks third in the official heirarchy as First Vice Prime Minister and Member of the Political Executive

Committee of the Central Committee of the Communist Party, has her birthday celebrated every January 7th. In January 1984, she was officially referred to as a brilliant scientist, a world renowned person of learning, a militant Communist leader, and a Doctor in Science and Honorary Member of prestigious scientific institutes and academies of many countries around the world. And tribute was paid her for working alongside "the most beloved son of the Romanian people; the founder of modern Socialist Romania; the greatest hero of peace, collaboration and understanding among people; . . . Comrade Nicolae Ceausescu."[7]

The worshipful tribute to Ceausescu went far beyond birthdays to include every national party occasion of importance such as the annual August 23rd victory over the fascists celebration, and the 65th anniversary of the union of Transylvania with the rest of Romania commemorated in 1983. Such national historical days have become glorifications of Ceausescu more than recognition of the original events.

Part of my own blacklisting by Ceausescu was due to my unwillingness to give him his desired veneration. Coming from a country that does not worship its leaders, and having been born in a state whose motto is *Sic Semper Tyrannis*, I drew the line. It is protocol to stand for a head of state who enters a hall for a national assembly meeting and who departs. And even for courtesy's sake, it is well to stand a few other times during a speech. But to stand every two or three minutes with everyone clapping in unison in homage to a tyrant's shouts of Long Live Communism's Victory, Long Live the Communist Party of Romania, and Long Live Ceausescu, seems clearly beyond the call of duty. But other diplomats and all Romanians were afraid to do otherwise.

Deeper reasons for his resentment, were my questioning of his "independent image," and my highlighting of human rights concerns. As Professor Stephen Fischer-Galati recounted to me, Ceausescu's brother Ilie expressed disappointment that I did not help protect Romania's "maverick image." The main roadblock in the way of Ceausescu getting everything he wanted from the U.S. was his terrible human rights record, increasingly highlighted by some of us in the American Embassy along with interested Congressmen and religious organizations in the U.S. The news about Romania's repression that filtered back to the U.S. hurt Ceausescu's image.

Ceausescu was especially astute at playing the game of divide

and rule when dealing with American and other Western representatives, especially in the area of human rights. Many Foreign Service officers working in the embassy in Bucharest were well aware
of the human rights situation in Romania and preferred to get the
truth out. But the overriding concern back at State was to protect
the MFN relationship with Ceausescu's Romania.

Ceausescu knew that the concerns of some of us in the embassy
were not the concerns of the leadership elite at State. And he played
on the difference. Since the embassy was perceived by official
Bucharest as more concerned with the plight of the people in Romania including human rights and emigration, the Romanian government dealt with those less concerned in the State Department.

Even with regard to the embassy, reports from and conversations
in Washington encouraged Romanians in Bucharest to attempt playing off embassy officer against embassy officer. This was followed
up by Romanians reporting to friends in the State Department on
who were the good guys in the U.S. Embassy from the overall relationship's point of view. The good guys were those less concerned
with human rights and the bad guys were those more concerned.
The rumored Romanian list reportedly showed embassy officers
who were more cooperative with the Romanian officials and less
preoccupied with human rights. It similarly showed an equal number of embassy officers including the ambassador who were more
concerned with human rights and religious matters.

There was a difference in State and embassy reporting on human
rights. In addition to the State revision of the Human Rights press
release and the Palmer-Malitza document regarding the
TCP/emigration issue mentioned elsewhere in the book, the 1984
CSCE Report reflects State efforts to soft-pedal human rights violations. Despite an embassy report detailing the worst known violation by the Romanian government in 1984—the brutal beating of
Catholic priest Geza Palfi—the CSCE Report omits any mention
of it. Additionally the report prematurely gave Romania too much
credit for releasing Father Calciu from prison when in fact he languished for months under house arrest unable to receive visitors
or telephone calls or even fill out emigration forms. This happened
after he had made his wishes for emigration to the U.S. known to
embassy officers outside the window of his apartment. Before being finally released he was reportedly moved outside the city to an
unknown address where he could not be contacted.

The convergence of interests between the State Department

leadership and the Romanian Communists dates back to the U.S.-Romanian Trade Agreement and MFN. The special relationship has continued despite the lack of internal reforms in Romania. And Romania's foreign policy has only gotten closer in terms of relations with Moscow. Why then has the State elite persisted in maintaining cordial relations with such a mad man? On his 67th birthday on January 26, 1985, *Luceafarul* said about Ceausescu:

> When Orion was spread upon the sky
> and luminous frost settled upon the villages,
> At Scornicesti, in the museum house, there
> came into—the world
> Our Nicolae with a laurel crown . . .
> There is no country more beautiful than our
> Carpathian Homeland,
> Nor any people harder working or more
> brilliant, nor any politician as great
> as Ceausescu, in honor of whom the people today
> stand tall.

The people in Romania know the shallowness of this, if not the State Department elite.

CHAPTER SIX:

Dissent by the
United States Ambassador

During my stay in Romania I felt obligated to take stands on certain occasions that I considered best represented the President and country I was serving. These positions were not taken for the purposes of overtly challenging the regime in Bucharest or damaging the veneer of "friendly" U.S.-Romanian relations. And even though the Romanian government was often irritated by my actions, they were basically solaced by the facts that I would not be there forever and that the active policy line from Foggy Bottom was not really supportive of me. Nevertheless they did not care to allow precedents to be set and other Western ambassadors to get the wrong ideas about what was permissible by Ceausescu. For my part I did not wish Ceausescu to be prodded to drastic action against me or for an international incident to take place. It was painful enough to watch the State Department leadership capitulate on a day to day basis to the Communist regimes while Ceausescu was engaged in playing the U.S. diplomats like a fiddle and in conscienceless murder around the globe. The record shows that Ceausescu has no compulsion about killing his opponents whether they were religious or political dissidents at home, or whether they were enemies traveling abroad—witness the cases of Paul Goma and Virgil Tanase in Paris and Emil Georgescu in Munich. Pacepa has recounted at length Ceausescu's talent for winning over his negotiating opponents through "discreet anti-Soviet allusions."[1] I observed the same facility in meetings involving Ceausescu with Haig, Max Kampelman, Malcolm Baldrige, Tom Lantos, and several others.

I took the steps because I considered that someone had to put down a marker for the human rights and dignity of the people in Romania, and for the values and principles central to America's heritage. President Reagan on an annual basis has delivered proclamations observing Captive Nations Week by saying that "we shall continue to speak out for their freedom (of those denied the benefits of liberty)," and in quoting Alexander Herzen "to shrink from saying a word in defense of the oppressed is as bad as any crime."[2] In addition I made symbolic gestures which while nonrevolutionary were significant enough to let the oppressed freedom fighters behind the Iron Curtain know that such American voices have not been silenced.

The only scheduled occasion when the U.S. Ambassador to Communist Romania can talk on Romanian Television is the Fourth of July. Communist spokesmen appear regularly on American TV. I arrived at the RomTV Station on the 3rd of July to tape a July 4th message to the Romanian people. In my first summer in Romania in 1982, I had drafted a brief presentation that quoted President Reagan mentioning liberty and belief in God as fundamental to America's history and greatness. I pointed out that President Reagan said: "July 4th, independence day for Americans, is the occasion for us to show our appreciation 'to those who came before us, to the same God who guides us all and to the spirit of faith and patriotism which still makes America the land of the free and the home of the brave.' " The Romanian officials did not like the looks of it. They instructed me to take God out of the address and put their god Ceausescu in. And they were visibly upset when I refused to do so. I quickly heard through the diplomatic and lower level government grapevines that my presentation had upset the Romanian leadership. Still, it was all made worthwhile when an embassy officer told me that a haggard Romanian worker came into the U.S. Embassy saying, the "U.S. believes in human rights, doesn't it? I know the Ambassador is a religious man because he spoke *frumos* (kindly) on July 4th on TV." Other Romanians grabbed me outside church services in the far north of the country weeks and months later saying that they had never heard God mentioned on Romanian TV since the Communists took over in the 1940s, and to know that these were the words of the President of the United States and his representative was dear and meaningful to them.

During my second summer in the country, I again mentioned God but not Ceausescu in my Fourth of July talk. Quoting Reagan I said: "As Americans have done for the last two centuries, we will celebrate our independence, and consecrate ourselves, with the grace of God, to the continuation and preservation of Liberty, Justice and Freedom." In 1983, the officials seemed more miffed and demanded a copy of my presentation several days before the television taping. I did not cooperate.

During my last visit to the TV studio, in July 1984, the Romanian officials were waiting to sandbag me. I went to the station at 10 o'clock, as scheduled, driving in the official limousine with my colleague on these occasions—the Press Attache or Public Information Officer of USIA, William Edwards. Upon arrival at the gate of the TV station, we were informed that we would have to wait 15 or 20 minutes, and then enter through the back gate. We waited and went to the back gate where we were kept waiting for another 15 minutes. Then they told us that we would need to return to the front gate. I said that if they did not let me speak as promised I would go back and advertise it to the world as an example of their unfairness and fear. The Romanian authorities relented, and I was escorted into the studio. Once there, however, they made a scene because we did not give them an advance text of the address. The TV manager tried to extract some concession in his office before proceeding to the taping room. He also stalled for time while he called back and forth on the telephone for further advice and instructions. It was a typical run-around. They had the last word by putting the Fourth of July address two hours early at 5:00 p.m., when most Romanians were still at work.

In my last Fourth of July address to the Romanian people, in 1984, I again quoted President Reagan: "All Americans can take pride in knowing that the Fourth of July stands as a lasting symbol of freedom and a beacon of hope for the oppressed of every land. . . . Let us pray that God will guide us and future generations in preserving the liberty that is the essence of the American spirit."

Attendance at church services is a private matter for us. But it was virtually impossible for me to go to Baptist churches in Romania—where Baptists are considered especially dangerous by the Communists—unnoticed by much of the populace. Although I represented the U.S. at the main Jewish synagogue on occasion, and attended other churches, including Romanian Orthodox ones, my attendance was usually at Baptist churches. I have never been in churches where the emotional and spiritual level of feeling was as high. The strength and power of the people's voices and touch and the pastor's messages were overwhelming. It was virtually impossible to attend such services without being greatly moved and totally drained. You knew the high price these people had paid for their faith and you felt inadequate in the face of it. At the same time you could not come out of the services without knowing that our God is far superior to the evil of the materialistic and atheistic Marxist-Leninists who have no conception of a human being's inner worth, spirit and dignity. And these believers were giving up opportunities for apartments, better food choices, cars and better lives for their children in school. As active Christians they were rejecting compromise with the Communist regime and making themselves subject to increased harassment and persecution from then on.

It became obvious that our attendance at church services in Romania could afford a small measure of protection or support for the believers. This was perhaps especially true of the Baptist churches we attended most often. In Bucharest, we sometimes attended the "Mihai Bravul" (Sfinta Treime) Baptist Church pastored by the Reverend Vasile Talos. An embassy officer who worked with religious dissidents in political reporting told me on August 3rd, 1982, that our attendance at Talos's church was the talk of the town and country. In November of 1982, I visited the Baptist Seminary that had been badly damaged by the 1977 earthquake. The government had taken advantage of the earthquake to destroy the effectiveness of the seminary. It had no heat, few lights, and in general was run down and in dangerous condition. Additionally, the government severely restricted the number of new students who could enter the seminary on an annual basis, to either zero or a few, even when the nearly one thousand Baptist churches nationwide had less than two hundred pastors and thus greatly needed more trained ministers.

In November 1982, I attended the Giulesti Baptist Church of the Reverend Bunian Cocar, who stayed in trouble with the authorities because of his outspoken evangelism as well as success. In the Giulesti Church which I attended with Kentucky State Senator Gene Huff and Representative Tom Riner—two fighters for religious believers in Romania—one parishioner got up and referred to the admonition in II Corinthians 5:20 that we are ambassadors for Christ. I subsequently said that in brief addresses before church worshippers and considered the instruction a big responsibility. It might be true, as Jeff Collins of Christian Response International says, that because of my attendance at Giulesti the church was spared from demolition until my departure. I know for a fact that it did me a lot of good to meet the courageous worshippers and their pastor, to symbolically offer my support, and try to boost their spirits.

While it seems unbelievable to us as Americans, the Romanian regime expected homage to its cult leader Ceausescu—even in churches. In most official churches as in other aspects of life, spokesmen felt compelled to pay some measure of tribute to Ceausescu and Romania's Communist leadership. When this was done by the leaders of the Orthodox Church on the holy occasion of midnight services for Easter—mentioning Ceausescu in the same breath as the birth of Jesus Christ—it was far more than I could stomach. At that moment of sacrilege, I left the service never to return. But in many official and virtually all non-official churches throughout the country courageous pastors and priests refuse to capitulate to the authorities by giving homage to the pagan god Ceausescu. In speaking in churches we never mentioned the name or position of President Nicolae Ceausescu.

We hosted Christmas receptions at the ambassador's residence, sent Christmas cards to friends, and spoke, when in the U.S., on the religious situation in Romania. In so doing, I probably made the State Department as uneasy as Ceausescu. In fact, I was advised by Romanian and American employees at the embassy not to use "Christmas" on greeting cards because it might offend some of the Communists in Romania. Their advice was to continue the tradition of many other ambassadors by using Happy New Year cards only and to stay away from "Christmas" on VOA and RFE broadcasts as well. The United States does not have an official or established religion, even though the majority of Americans adhere to the Christian faith. Since the Christmas cards were our tradition and sent as personal greetings—not official ones—I did not make the change. Similarly, we hosted at the residence—not in the embassy—Christmas receptions to which we invited friends, representatives of various religious groups in Romania (Christian and non-Christian), and others. In 1984, Ceausescu ordered Romanian religious and political officials not to attend our Christmas reception.

I was invited to speak at the White House in September 1984, but was advised not to talk about the religious situation. Robert Reilly relayed the message to me that the NSC might balk at me talking about any such thing for fear of upsetting the Communist

Romania that had just attended the Los Angeles Olympics (and thus defied Moscow, according to the mistaken State Department experts). I spoke on the situation in Romania and Eastern Europe, including the religious conditions, without tilting my address as regarding the "religious situation."

I was certainly frustrated by the extensive favorable coverage Romania and Ceausescu got by going to the Olympics. They became virtual heroes in the eyes of Americans at exactly the time when Ceausescu was actually moving closer to the Soviets and enforcing harsher human rights violations and an anti-religious campaign. A Romanian official at some risk told me that the Romanians had asked the Soviets several months earlier whether Romania should go to the Olympics and thus keep intact its image of "independence." I reported this private conversation to the State Department, but to no avail, because it ran counter to the State line.

In the August 1984 atmosphere of euphoria about Romania's attendance at the Olympics, all else was forgiven. MFN hearings in the Senate were virtual whitewashes of Romania's heightened human rights abuses and religious persecution. It coincided with the Romanian cover-up of Roman Catholic priest Geza Palfi's murder. And it was sickening that the Romanian government deluded the Democratic National Committee into sending a representative, Alan Schaefer, to go to Romania, where he was portrayed as a high-level American representative there to celebrate the 40th anniversary of Romania's Communist regime. Most other Western democratic parties and groups refused to participate in the Communist showcase event on August 23rd. But the Romanian Communist newspapers advertised the Schaefer appearance as official representation of the U.S. Democratic Party to the Communist front organization in Romania—Socialist Unity Front of the Romanian Communist Party. It just so happened that Schaefer had a daughter studying in Romania on a Romanian government fellowship. At the U.S. Embassy we argued against any high level official representation from the U.S. government, which caused Romanian resentment.

Another example of Romanian efforts to get homage paid to Ceausescu came during the negotiations for publishing my doctoral dissertation in Romania. Former colleagues of mine at the Nicolae Iorga Institute of History and other institutes in Bucharest urged me to publish my Ph.D. Thesis so that it would be more widely known among Romanians in general. The discussions involved in the publication process with the official Scientific and Encyclopedic

Publishing House provide further insight into the requirements of submission to authority placed on people working in Communist lands. My dissertation was harmless enough in that it was on a prewar, i.e. pre-Communist era subject: *British Policy Toward Romania, 1938–1940*. But even that era concerned the Communists because it was a time when many of the now Communist leaders were fascists. But my work focused more on foreign policy.

What the Communists required, however, was a tribute to their Communist chief, usually in the preface or introduction. I was specifically advised to put a tribute to the Communist boss on the first page, or, failing that, somewhere in my text. Refusing that, I was asked if I would praise Ceausescu while one of their scholars praised President Reagan on the same page. I tried to explain that we did not give such homage to our Presidents, and that, besides, it was a scholarly work with no political overtones. After that rebuff they tried to persuade me to include some mention of Ceausescu in the text, postscript, or footnotes. I told them that while no disrespect was intended, it was not the way we did things in the U.S., and that publication was not worth me having to make such a tribute. Not giving up easily, and apparently desiring to publish the book, the Communist historians responsible for tying together the book arrangements suggested inclusion of references to Ceausescu's works in the bibliography. I replied that the text of my book was complete and that it was not a political work. We settled on their inclusion of a postscript in which two Romanian historians quoted a few lines describing the Romanian people's alliance with Nazi Germany in World War II. There was nothing attributable to me in the book referring to Ceausescu. I was able to add a preface to the book in which I briefly described some hopes for U.S.-Romanian relations that emphasized liberty and "human dignity" (code words for human rights and individual worth), and respect for those rights.

The published book was well reviewed, and sold out immediately as do most such books when they are printed in Romania.[3] Following my departure as ambassador and my outspoken interviews immediately thereafter, I received several copies of my book in the mail. Some of the Romanian officials to whom I had given autographed copies of the book, returned the copies with letters of disavowal. In what was surely an orchestrated campaign the virtually identical letters accompanied the returned books. Those writing to me said they could no longer be friends with one who had attacked Romania—actually I condemned the Stalinist rule of Ceausescu and his official positions. Those who befriended me would have to hurry to distance themselves after my statements. What encouraged me was the number of books that were not returned. I can only hope that my friends have not paid too high a price for their friendship.

One of the most uncomfortable demonstrations came with the obligatory attendance at the numerous special anniversaries and celebrations of Communist milestones and Ceausescu days. It was uncomfortable in the sense that each occasion developed into a virtual worship service to Ceausescu. And grouped with the diplomatic corps in a prominent place among the tens of thousands present in the coliseums, made it more obvious when one did not stand with the rest.

So the paramount question faced was whether to stand or not to stand up for a Communist god, when the tribute went beyond that to a head of state, on to a god and Communist victory. Of course, there were diplomatic requirements to attend such Romanian government and Romanian Communist Party functions each year and to stand up upon the entrance and departure of the President. That I did as the official representative of the U.S. government. And perhaps it was a gesture of protocol courtesy to stand on a few other occasions during Ceausescu's and other leaders' speeches. But beyond that, what should be required of the representative of the most free and democratic country on earth is questionable.

It is necessary to understand the atmosphere of such occasions. At several minute intervals during the President's speech, party stooges would literally jump out of their seats with cattle prods and initiate the loud but rote cheering for Ceausescu. On December 1, 1983, at the celebration of the Union of Transylvania with the *Regat* (Old Country of Wallachia and Moldavia), for example, the occasion turned into a worship service for Ceausescu. The orchestrated Hitler-style devotion to the cult leader was anathema to me. During such jump-and-cheer for Ceausescu and Communism moments, I decided to draw the line by not standing. On occasion one or two other ambassadors stayed seated with me or stood late and sat down early (the Danish and Canadian envoys most often joined me). I felt that it went beyond the requirements of protocol to stand up for repeated homage to Ceausescu's divinity and to the Communist Party's victory over capitalism and the West. The other diplomats stood automatically—while complaining privately—with the Communist stooges robotized for the occasion. So my action got the notice of the authorities. They did not like it one bit, but an international incident was not made of it. The embassy's consular chief John Vessey III said that my not standing was the talk of the town. A Romanian National Assembly official told me that I was noticed not standing with the other diplomats.

At the opening of the Romanian Communist Party's 13th Congress on November 19, 1984, Ceausescu talked for over two hours on Romania's achievements—mainly economic—and future successes. The captive troops leaped to their feet for the beloved son referred to as the chosen one and leader of the greatest era in Romanian history. They screamed as usual: *Ceausescu si Partidul, Ceausescu si Poporul, Ceausescu la Congres (ul) Reales* (Ceausescu and the Communist Party, Ceausescu and the People, Ceausescu at the Congress reelected), and other such praise. In view of this experience, the United States government should establish guidelines that enable its representatives to refrain from such un-American and un-democratic actions, while of course carrying out the minimum protocol requirements needed for correct relations with such Stalinist regimes.

Early in my tenure as ambassador, I was successful in removing the Romanian national employees (who worked for Romanian intelligence) from the embassy chancery.* This action went against the preferences of the leaders at the State Department, who argued for "open embassies" and pleasing the Romanian employees. State Department officials tried to discourage me from taking this action. Romanian Communists opposed it because it diminished their possibilities of collecting intelligence information from the sensitive areas of the American embassy. In the wake of the spy scandal at the U.S. Embassy in Moscow in 1986 and 1987, belated efforts were made by Foggy Bottom to reduce or end the presence of national employees in American embassies throughout the Soviet Bloc. But in the early 1980s, such ideas for enhancing U.S. national security were not welcomed or appreciated.

We hosted numerous dinners, luncheons, and receptions on special occasions at the ambassadorial residence, sometimes inviting Romania's leading religious, cultural, and political dissidents. The biggest annual event at the residence was the Fourth of July celebration, which was attended by approximately two thousand peo-

---

*Our embassy in Bucharest was the first in a Warsaw Pact country to "secure" its chancery building by removing the "national" employees.

ple. It was at such receptions that we could more easily invite large numbers of pastors and priests, and writers and other cultural figures, as well as the expected officials, diplomats, and embassy employees. Many of those being harassed by the government later told us that their attendance at events at the residence helped give them a measure of "protection if not increased status in the eyes of the authorities." Such occasions gave us the opportunity to meet these courageous people. Also, embassy officers were able to get the latest information on the plight of the dissidents. The record shows, however, that most Foreign Service establishment ambassadors have not invited such "problem" individuals who might offend the Communist government.

The State Department has supported efforts by American ambassadors in places like Chile and Nicaragua, to establish contacts with Communists and others of the radical left. It appears that there is a greater willingness to have America's representatives contact Communists, than to monitor the plight of those persecuted by Communist regimes. The State Department stood ready to join their Romanian Communist counterparts in disavowing the anti-Communist U.S. Ambassador in Bucharest. The concern at State was more to prevent rocking the boat or offending Ceausescu, than to advertise human rights abuses or to aim for reciprocity in the bilateral relationship.

CHAPTER SEVEN:

Washington Meetings With President Reagan and Secretary Shultz

By the spring of 1983 I had been on the job for a year and a half. I was tiring of my battles with the State Department, and I decided to take my case higher up. I wrote a letter to Faith Ryan Whittlesey who was then the Assistant to the President for Public Liaison at the White House. In a letter which spelled out my frustrations and concerns I mentioned that I would be spending two weeks in Washington for annual consultations at the State Department. I mentioned that the State policymakers were determined to maintain an illusory relationship with Romania.*

In the letter to Whittlesey (and in similar letters to others), I noted that the President had recommended that MFN status be withdrawn or that Romania stop implementing its education repayment decree. In their efforts to appease Romanian President Ceausescu even as he became more repressive and irrational, State officials took the initiative in proposing a solution whereby the U.S. would reward Romania for its bad behavior.

It was Ceausescu's place to revoke the decree which goes contrary to the Jackson-Vanik Amendment. Also it was Ceausescu's obligation to improve emigration procedures and the human rights record.

In an attachment to the letter to Whittlesey, I included these points. The U.S. State Department offered Romanian President Ceausescu a capitulative deal of dubious promises if only he would

*See Chart #2 on page 39.

be so kind as to stop implementation of a decree which violates the Jackson-Vanik Amendment and thus jeopardizes MFN status. The U.S. should not promise to mute Congressional criticism of Romania's deplorable human rights and emigration procedural bottlenecks; as Ceausescu warned us that he would not want MFN continued unless the U.S. called off Congressional and press criticism. The U.S. should not promise to financially and economically reward Ceausescu for his increasingly repressive decrees and policies. The U.S. should not take the initiative in proposing a package deal to save face for Ceausescu, which will appear to the Romanians and the world as a U.S. bailout and backdown from principle. The U.S. should not promise to assist Romania attain multiyear MFN in the future without guarantees of improved human rights and emigration procedures, since independence from the Soviets is not attainable or desired by Ceausescu. And the U.S. should not promise to restore MFN for only non-implementation of the decree, because its existence on the books could be used later.

Finally I noted that while State was cooking up an appeasement deal, Ceausescu's regime was becoming more dangerous by: cracking down on religious believers; making emigration more difficult if not impossible for many; violating human rights to a greater extent by various decrees such as the typewriter registration law; taking positions in Romanian newspapers, radio and television more critical of the U.S.; cutting down drastically on needed imports from the U.S. and other Western countries; making doing business more difficult for American businessmen; transferring technology from the U.S. and West to the U.S.S.R.; sending spies and hit men abroad to manipulate and get rid of enemies; and warning the U.S. after the President's MFN announcement that he would not tolerate American criticism of his internal policies and that he needed a package deal of financial rewards in return for not implementing the decree—a scam he had no doubt craftily devised all along.[1]

Faith Whittlesey cared enough to do something about my concerns, by helping set up a meeting for me with the President. On the 11th of August 1983, I met with President Reagan, Vice President Bush, Judge William Clark, and Counselor Edwin Meese, for half an hour in the Oval Office. The session which was set up chiefly by Faith Whittlesey resulted from my expressions of frustration and resentment that the State Department line on Eastern Europe and Romania in particular was not open to change either via new evidence or other views. Additionally, pressure was kept on me to downplay human rights concerns, and to support the trade of sensitive technology to Romania.

It was made clear to me that America's maintenance of a cordial relationship with Romania, was of paramount importance. This special friendship or association had to be preserved, despite Ceausescu's tyranny, repression, and unpopularity. New facts we sent in from the field regarding Romania's collaboration with Moscow, less than independent policy and harsh human rights records, greatly upset the old boy network whose minds were long ago made up on Romania. The game had to continue to be played and the careers of those involved in the past policy formulation had to be protected.

President Reagan started the conversation by telling a joke to lighten the atmosphere, having no doubt been forewarned that I had a story to tell. His joke had to do with a Romanian chef he had known in Hollywood and the chef's recipe for a Romanian omelette. His awareness and knowledge of Eastern Europe did not seem to go much beyond that expressed by his interest in Vice President Bush's forthcoming trip to Bucharest and other matters. But he was obviously more comfortable talking about the humorous anecdote from his past, politics, and the general situation of the Communist world, than with specific problems and differences of opinion in-house. The re-election of President Reagan and Senator Helms in North Carolina were mentioned with the President noting interest in Helms winning. I thanked him for the opportunity to express my concerns. I spent most of the time detailing my concerns about State implementation of the old policy which I did not feel was consistent with Reagan's administration.

I told the President that his stand *vis-à-vis* the Soviets in general, and toward the Romanians on the education repayment tax, had won him much admiration among the Romanian people. I added that as a political supporter of his I was trying to do the best job possible representing his views and U.S. interests. I was working to add a little realism to traditional U.S. policy toward Romania and Eastern Europe and to accentuate American values and principles. I also said that this was particularly important where a repressive Communist government cares little for either human rights or religious freedom. I expressed my concern about the U.S. getting too close personally to Ceausescu and noted that I alerted the Vice President on this matter in preparation for this visit to Romania. My advice was to say some nice words about Romania and even perhaps U.S.-Romanian relations, but not regarding Ceausescu personally or the government. I informed him that our common friend Faith Whittlesey had visited us in Romania during the previous year, and I pledged to be a good host for Bush's visit.

In getting down to the bottom line of what I considered wrong with U.S. policy toward Romania, I said that the State Department bureaucracy was frustrating the implementation of the President's foreign policy. I pointed out that it is often "lonely" for Reagan supporters to serve in the State Department, and that political appointees like myself were under constant fire.

I let the President know my appreciation for his annual Captive Nations Week addresses, which gave hope to the Romanian people. Such courageous statements reflecting both principle and reality made him admired by the people in Romania. But I reiterated to the President that in the course of trying to reflect and carry out a Reagan foreign policy it was "lonely over there." This isolation was made worse by the pressures from Foggy Bottom. I mentioned that I was being pressured to approve the sale of sensitive technology to Romania that was not in our best interest. Judge Clark reminded the President that Defense Secretary Caspar Weinberger had briefed them on that subject and was supportive of my position. I also said that I was being pressured to downplay my concern for human rights.

Counselor Meese listed names and asked me to respond. Was it the Secretary of State? Was it Assistant Secretary Burt? Was it the Under Secretary of State for Political Affairs Eagleburger? I nodded in response to the last name. I mentioned the human rights situation in Romania and the need for greater realism dealing with Romania and Eastern Europe. Romania's leader was repressive, unpopular, and less independent than was earlier presumed. The President, who appeared surprised at all this and perhaps a little upset at hearing of division in the ranks, nevertheless indicated his concern, sympathy, and understanding.

Following the meeting with the President, I spoke individually with Clark, Meese, and Bush in their offices. Clark said that I was doing exactly what I should and that I had the support of the President himself. He said that I should get to know two individuals at the NSC—namely Paula Dobriansky and John Lenczowski—and continue to send in cables that reported events as I saw them. In correspondence between us, Clark was always supportive. In his letter of November 30, 1982, referring to the high tech issue, Clark said that the "considerations . . . raised will certainly have an impact on United States Government decisions on technology transfers to Romania." Meese was also supportive. He told me to keep up the good work and hang in there. Bush, however, inquired if I had told this to Secretary of State Shultz and wondered aloud how bad the situation was at State in my view. He seemed concerned only about the fact that I brought it to light, embarrassing Shultz, not the problem itself. Without doubt he immediately proceeded to contact his friend at State, and passed on to Shultz the grievances I had presented to the President.

Having ended my consultations in Washington with the meetings in the White House, I flew to Raleigh-Durham Airport and drove to the home of my wife's parents in Pinebluff, North Carolina. No sooner had I arrived that evening when I got a telephone call summoning me to return to Washington to meet with the Secretary of State the next day. Secretary of State Shultz and his Deputy Secretary of State Kenneth Dam were present. Shultz dressed me down for criticizing him before the President. I assured the Secretary that I did not criticize him personally, but criticized the department bureaucracy and other individuals. Shultz said that as the former head of a corporation he knew that he had responsibility for his organization and that any criticism of it was criticism of him. Shultz asked me for specifics about my complaints regarding Eagleburger, which I gave him. It was obvious that Shultz was a close ally of Eagleburger.

My general frustrations were expressed to Shultz in the following manner. I have worked through State channels and have done everything possible in the last two years to gain the support, good will, and respect of the career State Department people. I have a good relationship with those in the embassy. The Inspector General's team recently visited Bucharest and reported that morale was high and that we were doing a good job.

The inspection report showed that morale ranged from good to excellent in a post known for its low morale.* It reported that staff morale was good in part due to the ambassador who made improvements in recreational and community activities for the Americans and kept up a heavy representational schedule which included the Americans. Also the report noted the effective way in which the embassy was representing American interests. It additionally noted

*See pages 20 and 319 for mention of the inspection report.

the ambassador's knowledge and experience of the country from earlier stays and his language knowledge.

When policy is made I support it, but those of us at the embassy wanted to be heard in the process. I said that I felt the time had come for me to strongly express my concerns and suggestions regarding Romania and East-West relations. It is my belief that if we grant credits, aid, and high tech via favored nation treatment when Ceausescu was becoming more paranoid and repressive we would be making a big mistake. With an increasingly deplorable human rights record and a foreign policy not really independent of Moscow, our aid was going in return for next to nothing. In my view, in a process of reassessment of our policy, Romania was an example of a past policy of aid and trade not leading to increased leverage or internal liberalization or foreign policy acts of independence. Greater reciprocity and a *quid pro quo* would be desirable, I noted. But it seemed that the more we called for realism in our policy, concern for human rights, and no technology transfer, as well as reciprocity in the relationship, the more pressure we came under. Since Shultz had obviously not read the previous cables or shown concern or awareness of the efforts we were making, I had in mind three particular examples.

First, officials in the Eastern Europe office told me that Human Rights and Humanitarian Affairs Assistant Secretary Elliott Abrams should not head the 1984 U.S.-Romanian Human Rights Roundtable, because he had offended the Romanian government with comments he made during a Radio Free Europe interview. Nevertheless, Abrams ultimately did head the Human Rights Roundtable.

Secondly, I had said during a meeting between the Deputy Assistant Secretary of State Mark Palmer and Romanian Ambassador to Washington Mircea Malitza, that the United States should not give away its values and beliefs. When Romania's Ambassador screamed about the inclusion of the phrase—in a joint statement—"the United States strongly believes in free emigration," Palmer capitulated and watered down the statement over my protest. With that I walked out of the meeting in disgust.

Thirdly, I received an eyes only cable from Eagleburger filled with distortions. It clearly implied that I should not require the Romanians to live up to their fall 1982 commitments to Abrams regarding emigration procedures. The cable continued to spell out the policies of Eagleburger in case I did not remember what they were. I responded item by item in a return cable to Eagleburger.

Being in disagreement with Eagleburger's policies, I considered it necessary to take my concerns higher up.

The meeting with the Secretary made it obvious that little was known at the higher levels about the issues concerning Romania, and that State policy was handled out of Eagleburger's office. At one point Shultz said he thought Eagleburger was taking care of things there i.e. regarding Eastern Europe. Only two political appointees were above him at State—Shultz and Dam. It was Eagleburger's protégé DAS Mark Palmer and other colleagues in the East European Affairs Office and at the Romania Desk, who looked after most of the day to day details in U.S.-Romanian relations. These officials were all agreed on keeping the Kissinger-Eagleburger policy toward Eastern Europe in place.

Naturally the Secretary shared the events of August 11th and 12th with Eagleburger in the same way Bush had shared the events of August 11th with him. Eagleburger, to put it mildly, was livid about it. From the day of my appointment Eagleburger had ensured that I was left outside the power curve. Everything sent by the embassy in Bucharest to the State Department was treated as tainted. This had forced me to use whatever outside channels I could to get my views aired. It was not easy. Virtually every group, official or unofficial, visiting Romania was briefed at State that the "ambassador is bad news" and is considered off-the-wall by the State Department leadership. They were advised not to pay any attention to Funderburk. A friend in the department told me the word in the halls was that "Funderburk was on Larry Eagleburger's hit list." Press articles were leaked, or rather planted, by the State group to discredit and denigrate me. Articles appearing in *The Washingtonian* and *Mother Jones* grouped me with other "bad" political appointees as a right wing Helmsite based on pre-appointment descriptions. Not a word was said about my then two years as ambassador.[2]

Shultz had sat there Buddha-like showing little emotion or expression but conveying determination and pomposity. He ended the conversation by extending the olive branch of cuff links and pins so I "might feel more like part of the State Department." I gratefully took the trinkets but have yet to wear them. And they did not help give me a feeling of belonging to the club at 2201 C Street Northwest, Washington, D.C.

A series of meetings in Washington between the Romanian Foreign Minister and top American officials such as Vice President Bush and Secretary of State Shultz further heightened my frustration and dismay over the extreme eagerness to appease the Romanian Communists. The toughness of Senator Helms in his May 16th, 1983, meeting with Romanian Foreign Minister Andrei was followed by the comparative weakness of the State Department officials the next day. But immediately after the meeting with Helms, Vice President Bush saw Andrei. Bush mentioned that if the invitation to visit Romania was still open he would like to do so. Bush also said that he was glad the U.S. and Romanian officials were near agreement on the major divisive matter of the education repayment tax. Nothing that was said by Bush was tough or requested improvement in Romania's deplorable human rights, emigration, or general domestic situation.

The Andrei sessions with Shultz, Eagleburger, and underling Palmer were the most disappointing. On May 17th, Shultz mentioned specifically that two or three years was the U.S. understanding of Romania's newly imposed work/service requirement for an education obligation to the state. He further stated that any additional imposition of roadblocks in the way of emigration would be contrary to our understanding and would create problems. After the "obligatory" counsel to the Romanians under the circumstances, the Secretary turned the discussion to international topics of interest to show appreciation for Romania's positions and elicit Romania's advice. The Secretary said that he hoped the Romanians would pass a message to the Syrians to come to agreement with the U.S. As usual Andrei (echoing Soviet wishes) said that the U.S. needed to involve the Soviets in any agreement in the Middle East. Andrei made a point of saying—as if the Romanians were reading our mail or had a "plant" on the U.S. side—that Romania would like to purchase high tech items and would of course not transfer them. He said we had their assurances that they would not transfer high tech to the Soviets.

I had written many top U.S. officials in the fall of 1982, regarding the danger of providing Romania with high tech items. While Secretary Shultz was one of those to whom I wrote, I never got a reply from him.

Andrei also said that EXIM loans were important to Romania. Shultz and Eagleburger responded that they would contact William H. Draper, III, President and Chairman of the Export-Import Bank once again. They recommended that Andrei meet with Draper. Brief mentions were made of Middle East questions, Central America, China, and zero options. But Andrei saved his sharpest words for the negotiations on the emigration question, essentially trying to intimidate the Americans present.

Andrei warned that additional changes should not be made in the education repayment-emigration arrangement, and noted that last minute changes had already caused things to slip. While Andrei expressed concern in a blustery manner, he told Eagleburger that Palmer had done a good job and that the Romanian government was pleased with the State Department's assistance and cooperation. It clearly appeared that Andrei showed fake resentment that the U.S. would dare propose a change—even if minor. He stood firm as a typical negotiating tactic. At the same time Andrei did not mention that the Romanian officials had asked for more changes earlier which were granted! Eagleburger patting Andrei on the back figuratively thanked Bucharest for tough positions *vis-à-vis* the Soviets. He also noted that Yugoslavia needed and appreciated Romania's buffer position between them and the U.S.S.R.

The worst aspect of the negotiations with the Romanians was the concessionary position of State Department officials, who had played a key role in bringing about the arrangement. Mark Palmer, and Jonathan Rickert—the Romania Desk Officer—had generally worked things out with Romania's ambassador. Palmer had not insisted on a side letter which included assurances of non-implementation of the education decree, or a specified time for any education work/service requirements. Similarly, he had not pushed for a shorter specific emigration processing/procedural time, or for an end to harassment of those who applied for emigration. After all, Romania's Ambassador Malitza had said that there was no such harassment. Rickert's position was that the Romanians had accomplished one of the three main 1982 assurances of emigration procedural changes, i.e. emigration numbers were kept up at a good level, and the emigration was smoother—monthly numbers were more uniform than in the previous year when there was the typical jump just before MFN hearings. To Rickert, one out of three was not bad even though the processing time imposed on emigrants and the harassment meted out to those who had applied to leave the country continued unabated. Palmer and Rickert *et al* in the department generally played the game in order to carry out the script of Eagleburger to salvage MFN and the special relationship. They were apparently oblivious to unfulfilled Romanian assurances given to Congress and Elliott Abrams the previous year.

I was so shaken by what appeared blatant capitulation to the

Romanians that I typed a statement for State Department officials of observations detailing many of my concerns at that time. In my "Observations of May 18, 1983," I recommended consideration and inclusion of certain concerns (below) before signing a Presidential letter and a side letter of Ambassador Malitza in order to protect President Reagan's position and U.S. interests while keeping in mind Romania's failure to live up to 1982 assurances regarding emigration and human rights improvements. With regard to the main bone of contention in 1983—the education decree and emigration—I spelled out what I thought the U.S. side needed to say. Obviously this reflected the fact that the Romanians had gotten the best of the State Department negotiators, and my disappointment at not having more success in firmly representing American interests.

I wrote that the U.S. should make clear its strong support of the principle of free emigration. Also I pointed out that precise written assurances for the future and concrete evidence of changes including non-implementation of the education tax for those emigrating to any country in the world were necessary before the President could actively back MFN renewal. I felt that this was required in view of Romania's failure to live up to the written assurances of 1982 to Senators Helms and Jackson as well as Abrams, that emigration procedures including processing time and harassment would be improved significantly. Ambassador Malitza, for example, had expressed Romanian agreement to reduce processing time of applicants for emigration to nine months the first year and six months thereafter. However, a year later those promises had not been kept.

With regard to the future, I wrote that specific guarantees should be given that more educated and skilled emigrants would be permitted to leave and that no further barriers—beyond the existent economic and procedural—would be placed in the way of emigrants. Thus a specific minimal time could be delineated as a work or service expectation for those who had higher education in Romania so that some vague and general time could not be arbitrarily imposed as a means of restricting emigration. Finally, I said that the Romanian government should improve human rights conditions and facilitate the emigration of U.S. "representational" lists of applicants periodically given to Bucharest. In view of Congressional concerns, U.S. values and principles and past promises, the President's credibility and future leverage, the above concerns should be expressed to the Romanian government. I attached notes regarding

Romania's non-independent foreign policy, and the question of technology transfer. This document was undoubtedly one of the things which "provoked" Eagleburger into sending his threatening cable with off-the-wall charges to me in Bucharest shortly thereafter.

*Funderburk with Secretary of State Al Haig at airport press
conference, Bucharest*

*Funderburk with Vice President George Bush
& Romanian officials in Bucharest*

*Vice President Bush with Romanian Foreign Minister Andrei &
Ambassador Malitza (both on couch) in the Vice President's office*

*Funderburk with Secretary of State George Shultz
at the State Department*

Funderburk family (Britt, Betty, Deana & David) with Reagan

*Oval Office Meeting with Meese, Reagan, Funderburk,
Bush & Clark (l to r)*

Funderburk with Reagan in the White House

Under Secretary of State Lawrence Eagleburger with Funderburk in embassy chancery building

With Mrs. Funderburk and Mr. & Mrs. Max Kampelman in Bucharest

Washington Meetings With Lawrence Eagleburger, Elliott Abrams and Senator Jesse Helms

The Eagleburger Affair

The central figure in U.S.-Romanian relations during my diplomatic stint was Lawrence Eagleburger who served first as Assistant Secretary of State for European Affairs, and then as Under Secretary of State for Political Affairs—the third ranking position in the department and the highest ranking career diplomat position. Known either as Lawrence of Macedonia or The Eagle, Eagleburger was the epitome of the Foreign Service system. What distinguished him from the timid, lackluster technocrats in the bureaucracy was a knack for wielding power and his occasional flashes of boldness. One could sense his vindictive aspect, but he also projected a jovial and personable side.

Eagleburger was deeply involved in every aspect of American foreign policy *vis-à-vis* Europe in general and Eastern Europe in particular. In that part of the world Yugoslavia was his paramount concern, and, because of that, he took an important interest in Romania. He considered it his principal mission to maintain the differentiation policy set up by his mentor Kissinger. So MFN for Romania had to be retained at all costs.

The Romanian imposition of an education repayment tax decree, in 1983, precipitated the top crisis in U.S.-Romanian relations during my stay as ambassador. The decree announced that anyone who applied for emigration from Romania would be required to reimburse the state for each year of his or her higher education. The amounts required could in some cases exceed $50,000, a sum beyond the means of Romanians. The imposition of such a draconian tax measure was in direct violation of the Jackson-Vanik Amendment that was at the base of the U.S.-Romanian Trade Act and the MFN relationship. By heavily taxing emigrants and thus effectively putting near insurmountable obstacles in their way, the tax also violated several international agreements signed by the Romanians, such as the Helsinki accords.

Eagleburger took it upon himself to singlehandedly resolve the problem, and return the differentiation relationship on its normal course. In the process of trying to salvage the relationship, Eagleburger, as a worst case scenario, could see his orchestrated policy unraveling before his eyes.

On January 10, 1983, Larry Eagleburger arrived in Bucharest as a special Presidential envoy, delegated to go around me and the embassy to save the "special" relationship with Romania. Since it seemed that Ceausescu was hell-bent on a showdown, it was up to the U.S., led by Eagleburger, to save the relationship for Ceausescu and Romania. Eagleburger, as a friend, bluntly laid the cards on the table to Romanian Foreign Minister Andrei and President Ceausescu at a mountain retreat north of Bucharest. Andrei later described Eagleburger's treatment as that of a colonial power. At any rate the Romanians said that because they needed to save face. And following Rabbi Arthur Schneier's comment that Ceausescu needed some face-saving compromise, Eagleburger was no doubt feeling out the Romanians for hints of what the U.S. could do. Eagleburger was concerned about the dilemma the U.S. was in, and sought a joint solution to the problem. A few months later he sent Milton Rosenthal to Bucharest with the concession package of gifts if only Ceausescu would back off in terms of implementing the tax. Ceausescu would not even have to officially withdraw the decree, as long as non-implementation would be the result.

If Ceausescu had planned out such a crisis to divert U.S. attention from the other truly severe repression rampant throughout the country, he could not have done better. With America preoccupied with a probably bogus issue—the tax—Romania would get a free ride in obtaining MFN and have other rewards kicked in for good measure.

An abbreviated saga of the education repayment tax is as follows: The first case of implementation of the tax was on January 21st, less than two weeks after Eagleburger's visit. On January 24th,

Consular chief John Vessey III, notified me of the first confirmed-in-writing case of the decree's implementation. The Bucharest authorities required a payment of $7,400 for studies by Margareta Paslaru Sencovici. In a meeting with Congressman Tom Lantos' delegation on February 10th, Foreign Minister Andrei said the decree was irrevocable. Andrei added that the U.S. should "carefully" handle any publicity regarding MFN withdrawal.

I noted in my diary that we had probably reached a turning point in U.S.-Romanian relations and that it appeared the post-MFN period would soon be beginning. In a Voice of America editorial of February 13th, the VOA condemned the education tax *ransom* and said that Romania would no longer get MFN if the tax continued. But in a bombshell cable from Washington on February 24th, the State Department hedged on any MFN-withdrawal pronouncement. In view of state back-pedaling, I recommended that Washington stand firm. On March 4th, it was officially stated to the Romanians that MFN would be withdrawn on June 30th if the situation continued as it was.

In April, however, the State Department was hustling to prepare a package of gifts for Ceausescu so that he would back off in implementing the tax. Eagleburger did not want me to get in the way of keeping the MFN relationship with Romania. The State Department elite was determined to find a way to save Bucharest from itself.

Eagleburger sent me a threatening, *Eyes Only* cable dated May 28th. Eagleburger warned me to back off from human rights/emigration concerns. Perhaps his goal was to solve the education tax problem without any glitches. But he was saying that we did not have the right to *again* alert the department to potential problems associated with leaving the decree intact. Also, he erroneously said that I told the Israeli Ambassador in Bucharest that the U.S. would likely recommend MFN even without a Romanian-Israeli agreement on the matter. I had in reality told the Israeli Ambassador the opposite. Having had very good relations with both the Jewish community in Bucharest and the Israeli Embassy, I asked Ambassador Zvi Brosh over to the American Embassy for a private chat. When I explained the situation to him, he agreed that I had not said what Eagleburger claimed and that he would contact Washington and Tel Aviv to straighten things out. The problem was that he never did inform them of the truth.[1]

I wrote to Senator Jesse Helms and to Faith Whittlesey about the

Eagleburger threats and charges. Largely because of the efforts of
Faith Whittlesey, I was able to take my case dealing with the whole
Romania problem to the President. In a subsequent meeting with
the Secretary of State, I told Shultz about the Eagleburger
intimidation—for all the good that would do. Eagleburger continued
his attacks on me even after I left government service. During my
U.S. Senate campaign, he made several more charges in a newspaper interview which were not true. At the same time, he gave
the maximum individual financial contribution to the liberal Democrat running for the Senate from North Carolina. He did this despite the fact that he reportedly is a moderate-liberal Republican
originally from Wisconsin. Meanwhile, he works, appropriately,
as the head of Kissinger Associates, which among other things are
consultants in dealings with foreign countries including Communist
ones. Eagleburger had served as ambassador to Communist Yugoslavia, in addition to his other positions at the top of the career
ladder at State. In 1986 sales of Yugos—the Yugoslav made car
priced under $4,000 were going very well in the United States.[2]

Elliott Abrams and Human Rights

From the standpoint of a Reagan conservative in the State Depart-
ment, I found Elliott Abrams to be fair, courageous, and helpful.
As Assistant Secretary of State for Human Rights and Humanitarian
Affairs, Abrams was in a key position regarding U.S. relations with
Romania. In June of 1982, Abrams told me that he would support
my efforts to demonstrate greater concern for human rights in
Romania. At the same time, Abrams was a State Department employee subject to the directives of the highest officials in the State
Department, including Eagleburger whose interest in Eastern Europe was paramount. Abrams did what he could to support my
concerns—helped in drafting position papers and reports dealing
with human rights violations in Romania, and he spoke out at Human Rights Roundtables and in Radio Free Europe and Voice of
America broadcasts. Like me, he pushed for a tougher line than
the leadership elite of the European Affairs Bureau at State was willing to support. The European Affairs Bureau would water down
Abrams' statements or official department papers dealing with human rights and take a softer line less offensive to the Communist
regimes of Eastern Europe. For the most part, Abrams would advocate firm positions in debate and discussion within the department, but in the end, he would back the official department line.

As Eagleburger had put it: "up to the decision, fight; after, salute and march."[3]

We stayed in touch on a fairly regular basis both officially and privately. But two of the most important occasions involving human rights concerns in U.S-Romania relations were the 1983 education tax imposed by the Romanian government—which forced anyone applying for emigration from Romania to reimburse the state for his higher education, at a price that few Romanians could afford, and that, in any event, was a direct violation of the Helsinki accords and the Jackson-Vanik Amendment; and the U.S.-Romanian Human Rights Roundtable in Washington in February 1984.

In October of 1982, Abrams traveled to Bucharest for talks with the Romanian government. Abrams candidly told the Romanian officials that the more independence Romania showed in foreign policy, the warmer relations would be with the U.S. Abrams courageously related that most Americans do not think MFN is in America's best interest, particularly because of religious persecution and human rights abuses. The only problem is that astute Communists would recognize such language—if isolated to tough talk by Abrams and Funderburk—did not really reflect general State Department concerns. Thus it would have less effect if not joined by a consistently firm line by the U.S. government.

The Romanians were represented by Deputy Foreign Ministers Maria Groza and Aurel Duma, and Foreign Ministry Consular chief Gheorghe Badescu, among others. They stated, at the outset, Ceausescu's dictum that Romania is not a country of emigration. Romanian officials are experts in turning the tables by going on the offensive when charged with violations. Using Orwellian doubletalk, Badescu said that Romania had adhered to all international commitments and has always observed the Helsinki Final Act, but the U.S. was the only one in violation of Helsinki by requiring refugees to stay in camps against their will. One category of Romanians leaving passed through a center in Italy for about a week for both medical exams and processing. While perhaps a minor irritant, this has proved to be no real problem but in fact, a way to get those out of Romania in past years who were dissidents—religious or political refugees—without relatives in the U.S. The Romanians claimed that ten times more (than in reality) were actually returning to Romania after arriving in the U.S. The actual figure is not even 1%.

Abrams pointed out that one of the most emotional issues in the

U.S. was the policy of harassing and punishing those planning to emigrate. The Romanians gave several responses, none of them truthful. Duma said that 99% of those applying for emigration keep their same jobs. Former Romanian Ambassador to the U.S. Corneliu Bogdan said that Romania has full employment. Groza said employment can be found after losing a job but not at the same level. Groza maintained preposterously that there is no system of harassment just because one wants to leave Romania. Finally, in the Abrams discussion of persistent reports of religious persecution and violations of religious freedom, the Romanian response was predictable. Duma argued that basically there was no religious problem since the churches are full. But that contention is not even close to accurate even after taking into consideration the fact that thousands of churches were destroyed by the Communists and thus many people do not have access to churches. Duma also said that Romania has 14 recognized cults (denominations), and that only with the Baptists are there problems because there are so many divisions among them. So much for dealing with those who lie.

In a discussion regarding Romanian harassment and delay of those applying for emigration, the Romanians assured Abrams that they were not really considering an education tax along the lines of the 1972 Soviet proposal.[4] Despite such an assurance from the Romanian officials, it was only a few months later when Bucharest began implementation of the draconian measure. Following the first case of implementation on January 24th, the Romanian Foreign Minister stated on February 10th, that decree implementation was irrevocable. Back in October of 1982, following Abrams' visit to Bucharest, his interviews with VOA and RFE were broadcast. RFE tended to get down to the nitty gritty and broadcast actual emigration and human rights cases on the air which the Romanian government resented. By contrast, VOA was more conciliatory and deferential. But this time even in his VOA interview, Abrams lectured the Romanians on the need for "decent standards" in emigration if they wanted to keep MFN status. Abrams pointed out that Congressional anger, frustration and opposition were mounting, and that Romanian promises would have to be kept regarding their pledges to reduce harassment and delay practices toward emigration applicants. If Romanian promises are not kept, Congress and the President would not approve MFN according to Abrams.[5] The RFE broadcast was put in even more blunt terms and provoked the angry response of the Romanian government. The State Department, concerned about the tough talk of Communist "friends," tried to distance themselves from the Abrams statements while quietly assuring the Romanians that he had overstepped his bounds (in making such tough talk).

On February 1, 1983, I wrote a letter to Abrams similar to the ones I wrote to Judge Clark, Senator Helms and Faith Whittlesey, among others, while I was ambassador. These letters expressed my reservations about a U.S. policy granting MFN without reciprocal improvements in human rights and emigration. They refute the false claims made by Eagleburger and Assistant Secretary of State for European Affairs, Richard Burt, in a newspaper interview.[6] Specifically, I wrote to Abrams that the MFN relationship was not worth "ignoring American beliefs, values and principles, or the Jackson-Vanik Amendment," and that we should not "downplay human rights and emigration concerns in order to preserve the MFN relationship."[7] I said that I did not believe MFN was in the national interest from a security, strategic, or moral point of view, without a meaningful *quid pro quo* such as non-implementation of the education tax and substantial improvements in emigration procedures and fundamental human rights.[8]

On February 13th, a VOA editorial reflecting some of these concerns condemned the education tax implementation and warned that there would be no MFN if it continued. And on March 4th, the U.S. officially announced that MFN would be withdrawn on June 30th—after an effort was made back on February 24th to backpedal on the previous condemnation. In the meantime, Abrams responded to my letter by expressing his support for my concerns and recommendations. He said that the U.S. would end MFN and stand by its principles and laws for all the reasons I had stated. He also mentioned that we had similar views on a lot of foreign policy issues including Romania and that I had "consistently argued for greater realism in U.S.-Romanian relations."[9]

In preparation for the upcoming U.S.-Romanian Human Rights Roundtable in Washington, I wrote another letter to Abrams detailing my concerns that the resolution of the education tax might obfuscate the fact that human rights and general living conditions had worsened over the past few years.

A declining standard of living, worsening energy (heat, gas and lights) and food shortages, tighter security and a decline in health (increased alcoholism, poorer sanitation, worse conditions at hospitals and worse diets) had taken place. At the same time, religious repression, continued problems facing would-be emigrants, the non-resolution of the Father Calciu case, and heightened political and cultural repression, had created a deteriorating atmosphere in Romania in terms of fundamental human rights. I expressed my strong feeling and hope that the U.S. would make efforts to gain concessions or improvements in the areas of human rights, emigration and general conditions of life for the people i.e internal reform and liberalization, or otherwise our favored treatment and its concomitant aid would not be justified. Inasmuch as few changes can be expected under Ceausescu, it is even more incumbent upon the U.S. to firmly enunciate its immutable principles in terms of human dignity and our expectations for improvements in Romania. Finally, I stressed my pleasure in knowing that Abrams would be at the Human Rights Roundtable. Because, after all, Eagleburger and Palmer had noted their concern about Abrams' past tough talk and fear that his hard line might antagonize the Romanians.

At the U.S.-Romanian Human Rights Roundtable held in Washington February 27-29, 1984, Abrams told me that it was hard to talk to those who "lie, lie, lie." While the Romanian Communists presented a tough, united front with Deputy Foreign Minister Maria Groza, Director of Consular Affairs in the Foreign Ministry Gheorghe Badescu, and Ambassador Mircea Malitza, among others, the U.S. side was sharply divided in its perception of Communist Romania and in its goals for U.S. policy. Abrams was the head of the U.S. delegation which included myself; State Department officers Richard Combs, Roland Kuchel, Jonathan Rickert, and Judith Buncher, and U.S. CSCE representatives. It must be noted that Abrams, who should have been the logical choice to head the U.S. side, was not the pick of some State Department officials. In a conversation with a State Department Eastern European Affairs official, I was told that the concern was that Abrams would offend the Romanians because of an earlier presentation he had made e.g. the RFE interview. Therefore, it was with some apprehension that the State Department European Affairs Bureau agreed to let Abrams head the American delegation at the roundtable.

Communist officials know to use divide and rule tactics when Americans have widely differing views. American presentations ranged from CSCE Staff Assistant Lynne Davidson's hard hitting exposes of Romanian human rights violations, to USIA officer Alvin Perlman's supportive expressions of appreciation for Romania's "commendable efforts" and "positive and constructive manner."

Lynne Davidson noted that the CSCE received more letters of complaint about Romania than any other country in Eastern Europe, and that Romania has a serious image problem both to Congress and the U.S. public because of its poor human rights record. Since her presentation followed several be-kind-to-Romania papers, Ambassador Malitza responded strongly to Davidson's.

But the one which most bent the Romanians out of shape was that of Roger Whyte—Special Assistant to the Deputy Under Secretary for International Affairs of the U.S. Department of Labor, which was entitled "Human Rights and the ILO." Evidently the Romanians did not care to hear about ILO standards such as freedom of association for workers which Whyte stressed. He pointed out that Romania had ratified ILO Conventions concerning freedom of association. Finally Whyte said that the World Confederation of Labor had filed a complaint against Romania before the ILO because of Romania's crushing of the workers union formed in 1979. SLOMR, or the Free Trade Union of Romanian Workers, suffered the beatings, jailings and arrest and in some cases the disappearance of its members. The Romanian representatives said that Whyte was out of order because of Romania's membership in the ILO and transmissal of information to the ILO from Bucharest. They argued that all people have jobs, the right to strike exists, and Romania is in compliance with labor union formations.

While CSCE Staff Director Spencer Oliver reflected on individual cases candidly, whitewashes by Perlman and VOA Romania chief Ed Mainland were perhaps most typical of the disappointing sessions. Even one of Mainland's colleagues from USIA told me that Mainland had totally capitulated at the roundtable to the disappointment of many.

The Romanians present at the roundtable consistently stuck to their propaganda line—confident that they would get away with it. Thus Badescu said there is no question of losing jobs in Romania after applying for emigration. The truth, however, is that losing a job after applying to emigrate is more the rule than the exception. Badescu also made the ludicrous statement that the U.S., by protecting human rights, was giving credit to persons who have committed crimes against the Communist state but became political refugees when they reached other countries. Madame Groza made the dubious claim that Romania has health care, free education and adequate material support and pensions for all people. She said that whereas Americans mention violations, Romanians mention observance of human rights, reflecting different approaches. In response to Abrams' report of religious persecution and violation of religious rights—such as church closings, harassment of pastors and even demolition of churches like the one attended by Funderburk—the Romanians said that religious freedom is reflected by the existence of 11,000 Orthodox churches and 14 authorized cults. They did not, however, mention the thousands of churches destroyed since the Communist take-over.

In my presentation on emigration, I tried to address the basic problems in the big picture. The U.S. Embassy is inundated with the hundreds of Romanians who come into the consular section and with the hundreds of letters from Congress, human rights and religious groups and individuals. Americans are free to leave the U.S., and the U.S. did not create a backlog of Romanians trying to leave Romania. If there are basic human rights, economic and social opportunities, political and religious freedoms and an improving standard of living, why do so many thousands of Romanians want so desperately to leave Romania? The real origin of the problem, then, is the conditions of life which lead people to leave and the lack of free emigration from Romania. Some of the Romanians with approval to leave do not meet U.S. eligibility and some are undesirables. The U.S. believes in the right of free emigration, but does not have the obligation to take every immigrant from Haiti, Vietnam, or Romania who wants to improve his economic or other standard of living.

A most serious problem in U.S.-Romanian relations regarding emigration is the harassment of many of those applying for emigration. The harassment—often described in part as emigration procedure problems—included the loss of jobs-belongings-residences, delays of 1½ to 2 years or more before departure, high and numerous payments required, and loss of citizenship and/or the rights of a citizen. And those approved for departure were typically given only a brief few months before losing their passport exit visa validity. The Romanians stated their position on emigration with Badescu, saying that they did not agree with me regarding the question of jobs lost.

One example of the State Department elite weighing in to limit tough talk which might be offensive to the Romanian Communists, came with the preparation of the press statement to be released at the end of the U.S.-Romanian Human Rights Roundtable. It was Abrams and myself—not the department elite—who wanted included in the final press statement that the U.S. "reiterated its belief that human rights issues are central to the Helsinki Process, and restated its commitment to respect human rights and political freedoms and to press for full compliance with the human rights provision of the Helsinki Final Act and the Madrid Concluding Document."[10] Similarly the State Department's Eastern Europe Office did not want to include that the talks were held in the context of Helsinki and Madrid specifically to discuss human rights and basic freedoms.

Senator Jesse Helms

I stayed in periodic contact with Senator Helms with perhaps a few personal letters a year. And I met with the Senator about once a year in his Washington office. There were no cable exchanges through official channels except those dealing with immigration cases. Generally speaking we knew where each other stood on the issues and thus had no real need for frequent meetings or correspondence. The fact is that in Washington, Senator Helms works on a wide range of international and national concerns perhaps with some emphasis on Central and South American developments because of his committee responsibilities.

Aside from my presence in Bucharest, the Senator had long been a champion for the concerns of persecuted religious believers and political dissidents in Communist lands and had specifically gone to bat for countless individuals in need in Romania. During my tenure as ambassador, no one—with the possible exception of Senator Howard Metzenbaum of Ohio, which is one of the main centers for ethnic "Romanian" immigrants from Romania—sent more letters and cables in behalf of Romanians. Hundreds of pieces of correspondence came to my office at the American Embassy in Bucharest from the office of Senator Helms. He demonstrated a great interest in and concern for hundreds of desperate Romanians even though most—probably 95%—of the cases involved families living in states other than North Carolina. In other words, one did not have to have an association with North Carolina and thus be a constituent of the Senator, to enlist his concern and assistance.

Beyond the consular case letters and those religious-political-cultural figures punished by the regime who did not seek emigration, Senator Helms got involved in other ways as a champion of freedom fighters. Examples from letters and representations Helms made to the Romanian authorities are the following: "I am con-

strained to speak out for the human rights of this family and I trust
that your government will reconsider the very counterproductive
treatment that it has evidently been meting out to them" (May 12,
1982); "I am always more than happy to back up his efforts on behalf of the Christian believers in that afflicted country" (March 3,
1982); "I gave them a long list of individuals reported to us to be
among the oppressed" (July 6, 1982); and "I call this situation to
your attention in the sincere hope that you will use your good offices
to remove whatever obstacles may be impeding the unification of
this family, which is their human right" (November 30, 1983).
Helms has been in the forefront of Congressional figures who took
the time to do something to help the Romanian and other persecuted
peoples behind the Iron Curtain.

Other ways in which Senator Helms impacted on U.S.-Romanian
relations and the lives of persecuted Romanians included: his meeting with Romanian officials, sponsorship of legislation, and peti-
tions for pressuring the Romanian government to reform and the
U.S. government to develop a realistic and pro-American interests
policy. On June 29, 1982, Senator Helms told me that he would slap
amendment legislation to deny Romania Most Favored Nation treaty
status if real progress was not made in their domestic situation and
immigration cases.

A meeting between Romanian Foreign Minister Stefan Andrei,
and Senator Helms took place on May 16, 1983, in the Senator's
office. Earlier a Romanian official had mentioned that I could not
get a meeting for Andrei with Helms. So I relayed the request of
the Foreign Minister for such a meeting to Senator Helms via the
Embassy-State Department channels. Thus the May 16th session
was arranged for the afternoon following a Department of Commerce luncheon and before the meeting with Vice President Bush.
I had not seen the Senator for about eight months or talked with
him prior to the meeting. I entered his office with the Romanian
Foreign Minister, the Romanian Ambassador (Malitza) and Romanian Foreign Ministry North American Affairs Director Mircea
Raceanu. Present with Senator Helms from his own office were
aides Dr. Jim Lucier and Kathy Stoner. Helms said at the outset:
"I should not be meeting with you gentlemen or let you in my office because you have not lived up to the assurances and promises
of last year." The Senator went on to say that he would lead the
fight against MFN for Romania unless real assurances of resolu-

tion of the emigration and human rights cases could be provided along with an end to the education tax decree.

Ambassador Malitza said that he had provided the Senator with a letter, item by item, of the cases submitted, resolving them. But Kathy Stoner was there with a packet of documents on the unresolved cases. Stoner questioned: what about Father Calciu who is in prison or dead, who knows? Andrei and Malitza said that the Calciu case was another matter and that as they had said before, it would be resolved when Calciu applied for emigration through the government. This was the official Romanian line. Jim Lucier, showing close awareness of the case, said in other words that Calciu would have to admit guilt for the charged crimes. It was the same old sham presentation by the Romanians: that Calciu was in good health and did not want out. Stoner pointed out that many other cases were unresolved, and that Malitza's promises in the letter were not lived up to by the Romanians. Helms said that he had only reluctantly agreed to hold the meeting in the first place because of his regard for the U.S. ambassador who had access to him anytime he wanted it.

Following the clash, Senator Helms said that he would wipe the slate clean and start over again. He asked for a letter of assurances which would be lived up to. Otherwise, he would lead the fight against MFN. Andrei, who was visibly upset, said that he was late for a meeting with the Vice President and had to leave. I think it is safe to say that Malitza and Andrei had probably never heard more frank and firm talk than in their meeting with Helms. Such action by the Senator helped support my position in Bucharest. He could be tougher than I could talking with them because I had to return to Bucharest to work day to day. If only the U.S. presented a tough united front to the Romanians, much could be accomplished in the relationship. Because there is little doubt that in the final analysis the Romanian Communist leaders—like the Soviets, having risen to their positions by sheer ruthlessness and shrewd skills—appreciate strength and toughness shown by an adversary. Deep down they do not respect the stereotype State Department officer who too eagerly gives them what they want and understands them only superficially.

After the meeting Helms asked me if he was tough enough on them. I responded that he had been and that I was thankful for it. Stoner added that Malitza was the lyingest s.o.b. she had ever seen.

I thought to myself then: thank God Helms was not afraid to say what needed to be said and what others may not want to hear. Both the Romanians and State Department officials undoubtedly considered that I was behind Senator Helms's words with the Romanians. They did not understand that Helms did not need advice or instructions on what to tell the Communist regime in Bucharest. The next morning, prior to the Secretary of State's meeting with Andrei, I was told by State Department officials that Andrei was breathing fire and ready to explode after the session with Helms. In the meeting with Shultz, Andrei did show some anger. Thus, it had its desired effect in my book.

In a letter from Helms to Andrei, following the meeting, Helms noted that he had previously expressed that U.S. concern over emigration procedures was broader than interest in individual cases. Helms further added that while the education repayment tax had been rescinded—actually nonimplementation was pledged—the overall situation in Romania had worsened. The same emigration problems of harassment during lengthy processing were in effect. Helms reminded Andrei that Malitza had promised specifically to improve the procedures. And Helms astutely stated that "the imposition of a totally new education tax must be viewed as a cynical 'bargaining chip,' an attempt to make the emigration process so onerous that even a return to the status quo would seem to be a relief."[11] The Father Calciu case was mentioned with Helms holding Andrei to the Romanian promise to allow a representative from the American Embassy in Bucharest to visit Calciu. Finally, Helms had included another list of persons unable to emigrate from Romania who had asked for help. And he added that only significant progress on the matters mentioned would convince him and his colleagues in the Senate not to go forward with legislation to disallow MFN for Romania.[12]

The Romanian government followed its usual cynical practice of making a few minor concessions just before MFN renewal time, and then acting harshly against dissidents after winning MFN during the summer. Senator Helms, in response, started the process of rallying Senate opposition to Romanian MFN.

Senator Helms wrote that "the conduct of the Romanian Communist government is an outrage." He said that Romanian Ambassador Malitza was told that there were a number of Senators ready to "take the strongest possible action against Romania if this sort of persecution of Christians does not stop." Helms continued by writing that "these people are totally devoid of character, and I have recommended to the President and the Secretary of State that we refuse to tolerate the senseless behavior of the Romanian government. As usual, however, the State Department underlings are being dilatory as they always are when Communists are involved."[13]

On the eve of Senator Helms's reelection in 1984, his campaign announced on October 25th, the endorsement of the Senator by 22 U.S. ambassadors. The unusual action by so many active Reagan Administration officials produced a spate of articles in the national and North Carolina press. The background in my case was simply that Jim Lucier, in the Senator's office, asked some months earlier if I would lend my name to the list of ambassadors endorsing the Senator's reelection campaign. I said that of course I would. Later, in speeches, I pointed out that for the future defense of the Free World in its struggle against Marxist-Leninist tyranny, it was more important for Senator Helms to get reelected than it was to fret over any diplomatic tradition. The complete list of those endorsing Helms is as follows:[14]

Abshire, David	NATO
Anderson, Thomas	Barbados
Davis, Arthur H. Jr.	Paraguay
Dobriansky, Lev E.	The Bahamas
Douglas, Howard Eugene	Ambassador at Large (Refugee Affairs)
Funderburk, David B.	Romania
Galbraith, Evan G.	France
Gerard, Jean	UNESCO
Hewitt, William A.	Jamaica
Jordan, David	Peru
Keating, Robert	Madagascar
Lodge, John Davis	Switzerland
Middendorf, J. W., II	OAS
Piedra, Alberto	Guatemala
Robinson, Paul H. Jr.	Canada
Ruddy, Frank	Equatorial Guinea
Tambs, Lewis A.	Colombia
von Damm, Helene	Austria
Walker, Richard L.	South Korea
Whittlesey, Faith Ryan	White House Public Liaison Director, former Ambassador to Switzerland
Williamson, Richard	International Organizations in Vienna
Winsor, Curtin	Costa Rica

Personally, I knew Ambassadors Douglas, Walker and Whittlesey, having in fact been a student of Richard Walker while doing Ph.D. work at the University of South Carolina. Beyond those three, I had once or twice met Ambassadors Galbraith, Tambs, and Winsor, but did not know at all the others on the list. Since all of the ambassadors endorsing Helms were non-career "political" appointees of the Reagan Administration, they were not subject to laws which restricted involvement in politics by U.S. government employees. Non-career federal employees were not subject to the Hatch Act, barring political participation.

A State Department publication entitled "Practical Ethics: A Briefing Book for Chiefs of Mission" and dated November 1984, was sent out to the embassies. A section on participation in political campaigns said that while ambassadors were exempt from the Hatch Act obligation to desist from active partisan political activity, other "Hatch Act constraints, such as restrictions on funds solicitation, apply, and the White House-issued guidelines included "prohibitions against making contributions to the official 'Reagan-Bush '84' committee, taking an active or visible management position in a political campaign, conducting fundraising events, or soliciting campaign funds on Government property."[15] A cable was sent to the embassies from the Secretary of State stressing the guidelines and that ambassadors, as federal employees, had their official duties as the primary task to complete. Also, the USIA Wireless File of November 29, 1984, carried an article by the *Christian Science Monitor* on the "Rising Tide of Noncareer U.S. Envoys Worries Experts." The article said that professional State Department employees (diplomats) were both "angry and embarrassed" at the endorsements of Helms by the ambassadors. The American Foreign Service Association chief said that State Department careerists considered the endorsements a mistake which "struck a real nerve" with them.[16]

During the last week of October 1984, I returned to the U.S. at my own expense, stopping along the way to deliver the keynote address at the annual European Baptist Convention (English language) held at Rolduc Monastery, Kerkrade, the Netherlands. In Washington, I spoke before a White House audience of East European ethnic groups on "U.S. Foreign Policy Toward Eastern Europe," and before Stanton Evans's Monday Club of conservatives. On October 30th, I made an appearance with Faith Whittlesey at a Senator Helms press conference at Raleigh-Durham Airport. I was quoted in the *Greensboro News and Record* as saying the endorsements of Helms were a distinctive tribute: "It is unprecedented and remarkable that over 20 ambassadors went to the trouble, despite whatever flak they might get from the knee-jerk liberal press, to put their names on the line in support of this Senator."[17]

Articles in national publications referring to the endorsement of Helms by the 22 ambassadors included such topics as "Mr. Helms's Foreign Legion," "Jesse the Helmsman," "State Department in a Dither Over Helms," "Undiplomatic Diplomats," and "Independent Envoys Pose Problems for U.S."[18] There were also a few articles which defended the non-career political appointees point of view, such as "Regaining Control of the Department of State" by James T. Hackett of the Heritage Foundation, "Choosing Envoys: Career Officers Vs. Political Appointees" by Smith Hempstone, "Galbraith Derides U.S. Career Diplomats as Timid" describing Evan Galbraith's blast at State, and "What Galbraith Meant About Guts in the Embassy" by William F. Buckley, Jr.[19]

There were the official "warnings" (often termed as recommendations) by the State Department about political involvement by ambassadors in cables and publications sent in the wake of the endorsements of Helms. And there were the whispers, rumors and leaks by State Department officials hinting the department's displeasure over the Helms endorsements. Department careerists used the ambassadors' endorsements as yet another means to keep the pressure on the political diplomats, with suggestions that many if not most of them who signed on for Helms would be replaced or squeezed out. Hearing rumors passed by official visitors and reading articles attacking the endorsement action by the 22 ambassadors did not have a pleasurable effect from the isolated position of Bucharest. And the furor over the affair may have left me feeling more solitary in Eastern Europe, since I was the only ambassador posted to a Communist country who endorsed Helms. But while there were official publications and cables reaching Bucharest from Washington on the subject and the not so atypical rumors coming out of Foggy Bottom, there was never a direct message containing any form of threat or job pressure on me from the State Department. Many in the department had hoped for the defeat of Helms and were thus disappointed in November, 1984. But they were relieved that the Senator would not, at that time, become the chairman of the Foreign Relations Committee.[20]

There was nothing that better showed the convergence of interests between the State Department elite and the Romanian Communists than the occasions of high level visits to Romania. The fact that so many top American officials visited Bucharest, and the way in which the visits were used by the Romanian Communists and the State Department, speak volumes about a flawed U.S. policy.

High Level U.S. Visitors to Romania: From Secretary of State Alexander Haig to Vice President George Bush

Secretary of State Alexander Haig

During my stay in Romania, the State Department's differentiation specialists sent scores of high level visitors to Bucharest to supposedly tease the Russian bear, "confirm" differentiation, help shore-up Ceausescu in his foreign policy "independence," and satisfy both the Romanian Communist leaders and the leadership of the State Department itself. The U.S. went to "Canossa" Bucharest far too many times. Each of the visits illustrated to me that the interests of the Communists and Foreign Service elite have apparently dovetailed. Many of the visitors fell into the trap of play-acting, expected by both Washington and Bucharest. Caught in the middle, some of us at the U.S. Embassy in Bucharest struggled to convince the visitors that U.S. policy should more realistically reflect the democratically expressed ideals of American people, and the yearnings for freedom of those living under Communism.

Every visit eventually turned into a struggle between the State Department, which briefed each visitor in Washington before departure on the wisdom of differentiation and U.S. support of the Ceausescu regime, and the ones at the U.S. embassy allied with me. As time went by in Bucharest and we saw more of the reality in terms of both intelligence information and life under Ceausescu's Communism, our view increasingly became one of questioning the wisdom of differentiation. As conditions of life worsened and

Ceausescu's government became more totalitarian and repressive, the pain and suffering of everyday life in Romania had an impact on us. It was a factor in our desire to do something for the plight of the freedom-loving majority, the persecuted, the dissidents, the believers, and even the anti-Communist government employees. And having seen a reality different from that on which U.S. policy was based, it became important for us to try to influence and in effect change U.S. policy.

U.S. long term interests—"futures"—as well as present ones required a different policy. A U.S. policy which is tough with friendly strongmen like Pinochet or Chun should be at least as tough with Communist adversaries like Ceausescu. Actual U.S. policy, based on the supposed value of friendly ties with Russian neighbor Romania, was afraid to antagonize or even challenge Ceausescu in terms of his terrible domestic regime. The usual explanation was that the domestic repression was the trade-off we had to bear in order for Ceausescu to get away with his foreign policy divergences from Moscow. After all, Moscow would not tolerate his international affairs "independence" if he did not have total Communist party control over the society. We became convinced that the U.S. was getting the worst of the deal with Romania. Of course the Romanian people were not faring very well either.

For a minimum I came to believe that the U.S. should devise a more realistic policy which recognized Bucharest's Warsaw Pact membership, did not trade high technology to the Romanians, and extracted significant concessions in terms of human rights, emigration, and even internal reforms such as better conditions for religious believers. As many visitors from Washington trekked into Romania to do homage to Ceausescu's cult and foreign policy "independence," I tried to balance the ledger. Inasmuch as the Romanian government knew that the ambassador was a hard-line conservative anti-Communist, it was important for the U.S. to present a common front to the Romanian regime. In this way the ambassador would not appear to be out on a limb isolated from official Washington.

Thus it was important to try to persuade the visitors to take a tougher line with Ceausescu. A few of us at the embassy made our own individual efforts, even though we never discussed or planned a coordinated approach. The experiences and reading of the situation by a few of us beginning in 1983, led to very similar assessments of what was best for the U.S. and the Romanian people. Because of a more democratic style in the semi-Country Team—or several key embassy officers who constituted part of the Country Team (literally the heads of the various sections, departments or agencies of the U.S.G.), a visitor would get the whole gamut of opinion and views of the Romanian scene. Thus, if the chief political officer would present a bleak picture of the political scene in Romania and suggest a tougher approach, the USIA chief might instead recommend not rocking the boat with Ceausescu in order to retain the cultural concessions we had already won. We knew that the visitor had gotten only one side in Washington, i.e. the value of differentiation and Ceausescu's foreign policy maverick status being preserved by treating him gingerly and generously.

Using the experience and expertise of a few of our chief officers—even if not uniform in view—we hoped that the visitor would inject into his conversation with Ceausescu or Foreign Minister Andrei, American concerns over certain human rights cases or reported religious persecution. We hoped that the visitor would have the courage and good judgment to refrain from groveling at Ceausescu's shrine and introduce a little plain talk about U.S. values, beliefs and political system expectations. Also it was hoped that the visitor would let Ceausescu know in no uncertain terms that Washington cannot for example sell MFN for Romania to the Americans without getting real concessions consistent with our ideals. This was not easy when many individual visitors thought they were essential parts of the policymaking process, witness the constant parade of religious group leaders, businessmen and other interested individuals like former Congressmen or Presidents.

There was also the problem that most visitors in the past told Ceausescu what he wanted to hear for the most part. Those few who dared to express a degree of candor and/or toughness might suffer the wrath of Ceausescu's little game of pique. Ceausescu routinely played off against each other Americans who had different policy ideas. In this game Ceausescu had the cooperation of the State Department elite. Beyond this, the Romanians shrewdly learned which Congressmen, religious figures, businessmen and U.S. government employees of various departments were most valuable in getting what they wanted. Bucharest skillfully used some visitors to denigrate or discredit Americans who questioned the pro-MFN for Romania policy.

The parade of U.S. dignitaries included Secretary of State Alexander Haig, U.S. Ambassador to the CSCE Max Kampelman, Deputy Defense Secretary Frank Carlucci and Vice President George Bush. These were among the leading American visitors to Romania between October 1981, and October 1983.

The first of the major U.S. official visitors to Romania was then Secretary of State Al Haig. He certainly came blowing into "backwater" Bucharest on February 12, 1982, with a take-charge demeanor. American conservatives had expected much more from Haig, thinking that he was a hard-line anti-Communist who could put our foreign policy back on a more realistic pro-U.S. track. But from the inside, except for his tough rhetoric *vis-à-vis* Havana or Moscow, he made little difference in the direction of U.S. foreign policy. A major aspect of this failure was his unwillingness to change the State Department elite stranglehold over foreign policy. Evidently he placed more faith in the status quo of Foreign Service bureaucrats. That was the practical effect of his Foggy Bottom inaction, even if he wanted great change but saw that he could not alone frontally take on State as retired General John Singlaub told me in Switzerland in July 1986. In State terminology this meant that behind the scenes incremental changes would have to suffice. Haig usually fought *against* non-career political appointees to top State Department positions while championing those candidates from the career service. This meant no change in day to day policy implementation. Considering this reality about Haig at the State Department, it should come as no great surprise that he played the game for the most part during his trip to Bucharest. Perhaps he was more candid with Ceausescu and Andrei than most visitors, though not as frank as he has claimed.[1]

Before the meeting with President Ceausescu, a standard preliminary session with Romanian Foreign Minister Stefan Andrei was held. Subsequent visitors continued the Haig pattern of delivering the tougher messages—usually related to human rights and emigration concerns—in earlier meetings with Andrei. Haig consequently handed Andrei a consular list of individual cases, but spared the Romanian chief the embarrassment of worrying about such "trivial matters." The list included immigration cases such as that of Andrei Coler—a case Vice President Bush took a personal interest in, marriage cases such as that of Eszter Szekely of Cluj-Napoca, and humanitarian cases such as that of Friedrich Klein and family of Medias. Romania's track record in resolving such cases, especially the humanitarian ones, was not good.

Following the Romanian discussion pattern, the preliminary

meetings hosted by Andrei were apparently designed to get out the specific requests and grievances of the Romanians and put the American official on the defensive. It was also intended to feel out the guest to see if he had any surprises—something Ceausescu found intolerable. While Andrei also fathomed himself a genius and liked to piously pontificate about the world scene and Romania's correct solutions, his lecture to Haig dealt more with bilateral relations. The most common Romanian thread in talks with Americans was to shame the U.S. officials by admonishing them for not doing more for Romania. Thus Andrei recounted Romania's economic difficulties which he said were made more difficult by America's unwillingness to help. Romania needs, Andrei said, more economic assistance in the form of CCC credits, approval of joint venture licenses, Eximbank credits, withdrawal of anti-dumping suits on steel exports to the U.S., the Landsat satellite, IMF and World Bank credits, and increased assistance via the joint U.S.-Romanian Economic Commission. Andrei said that "a friend in need is a friend indeed," meaning that Romania needs it and now is the time for the U.S. to help.

Haig stressed the importance of maintaining differentiation and the need for Romania to demonstrate independence from the Soviets. That more than anything else—although rescheduling the debt would help—would boost Romania's stock in the West and assist in influencing the attitudes of those "sterile" thinking friends who lump the Soviet Bloc together and believe U.S.-Soviet relations determine bloc ones.

In the Haig-Ceausescu meeting the focus was on an exchange of views regarding the full spectrum of international issues and hot spot items, something Ceausescu enjoyed most of all. Ceausescu impressed most visitors with his knowledge of world affairs and his ability to nuance his presentation to make the listener feel he may just not be a true Warsaw Pact believer to the same degree a Bulgarian or Russian is. Ceausescu played the same game with each visitor, hardly varying his regular spiel. But each time it was novel to the visitors—who seemed impressed. He lectured the U.S. officials on every occasion to feel guilty about America's past sins and failure to help solve all of the world's problems such as those of the Third World. The monkey of responsibility was put on our backs because after all with our massive wealth and bank domination over other countries, the U.S. not the Soviets owed the world penance. Always Ceausescu would stress the rights and sovereignty

of smaller nations such as Romania and the duty of the great
powers—read the U.S.—to refrain from interfering in their internal affairs. Ceausescu especially liked to fathom himself as a great
role player on the world scene, more brilliant than anyone else. He
appeared more interested in discussing, with firsthand expertise,
the Middle East events. Of course these conversations were with
the U.S. Much of Ceausescu's success derives from his shrewd actions in tirelessly meeting with any leader or *potential leader* of
countries around the world—especially Western nations—and treating them in royal style. Many individuals struggling at the time
remembered Ceausescu's hospitality after they reached the pinnacle
of power. Richard Nixon is perhaps the best example of this strategy
which payed off handsomely for Ceausescu.

The Haig-Ceausescu marathon meeting revolved more around
the international scene—global issues in Romanian parlance—than
about bilateral relations. While the discussion ranged from southern Africa to the Middle East to Central America, the focus was
on the Polish situation and Soviet-American arms control type questions. Unlike Haig's description of Ceausescu sounding like a non-
aligned Third World leader, Ceausescu's ideas on arms control,
missiles, Geneva and Madrid mirrored those of the Soviets.
Ceausescu's emphasis on rationalizing the Polish developments
reflected his extreme anxiety about Solidarity's strength and the
church's influence in Poland. Even though Ceausescu had things
under control in Romania, he feared a spillover from Poland.
Ceausescu charged that the Roman Catholic Church contributed
to the problems of Poland and the weakening of the country. He
said it is past time when the Vatican can control national affairs.
Of course, he argued, Romania favors religious freedom, has fourteen recognized cults, and has six cult representatives in
Parliament—a totally meaningless rubber stamp body used for propaganda purposes. According to Ceausescu that made Romania more
advanced than the U.S. regarding religion.

He continued to express his fear of the Polish situation by saying that events in Poland are directly linked with Vatican policy.
Insight into Ceausescu's thinking can be derived from the claim
that the martial law situation in Poland was precipitated by Solidarity which was created by the Roman Catholic Church. In his words
Solidarity was hatched by the Roman Catholic Church starting in
the cathedrals with the assistance of the Catholic priests. Imperialist circles of Solidarity were acting to overthrow the Polish govern-

ment, necessitating the measures to restore order. When Ceausescu said that events in Poland were directly linked with Vatican policy, one could clearly see the Soviet thinking behind an attempt to assassinate the Pope—threat to the unity of the Soviet empire in Eastern Europe. The Romanian chief repeatedly told Haig that Jaruzelski should be aided, not punished, by the Americans.

Ceausescu lectured the U.S. to take a more positive position at Madrid, to stop deployment of new missiles and to destroy existing ones, and noted positive aspects of the Soviet inclusion of the territory up to the Urals for missile withdrawal. He said that the U.S. must adapt more quickly to the realities of the world by supporting forces of independence and not old conservative forces. When Haig said that the U.S. was a nation established by revolution, Ceausescu answered by noting that Marx said Lincoln was an example of a President coming from the working class. Haig retorted by saying that the U.S. would support historic change when it represented the will of the people, as was the case in America's past—when it was not decided by Moscow. Finally Ceausescu said that the U.S. was exaggerating the role of Khaddafy who is one chief of state you can discuss things with and who can take a moderate position. Haig gave the Reagan Administration position on each of the items brought up by Ceausescu.

During his two day stay in Bucharest, Haig mentioned to me that William Safire was always a liberal, George Will was too pro-Israel, and Cap Weinberger was busy contradicting him and encouraging Begin to act belligerently. Haig further noted that Richard Perle shoots everything sent over out of the water, and Richard Pipes apparently has a vendetta against Romania or thinks Romania is a satrapy of the Soviet Union! According to Haig the anti-differentiationists were amazingly not any longer the conservatives but rather the liberal Jews and the pro-defense Jackson-type Democrats. When I asked him if he thought that Judge Clark at NSC would help things *vis-à-vis* the Soviets and Eastern Europe he seemed generally unenthused in his reaction. Then I said: now you have your old aide McFarlane as deputy. Haig unenthusiastically said something to the effect that he is O.K. My impressions were that Haig considered Ceausescu does not matter individually, as much as Romania and its strategic position. Haig also indicated to me that he felt Ceausescu understood what he was cryptically saying.

The last chapter in the Haig-Romania story came on the day before his resignation as Secretary of State. The last major foreign visitor to see Haig in office was Romanian Foreign Minister Andrei who met with Haig on June 24, 1982, at the State Department. Perhaps one with a crystal ball could have read between the lines of Haig's parting words at 4 P.M. on June 24th. Haig said to Andrei ironically that there will be a differentiation policy or "I will leave as Secretary of State." As we departed from Haig's office, Haig put his arm around me and said: "I am sorry that we were not much help to you out there; keep the faith." Probably he meant that he wanted to do more to help Ceausescu and a closer U.S.-Romanian differentiation relationship. At least that is the way I read his line at the time. A few businessmen including shoe manufacturers were interested in setting up shop in Romania. It was likely with that in mind that Haig had said that with the successful completion of talks with the Romanian officials the U.S. had a love feast planned for the Romanians later in the summer.

I was present at the State Department in Washington on the historic day of Haig's resignation. After meeting with Elliott Abrams and Richard Pipes, I witnessed Haig's announcement at 4:30 P.M., June 25th. At 5:00 P.M. at the White House I was again with Romanian Foreign Minister Andrei in a meeting with the Vice President. Bush, as if to assure the shocked and shaken Andrei, promised that the U.S. would continue differentiation and the same overall policy toward Romania.

U.S. Ambassador to CSCE Max Kampelman

The visit to Romania by Max Kampelman, U.S. Ambassador to the CSCE, was a combined private and official visit. No major Western government figure like Kampelman can travel to Romania on a personal visit without holding talks with Romanian officials. Thus it was when Kampelman traveled to Romania September 15-18, 1982, as a jumping off point for seeing ancestral sites in bordering Soviet Moldavia—earlier a province of Romania with a Romanian-speaking majority. He crossed the border to visit the home and grave sites of his parents who had come to the U.S. from Cernauti (Chernovtsky) in Romania's Bucovina region.

Kampelman had shown courage in defending U. S. interests in talks with the Soviets and bloc allies. In a civil way that did not alienate the adversary but rather gained his respect, Kampelman called a spade a spade. At a Chiefs of Mission Conference in London in December 1982, he told American ambassadors to European countries that "the Soviet Union represents the most serious threat to our society and values in this century." The Soviets camouflage their imperialist policies with the rhetoric of peace and democracy, he said, and have built military strength well beyond the needs of defensive military power. Kampelman said that Madrid is really a side-show which has not improved things, as the Soviets maintain over 100,000 troops in Afghanistan, allow few people to emigrate, and have worsened religious and political persecution. He perceptively stated that the Soviets believe they can win by outlasting us. They realize the need to mobilize their resources to "win"—a word they do not shy away from. The national game of chess in the U.S.S.R. reflects their patience and resolve to win: no move is made without considering all other moves. On the other hand, an American national game like poker has each hand being played for itself. These differences point up a real problem for Americans. Kampelman noted that as we are in a constant battle for the hearts and minds of men, our message of democracy, human rights concerns and Western values must be transmitted to the three audiences of the Kremlin, the CSCE delegates and public opinion on both sides of the Iron Curtain.

With regard to Romania specifically, Kampelman in concurring with our embassy assessment pointed out that the U.S. cannot afford to be faced down on principles it has publicly espoused. Also the U.S. should not have just limited human rights concerns, and must back up the warning to the Romanians by U.S. officials. Otherwise the credibility of American officials is undercut, putting them in a bad position in future dealings with the Romanians. He was referring to warnings made to the Romanians regarding the education repayment tax by some U.S. officials, which were undermined by State Department assurances.

In a meeting in Munich the first of April prior to his visit to Romania, Kampelman acknowledged that he was well aware of Romania pushing for Bucharest as the next site for the CSCE meeting—sequel to Helsinki-Madrid. He added that since Romania's human rights record was awful, Bucharest would not be appropriate for the CSCE meeting site. It was a relief to hear that. Two weeks before his visit to Romania, Kampelman told me in Munich that he would carry a tough human rights message to the Romanians and that I should stand with him for an anti-detente policy on East-West issues.

During his visit to Romania, Kampelman was rather firm in his conversation with Foreign Minister Andrei—unusual for American officials. When the handful of courageous U.S. officials took a hard line it provided a degree of buffer support for me and those who were helpful in the embassy. In the September 18th meeting in Bucharest with Andrei, the Foreign Minister said that he did not want to be responsible for a deterioration of U.S.-Romanian relations. In retrospect this statement by Andrei may have been somewhat prophetic as he got the axe not long after I departed from Bucharest. Andrei in a periodic dig at me before visiting American officials "jokingly" said that it was during my one year tenure as ambassador that U.S.-Romanian relations had deteriorated. Since he was also Foreign Minister during that year of slipping relations and increased tension, he said he did not want to be blamed for it.

Kampelman told Andrei that Romania had problems in two places: one in the White House and the other in the Congress. Saying that the State Department highly regards Romania—in Congress it relates to cases. While the view of a Romanian independent foreign policy usually overrides such irritants as human rights cases, there are those who respond to human considerations and solutions. Family reunification and other emigration problems are concerns of some Congressmen along with such *cause célébre* cases as Father Calciu's. The Swiss want to take Calciu and help resolve the problem. After all, Solzhenitsyn left and said a few words for several months, but after that it was over and quiet. Kampelman continued by saying he had an additional list which included Calciu, and that the basic issue in 1983 would be MFN renewal. U.S. business interests which in the past helped get MFN through, will have serious problems this time because the White House has been enlisted in efforts to stop it.

The White House has been affected by those in the administration who have grown up in the U.S. as strong anti-Communists, Kampelman said. They want a war of words, not a real war. To them Romania has the reputation as being a tough totalitarian regime which looks repressive and which takes away the jobs of those who apply for emigration. Andrei replied that of course none of that was true. Kampelman went on to say that such an image added up to Romania being often viewed together with the Soviets. Since the White House needs each vote in Congress, a recommendation by Kampelman was to show more receptiveness to individual cases.

After all, individual cases do not affect Romania's national security. Romania might try getting rid of them and taking credit for it. He said it would also be useful for Romania to support the U.S. when possible on international matters where Romanian national interests would not be in jeopardy. The Jewish community in the U.S. has helped with MFN but it is not alone, Kampelman noted. Probably no one else more thoroughly aired U.S. concerns in such a skillful way (appreciated even by the Romanians) than Kampelman had done. Thus his expert reputation as a negotiator with the Communists was demonstrated again.

In sum, in the Andrei meeting, Kampelman was a tough advocate for human rights although he joined most other American officials in avoiding anything difficult or tough in conversation with President Ceausescu. With Ceausescu being spared first-hand any hint of criticism or bad news, one wonders if he ever got the word at all. Kampelman was all in all an excellent spokesman for the Reagan Administration.

Deputy Defense Secretary Frank Carlucci

Frank Carlucci must have had ideas of getting Ceausescu's attention. On the first of September 1982, Carlucci had made it clear to me that during his trip to Bucharest he planned to let Ceausescu know the concerns of the U.S. included: technology transfer, Warsaw Pact coordination and human rights violations. He intended to play the game with intrigue added, but also to take a tough message to Bucharest. Unlike most visitors who went to Bucharest, Carlucci may have had his own game to play. In any event, he considered that his trip had a special role to play, and that the value of the trip would be enhanced by intrigue.

Ceausescu and gang, masters of disinformation and conspiracy, did not know what to make of Carlucci's swing. They knew that Carlucci as Deputy Defense Secretary and former Deputy CIA Director was a mysterious intelligence figure probably up to no good for them. As usual when visitors arrived Ceausescu got the readout from the preliminary meetings with the Foreign Minister or Defense Minister. After Carlucci's arrival on October 11th, 1982, he met with both the Foreign and Defense Ministers. In the Ministry of Defense session we were first informed that Ceausescu would meet Carlucci—which in fact was usually the case for a visitor of his stature. Fifteen minutes later we were told that it was a mistake and the Foreign Minister—not the President—would meet Carlucci. If Soviet heat on Ceausescu did not play a part from the beginning, it was Ceausescu's pique at the approach and style of Carlucci from the time of arrival into the initial meeting. Carlucci talked tougher and showed strong self-confidence.

In Bucharest, Ceausescu was going to play the game his way and not let anyone think they could with impunity talk tough to him. Ceausescu certainly showed his hand by refusing to meet with Carlucci after initially agreeing to do so. It was a double insult to the United States government and to Carlucci. Carlucci's aides said it negated the whole trip. It was excused from having any negative consequence or special meaning by Romanian Deputy Foreign Minister Maria Groza and Foreign Ministry North American Affairs Chief Mircea Raceanu.

While I welcomed such a visitor who told it like it was and placed a marker for U.S. interests, in isolation it had little impact in convincing the Romanian Communists of any American resolve. Those of us working inside the U.S. embassy for such American interests knew what "lonely" meant. Carlucci tried to put the best face on the visit describing it as worthwhile despite not seeing Ceausescu. He also volunteered that "he came away with a greater understanding of the challenge you face there as Ambassador."[2]

The Bushcapade:
The Vice President in Bucharest

George and Barbara Bush are two of the nicest people you would ever want to meet. The Vice President is decent, genteel, intelligent, sincere, and experienced in government. His loyalty to the President and the Republican Party are unquestioned. And perhaps no other political figure has shown greater sacrifices and commitment in serving his country. Bush has served as an elected member of the U.S. House of Representatives, Chairman of the National GOP, Director of the CIA, U.S. Ambassador to the UN, Chief of the U.S. Liaison Office in Peking and Vice President. He has paid his dues to the GOP. Even though he does not have the charisma of Ronald Reagan or his dynamic speaking style, he is a likeable person you want to respect and appreciate.

This same Bush is part of the Washington woodwork. He is the insider's insider and if not a creature of the government bureaucracy, one who is totally comfortable with the bureaucrats and bureaucracy. This is one characteristic which has not endeared him to conservatives. He has been too susceptible to the pro-compromise, conciliation and cooperation initiatives of the State Department.

The Vice President's trip to Yugoslavia, Romania, Hungary, and Austria, clearly showed Bush playing his role as a good soldier for the State Department. Similarly his Bushcapade through Eastern Europe, if anything, went overboard in unnecessarily boosting the stock of the Communist regimes there, while disappointing the people seeking freedom and a better life. The mere fact of Bush trekking to the three B's (Belgrade, Bucharest, and Budapest) was in response to the State Department's wish to reaffirm differentiation with the highest possible ranking U.S. government official. Certainly the timing regarding Romania was atrocious, coming as it did when repression and persecution of religious believers and political dissidents were increasing. And the occasion was not used to gain some real *quid pro quo* for the U.S.

After overnighting in Belgrade with the Vice Presidential party, I flew into Bucharest during the early morning of September 18, 1983, on Air Force Two with Vice President Bush. In the Belgrade Intercontinental Hotel the night before and on Air Force Two the State Department-NSC officials were cavalierly putting the finishing touches on the soon to be announced public reaffirmation of U.S. differentiation policy *vis-à-vis* Eastern Europe. Inasmuch as I was allowed to brief the Vice President before his arrival in Bucharest and meetings with Foreign Minister Andrei and President Ceausescu, I stressed the need for a tough statement of U.S. principles and interest in human rights, better conditions of life for the people of Romania, and freer emigration. Instead during a White House meeting of June 25, 1982, Bush had expressed his satisfaction with U.S. differentiation policy toward Romania, and vowed to help continue it.

The Bushcapade in Bucharest was disappointing to some of us at the embassy. It cut the rug out from under our efforts to get human rights concessions from the Romanians. Instead of supporting the U.S. ambassador in Bucharest, Bush allowed the State Department to maneuver him into pacifying Ceausescu's wishes. U.S.-Romanian relations in 1983 had been marked by the Romanian imposition of an education repayment tax which violated Jackson-Vanik and the MFN agreement. U.S. appeasement efforts included attempts to plead with Ceausescu to drop the tax and thus keep the MFN relationship intact. The irony was that the only ones who seemed desperate to keep that relationship were State Department officials. Thus the background to the Bush visit was Romanian repression followed by U.S. pleas and a behind-the-scenes package to satisfy Ceausescu. MFN would be salvaged for Romania and other goodies would be thrown in if Ceausescu would drop the tax. One of those sops to Ceausescu was a visit to Washington by Foreign Minister Andrei and Bush's visit to Bucharest.

Part of the concession package was apparently worked out by Eagleburger who sent businessman Milton Rosenthal to see Ceausescu in April, 1983. Rosenthal carried a message for a deal (with the concession package) directly to Ceausescu, bypassing the U.S. Embassy in Bucharest. The package reflected the State Department efforts to salvage MFN for Romania and to get the Vice President to see Andrei for delivery of the gifts. The Romanian Foreign Minister's visit to Washington in April of 1983 was the first part of this process.

Bush sandbagged the embassy in Bucharest during his visit. During the scramble of negotiations regarding the details of meetings between Romanian President Ceausescu and visitors such as Bush, the Romanians played their hands predictably. Romanian officials tried to ensure that U.S. Embassy diplomats such as the ambassador or his deputy (DCM) would be frozen out of key meetings. They were better able to accomplish this because of the press of time, the overt confusion which always permeated the atmosphere of Romanian negotiations, and the desire on the part of American officials to do the bidding of the hosts on such matters. Not every U.S. official, however, fell for such an old trap. Bush did.

To make matters worse and convey the wrong signals, Bush did them one better. First the Vice Presidential team told the Romanians that the ambassador would be included at the meeting and dinner involving Bush and Ceausescu. In the past when a visitor had insisted the Romanians had gone along, as they even indicated they would in this case. But at the last minute the Vice President succumbed to their classic whispered pressure. Bush caved in by ultimately agreeing to let the Romanians exclude the ambassador and DCM from the meeting and dinner. Not that we wanted to eat another meal with Ceausescu. But it left two Americans and four Romanians, a crucial imbalance accentuated by the fact that no experienced officer in the field was present even as a notetaker. Only Bush and his aide were present, but no American official who had lived and worked in Romania. Bush had acceded to State Department advice to accommodate Ceausescu. Earlier reports and conversation had shown that Ceausescu did not like my concern for human rights and U.S. security interests—making it tougher for Bucharest to get high technology. He did not want the ambassador or DCM to be present during the Bush meeting because of such concerns. Thus the State Department, with the Vice President and in this case the Romanian Communists, had again succeeded in squeezing out the ambassador and his deputy to the detriment of the best American national interests.

The second string on the night of September 18th assembled for dinner with the Romanian Foreign Minister. Bush aide Admiral Daniel Murphy and myself along with others got to hear Andrei's lecture. Andrei said that when the government of Romania needed help most and requested it from the U.S., it got nothing. Specifically CCC credits, powdered milk and EXIM assistance did not arrive in Bucharest but instead Romania's debt was dramatized in *The New York Times*, according to Andrei. Romania has learned— he said—its lesson and will not in the future turn to anyone for credits. Most importantly, Ceausescu very much wants an invitation to visit the United States and Reagan.

In the Bucharest meeting between Bush and Andrei (with Romanian Vice President Gheorghe Radulescu) and no doubt also in the Bush-Ceausescu meetings, Bush stressed the value of good U.S.-Romanian relations and America's appreciation for Romania's "independence." Bush also touched on international points of agreement and general U.S. foreign policy positions on hot spot issues of the day. Inasmuch as Ceausescu does not like to hear bad news and the State Department knows and respects that, woe be it for George Bush to bring any to him. Instead Bush said the U.S. appreciated Romania's contributions at Madrid (CSCE), Romania's efforts in resolving the education tax problem, and Romania's willingness to meet with the U.S. at a human rights roundtable in February 1984. Bush added that Washington was prepared to favorably consider EXIM credit for Romania's Cernavoda nuclear power project and CCC credit guarantees. By contrast Bush mentioned fleetingly U.S. concern for family reunification cases, freedom of emigration, and human contacts.

Bush's single concern regarding human rights and emigration was his personal interest case of Andrei Coler's emigration to the United States. Former Pennsylvania Governor Milton J. Shapp's son,

Richard, married a Romanian of Jewish origin whose brother and family were reportedly being harassed as applicants for emigration. Shapp contacted Bush and got him interested in the case of Andrei Coler and family. When their efforts were unsuccessful for several years, Shapp gave testimony to the House of Representatives Ways and Means Subcommittee on Trade urging Congress to deny renewal of MFN for Romania. Because of the Vice President's interest and other particulars of the case U.S. Government officials worked to resolve it. When Andrei and Elena Coler (with daughter Alexandra) were finally allowed to leave Romania some time later I received a letter from them which said: "We feel grateful not only in our name, but also in the name of other people too, people forced to live a life which is not of their choice and whose only hope in a change is the American policy toward Romania."

Bush had personally mentioned the Coler case in meetings with Romanian Foreign Minister Andrei but that was the extent of what he said on human rights and emigration.

The Romanian government was extremely pleased with the Bush visit because he let the Communist regime handle the arrangements for the meetings the way it wanted to. Also his very presence served the main purpose of boosting Ceausescu's stock before the Romanian people and his image as a maverick before the world. And his visit enabled Ceausescu to continue his game of personally wooing U.S. and Western leaders with his bush-league globe trotting. Finally his trip held out the hope to Ceausescu that additional high level visits between the leaders of the two countries would be forthcoming. Following the stops in Bucharest and Budapest, Bush's speech in Vienna openly reaffirmed differentiation and praised Romania's foreign policy. Ceausescu, thus, could tell the world that the U.S. favored him and by implication, his government. This meant the most tyrannical regime in the Soviet Bloc was again blessed by the United States. America can do better.

The Bush Speech in Vienna of September 21, 1983, following bad advice from the careerists like Palmer, sent the wrong signals to Eastern Europe and the world about U.S. policy. By saying that the U.S. would "engage in closer political, economic, and cultural relations with those countries such as Hungary and Romania which assert greater openness or independence," Bush diminished what the U.S. stands for and blurred distinctions between countries in the region.[3] The statement implied no difference between countries which have dramatically improved human rights, emigration and internal openness, and those which "supposedly" have foreign policies which do not parrot the Soviet line. Thus Hungary and Romania were grouped together. This upset the Hungarians. But to say that Communist Hungary, which has a better record of internal reform and human rights, is comparable with Romania, which has one of the worst records of domestic repression and violation of basic human rights, is ludicrous. One study shows Romania and the Soviet Union tied for fourth as the worst country on human rights with only Iraq, North Korea and Ethiopia worse.[4]

It is likewise untenable to imply that a more humane internal policy and practice (in Hungary) approximates a questionable foreign policy independence (Romania). Romania's votes closely follow those of the Soviets at the UN, and Romania follows the Soviets in aid to terrorists and Marxist-Leninist guerrillas around the world.

Bush said that the U.S. stands for the social, humanitarian and democratic ideals of Western civilization and for fundamental freedoms and human rights. Communist Romania does not stand for those ideals and does not carry out a policy which acknowledges or reflects such rights and freedoms. When the U.S., despite this reality, boosts Ceausescu's stock and honors Romania as one of the two favored countries in the Soviet Bloc of Eastern Europe, it is not being true to what it believes. Of all regimes why should the U.S. strengthen cooperation with Romania? Bush elected to be point man for the shenanigans of the Kissinger-Eagleburger clique in the European Affairs Bureau at the State Department. The differentiationists at State were pleased with his visit to Bucharest.

U.S. Visitors to Romania: From Secretary of Commerce Malcolm Baldrige to Chairman of the Joint Chiefs of Staff John Vessey Jr.

Secretary of Commerce Malcolm Baldrige

Secretary of Commerce Malcolm Baldrige's friendship with the President may account in large measure for his longevity in the Commerce position. Otherwise it would have seemed odd to keep on year after year the one who presided over the nation's biggest trade deficit in history—with the export-import gap widening. But Baldrige surely deserves some of the "credit" for trying to boost exports to Communist countries. The unfortunate reality, however, is that despite all the efforts to boost exports from the U.S. to Communist countries like Romania, under Baldrige it was imports into the U.S. from them which dramatically increased.

The Commerce chief is a key player in U.S.-Romanian relations because Romania's principal commercial objectives have been to: (1) increase "subsidized"-MFN exports to the U.S.; (2) get other U.S. economic assistance in tourism, marketing and industry; and (3) acquire Western high technology for military application, export, and Soviet needs. The political relationship with the U.S. was very important to Ceausescu's image and world figure role. But more importantly he needed hard currency to live high e.g. with caviar and champagne, to further world Communist aims of the

Soviets-Romanians, and to maintain virtual total economic control over the hapless Romanian people. And his political standing internationally directly impacted on his economic needs. U.S.-MFN and its related benefits helped Ceausescu's aims immeasurably while doing little for the U.S. and even less that was positive for the Romanian masses.

Thus in U.S.-Romanian economic and commercial relations, exchanges took place on a regular basis. Annual U.S.-Romanian Economic Commission (U.S. Government) and U.S.-Romanian Economic Council (private business encouraged by the USG) sessions occurred. In addition the annual Bucharest International Trade Fair held every October included a U.S. exhibit and sometimes special visitors like Baldrige. Other talks and visits occurred periodically involving matters of finance and trade. Thus there were many opportunities to observe Baldrige and other trade-promoters in action with the Romanians. Their preoccupation of maintaining or bettering Romania's MFN and GSP position led to Romania getting favored treatment that was much more "favored" than it should have been for such a repressive Warsaw Pact regime. For example, Commerce has protected the East bloc regimes like Romania from American imposition of anti-dumping trade laws. U.S. steel companies brought lawsuits which condemned "duty-free" import of steel from such government controlled subsidized industries in Communist countries. Nevertheless, Romania and some other bloc countries were allowed to unfairly dump steel and steel products in U.S. markets.[1] As ambassador I saw Romania get off the hook of anti-dumping suits, defended by Commerce in alliance with the State Department. Because of Romania's escape from anti-dumping suits, and an increasing bilateral trade balance in Romania's favor, talk of trade sanctions against Romania increased. Some of it has focused on the inability of the U.S. to compete with goods from Communist countries which have non-market economies and which engage in extensive slave labor practices.

Baldrige's visit to Bucharest in October of 1983, typified his actions favoring Romania. In a meeting with Romanian Foreign Trade Minister Vasile Pungan, Baldrige encouraged the Romanians to set more realistic goals in U.S.-Romanian bilateral trade. Baldrige said that the use of incentives to stimulate growth and increase productivity could be helpful in the agricultural and industrial sectors. Also he noted that Romania's government should recognize emigration and human rights concerns of Congress as an aspect of the MFN process. He pointed out that an exchange rate change could help Romania's exports. Nevertheless, his meeting with Ceausescu, also on October 5th, more closely epitomized his stance *vis-à-vis* Romania.

In the Ceausescu-Baldrige meeting, Romania's President laid forth his list of particulars while blaming the U.S. for whatever problems existed. He said that the U.S. could do a lot to create a good climate for trading. Problems in U.S.-Romanian trade as expressed to him by leaders of U.S. companies were: (1) MFN on an annual basis instead of multi-year; (2) U.S. measures hampering trade relations; (3) Romania's inability to get licenses from the U.S. government; and (4) lack of cooperation between companies, or rather the failure of American companies to assist Romania enough. Ceausescu went on to say that the U.S. should engage in free trade without political conditions and give up economic restrictions which contribute to worldwide economic problems. He criticized the U.S. for promoting high interest rates, and said it was America's responsibility to change its policy by lowering interest rates and aiding the developing countries of the world. He lectured that obligations come with being the leader, and that the world waits for the U.S. to fulfill its obligations.

Citing examples of acrylic yarn which had the wrong quality for the U.S. market and tractors which lacked proper services-parts, Baldrige suggested that Romania could use better marketing techniques to compete in the U.S. market. Baldrige noted that he had supported MFN in the past and that multiyear MFN would be a long term process requiring some movement on Romania's part and some convincing of Congressmen. Baldrige explained that U.S. policy is to treat Romania as a friendly country because Washington has a differentiation policy. Ceausescu responded that he appreciated Baldrige's constructive attitude regarding MFN and Romania, adding that he was sorry that he did not have the same influence in the American Congress as in his own. When Baldrige said that a major concern of the U.S. was the transfer of high technology to the Soviets, Ceausescu professed that Romania was not seeking military technology or items with any military value. Baldrige pledged to help Ceausescu with the Control Data Corporation case, the IMF, and in cooperative bilateral areas such as tourism, banking, agriculture, and overall trade increases.

Ceausescu made such assertions as: the Romanian government does not control its companies; Romania is a developing country which only desires balanced trade; and Romania does not need and does not intend to ask for further credits. Presumably he meant that Romania and Ceausescu were ready to go it alone.

Even though Baldrige presented a rather balanced picture to the Romanian leaders, an incident during his visit to Bucharest reflected his willingness to play into the hands of the Romanians. It might seem petty and insignificant if it were not such an integral and symbolic part of the way Ceausescu operates. Whether it was Ceausescu, Andrei, or Pungan, the Romanian officials preferred bush league shennanigans to predictable civil behavior. Their last minute switches from planned schedules represented their desire to win over American leaders by dealing with them one on one.

The other aspect of the Romanian strategy was to keep more knowledgeable and experienced officers of the American Embassy from being a part of any more than was absolutely necessary. Thus at the last minute the embassy was informed that Foreign Trade Minister Pungan wanted to change the schedule and take Baldrige to the Bucharest Trade Fair in the morning. Commerce officials Frank Vargo, Edgar Fulton and Jay Burgess adamantly insisted that the schedule—carefully negotiated and worked out over many weeks—had to be followed. Pungan's office had been notified to go directly to the Trade Fair without picking up Baldrige at the Intercontinental Hotel. The Romanians ignored the prearranged schedulers of the Commerce Department, sandbagged the embassy, and got Baldrige in the car with Pungan. Other American officials were kept out of the picture. To further show how the Romanians operate, Pungan told me that the U.S. Embassy informed him he was to speak at the Trade Fair. This could hardly have been true but nevertheless created confusion over whether Pungan would in fact speak at the American exhibit opening. There were other similar incidents involving positions in car caravans, receiving lines and official photo occasions which typified Romanian officials having it their way, changing things at a whim, and dealing only with the top personality in any entourage to better control the situation.

Congressional Delegations (Codels) of Congressmen Gary Ackerman, Mark Siljander, Tom Lantos and Sam Gibbons

A *codel* in government terminology—where the several letter abbreviation reigns supreme—is a traveling Congressional delegation, including one or more members of Congress and staffers. While there was a steady stream of high level visitors to Romania between 1981 and 1985, very few Congressmen made it to Bucharest. If a Congressman wanted to go on a boondoggle in Europe it might be to London, Paris or Rome. If a few members ventured to Eastern Europe it might be to Greece, Turkey, or Yugoslavia. Warsaw Pact countries got precious few Congressional visits and few of those were to Romania. Unless your background or ethnic heritage traced back to the area, a visit to Romania was usually a serious-minded one for business, not pleasure. And even then, in most cases, such a visit combined stops along the way limiting the Bucharest stay to as short a time as possible.

Gary L. Ackerman of Queens District, New York, and Mark D. Siljander of Holland District, Michigan, traveled to Romania without other Congressmen, but with their own missions. Congressmen Ackerman blitzed into Bucharest solo with his own foreign policy mission of returning with a constituent's spouse. The embassy consular section had taken care of most of the paper work with the Romanian authorities before he arrived in Romania. Vowing not to leave Romania without accomplishing his objective, Ackerman apparently wanted to do something rather dramatic and reap the favorable publicity back in New York. He could, upon the successful resolution of such a family reunification case, claim that he could deliver and that he was concerned about human rights—or at least the release of this one person. And despite his antics and limited objective, inasmuch as it helped get one person out of Romania reunified with her family, it was a worthy accomplishment. Apparently Ackerman left Bucharest with the assurance that the woman would also depart Romania within a day or so. Perhaps in part for the Romanians helping him play the game, he continued to vote for MFN for Romania in June 1986 and April 1987.

Congressman Mark Siljander visited Romania in December of 1984, traveling with an entourage that included his wife, a White House official, and representatives of Pat Robertson's 700 Club. Also Christian Response International Executive Director, Rev. Jeffrey Collins, came with the Siljander party. Siljander had at least two major reasons for going to Romania. On his maternal side his ancestry traced back to Germans and Romanians in Transylvania, and thus he had a personal interest in seeing the land of his ancestors. Also as an activist in the fundamentalist Christian cause, Siljander was deeply concerned about and interested in the plight of persecuted Christians behind the Iron Curtain. While in Romania he went to several churches and met with Christians representing various denominations. Because he was traveling with some individuals who knew the country and some of its religious figures, he was also able to see some out-of-the-way places not usually visited by American dignitaries. Notably, he attended a worship service in a snow fall and amid the rubble of a government destroyed church near Bistrita in Transylvania. As recounted to me by White House official Carolyn Sundseth, that outdoor service with several hundred brave souls risking their lives, was the most memorable and moving aspect of the whole visit.[2]

It should be noted that the Romanian government tried to head off the visit in the first place. Since the Romanian Ambassador to Washington, Mircea Malitza, had not discouraged the visitors he had staked himself out for some trouble. When people of such stature come to Romania, the Bucharest-based officials like to have total control over the situation. They prefer a long advance notice and a complete itinerary with places and individuals to be visited. The Romanian officials did not want the Siljander group to come but felt under pressure to let them visit anyway. They did not know what to make of the group because of the White House representation but considered that they had to be dealt with. Thus they tried to strictly arrange the visit to keep the fact-finding group from seeing the real situation. Efforts were made to ensure that many of those religious figures to be visited were far out of town and unavailable. Some meetings were cancelled as the individuals were suddenly not able to make the sessions. They included government "religious" officials and dissident figures. These government actions were in fact the rule rather than the exception for such visits.

In addition to the group seeing much more throughout the country than the government wanted it to see, an incident occurred revolving around dissident priest Father Calciu. Father Calciu was the top symbol of Romanian Orthodox opposition to the Communist regime. He had been in jail for many years and was in declining health. His case became a symbolic one to those in the West fighting for improved human rights in Romania. Trying to resolve the Calciu case was in fact the top priority human rights case of the American Embassy. His name was consistently put at the top of the list of American requests. The embassy helped arrange for the Siljander group to see Father Calciu personally. Calciu had just been moved from jail to house arrest in Bucharest. I went to the Romanian Foreign Ministry with Congressman Siljander to talk about the Calciu case and facilitate arrangements for seeing him. The Romanian Foreign Ministry officials refused to see Siljander, who accompanied me when I was delivering a demarche on Calciu. Along with another U.S. Embassy official I found this conduct by the Romanians incredulous. It was certainly undiplomatic, if not also self-defeating, to shun an American government representative who had been invited—even if reluctantly—to visit the country. Those of us at the embassy lodged a protest.

It was learned later that the Siljander visit and the focus it put on Romanian religious repression, was a factor in the recall of the Romanian ambassador in Washington not long after that. The recall of Ambassador Mircea Malitza was significant in U.S.-Romanian relations because the resourceful, English-speaking Malitza, was replaced by a more typical Communist representative who lacked skills of diplomacy and language. Malitza was effective for Bucharest because of his smooth, sophisticated way of projecting things. He had a knack for putting the best face on the worst Warsaw Pact regime. His enthusiastic defense of Ceausescu's government may have been at least partly related to his enjoyment of the trappings of "decadent" Western life in Washington. Because of his skillful whitewashing of Romania's repressive actions against political and religious dissidents, he effectively prolonged the hope of exposing the reality, and improving conditions in Romania. Malitza, however, carefully answered letters sent to his embassy regarding immigration cases, giving the impression of concern. And perhaps he had a hand in getting more Romanian cases resolved which occurred under his watch. But his main legacy from a pro-freedom point of view is that he deftly covered up the increasing tyranny of one of the worst regimes in Europe, thus fooling many American officials who gave more support to Bucharest because of his efforts.

The two main Congressional delegations to visit Romania between late 1981 and the summer of 1985, were those in 1983 led by Congressmen Tom Lantos and Sam Gibbons. According to *Politics in America*, California Democrat Tom Lantos, who was born in Budapest, Hungary, of Jewish parents, had a reputation as a strong anti-Communist.[3] After his visit to Romania in January of 1983, I wondered how he got that reputation.

The Lantos delegation included Congressmen Don Bonker, William Frenzel, and Tom Lantos, along with the wives of several other

Congressmen, and State's Assistant Secretary for Congressional Relations Powell Moore. I noted in my diary on January 19, 1983, that the delegation gave a disgraceful performance which undercut U.S. efforts at reciprocity in the bilateral relationship. It even undermined the efforts of Lawrence Eagleburger, who led State endeavors to maintain differentiation and MFN for Romania. Eagleburger had just arrived in Romania a little over a week earlier to try to save the special relationship with Romania by persuading Bucharest to withdraw the education tax decree.

In this crisis context, the effect of the group's presentations was to reassure the Romanian government not to worry about its most serious violation of Jackson-Vanik, MFN and Helsinki. Mrs. Annette Lantos unbelievably said that she thought the Romanian decree was justified and legitimate. She also said that she thought Romania and Bucharest looked wonderful—from her car window— and she was anxious to return to one of her favorite places. Congressman Lantos said that if offered ambassadorships to Brussels or Bucharest, he would take Bucharest. They did not, however, have to live in Romania, and witness the day to day harsh reality of suffering. And Ceausescu was especially adept at playing on other large egos. The traveling U.S. Air Force crew said that they had never had a greater ego aboard than that of Lantos.

The key meeting of the Lantos delegation was the two-hour session with President Ceausescu on January 19th. Ceausescu gave his usual line: "you need me more, so I'll go it alone if necessary," which put the guests on the defensive. Ceausescu said that Romania had lived without MFN before and would live without it again if need be. He claimed that he would accept no conditions in order to keep MFN. He argued that the U.S. would lose more if MFN was withdrawn. Other Ceausescu statements sought to justify the imposition of the education tax decree, and to maintain that emigration was not part of the U.S.-Romanian Trade Agreement. Congressman Frenzel mentioned concern over the MFN-trade relationship with Romania, and the problem created by the education decree. Frenzel also stressed his hope that MFN would not have to be withdrawn.

Lantos emphasized the great wisdom and leadership of Ceausescu in international affairs, especially disarmament and peace. He praised the so-called independent foreign policy of Romania. And unlike Eagleburger, he said that if the decree was implemented chances of passing MFN would be *reduced*. Also Lantos almost alone among U.S. officials of any stripe said that he hoped Romania would get multiyear MFN, i.e. guaranteed for several years and thus eliminate the burden of annual MFN review by the U.S.* Lantos affirmed that the Hungarians were treated no worse than the Romanians and thus their complaints of cultural genocide were not justified. The Lantos's expressed surprise that nothing derogatory was mentioned about their Hungarian background. To top it off, Lantos said that if a Democrat President was elected in 1984, he would persuade him to visit Romania in 1985. Others in the delegation told me that they were surprised by Lantos's extreme homage to Ceausescu and said that he was usually tougher than on this occasion. My concern was whether Ceausescu got the impression that being so praised he would not then have to worry about getting a deal to pay Romania for emigration through Congress.

The way Lantos played the game is perhaps best indicated by the following examples. In the meetings with Romanian officials, he praised Ceausescu's independent foreign policy. Outside the meetings, he admitted that Romania's foreign policy was not so independent. Inside the meetings, Lantos said not a word about human rights. The meetings constituted the time he could have been some help to the thousands imprisoned, persecuted, and not allowed to emigrate. After the sessions, Mrs. Lantos handed me a list of families they wanted us to help get out, saying to my wife that one of her principal concerns back in the office in Washington was to get three Romanian families out of Romania since their relatives frequently visited the office. But the task of getting them out was made much more difficult by the public performance of Lantos in Bucharest. Back in the U.S., the Congressman was the first to advertise politically, the accomplishments made, and concern shown, during the trip.

Probably the one bright spot during the Ceausescu meeting with the Lantos delegation was Congressman Bonker's performance. On two occasions, Bonker said that the holocaust occurred because no one spoke out. Bonker spoke out with a modicum of firmness. In response to Bonker's statement that he was concerned about human rights and reports of religious persecution, Ceausescu answered that Bonker was misinformed. Ceausescu said that unlike the U.S., Romania pays its priests and pastors part of their salaries. During Bonker's presentation, Ceausescu looked down and

---

*Lantos, however, voted in April 1987, to suspend MFN for six months.

rifled through the Capitol Hill guidebook given him by Lantos and was visibly irritated. As on other occasions when he was hearing uncomfortable things, Ceausescu stuttered and clicked his mouth and jaws while stumbling for words to come out. Even though Bonker worked directly with human rights issues, and Lantos was apparently preoccupied with establishing his credibility with Ceausescu, concern expressed by all members of the Lantos delegation for human rights, emigration, and the education tax decree would have strengthened America's hand *vis-à-vis* Ceausescu. Similarly, U.S. interests and those of the suffering people in Romania would have been better served by a joint expression of such concern.

In December 1983, the most influential Congressional delegation to come to Romania under my watch, arrived under the leadership of Sam Gibbons. It was a stop-over because it was hard to get many members of the delegation to leave Greece for Romania, especially during the onset of winter. The mild and courteous Southern gentleman Gibbons was joined by Barber Conable, William Frenzel, Douglas Bereuter, Sander Levin, and the wife of James R. Jones. Gibbons of Tampa, Florida, was the key member of the House of Representatives dealing with MFN and trade matters with Romania. Hence the strenuous efforts of the Romanian Communists to lobby Gibbons, who heads the House Ways and Means Trade Subcommittee. Gibbons was already pro-MFN for Romania, and if anything, his day in Bucharest wined and dined by Ceausescu, only reinforced that view. Gibbons appeared to take the words of the Romanian leaders at face value. Ceausescu's typical performance during the visit was apparently effective with the Congressional delegation.

Ceausescu made several incredible statements, including notable Ceausescuisms related to religion, politics and the Soviets. He said that Romania's religious policy is more liberal than that of the U.S. Lecturing, Ceausescu said that Romania did not need any more American type religious groups, such as a third Baptist cult in Romania. Every institution or group has to be registered by the state, he pointed out. Clearly reflecting his limited understanding of multi-party political systems, he noted that all countries have differences in the way they handle things. West Germany, for example, not long ago banned a fascist political group and did the right thing according to Ceausescu. But he said it indicates that all political parties are not freely permitted. Don't you wish you had only one political party in the U.S.?, Ceausescu seriously asked. He then laughed at length, obviously believing that they agreed with him that it would be easier and preferable with only one party. He went out of his way to explain and rationalize the positions of the Soviet Union. He said he knew Andropov was a good man who wanted peace because he (Ceausescu) knew him well. The U.S.S.R. wants peace and Andropov wants peace, according to Ceausescu. Thus the U.S. should return to its pre-deployment position of a month before, since the intermediate range missile deployment in West Germany only provoked the Soviets by showing force.

Discussing other matters, Ceausescu talked about Romania decreasing military spending and increasing both the GNP and standard of living by 7-8% the next year. Ceausescu shrewdly attempted to throw the monkey on America's back for Romania's anti-emigration policy. He claimed that there were over 2,000 Romanians waiting to emigrate but the U.S. would not give them visas. Many wait two years and it is a humanitarian concern, Ceausescu claimed. Obviously no one had told Ceausescu that Romania only allows a "handful" of its people to leave and only then after years of waiting without jobs, apartments, and citizenship status. Ceausescu did not reflect awareness that the U.S. has over 230 million people who can have papers and emigrate when they want without being punished by the government.

It was hardly necessary for Ceausescu to lecture the Congressional delegation on how much the U.S. needs MFN for Romania and Romania does not need it. Gibbons wanted continued subsidized trade even though current exchanges were overwhelmingly in Romania's favor. Additionally, Gibbons promoted MFN for Romania without even trying to get a *quid pro quo*. No doubt his position related to his perceived advocacy role as chairman of the House Ways and Means Trade Subcommittee. He also fully accepted the State Department argument for differentiation favoring Ceausescu's Romania. At the embassy, Gibbons privately told me that it was his understanding that Henry Kissinger started the flirtation with Ceausescu a decade ago to cause a little worry for the Soviets. He had Kissinger's view right, but the "little" worry caused for the Soviets was "microscopic."

I noted in my diary that whereas Gibbons determinedly wanted favored trade status for Romania, he did not express real concern about human rights. In observing American Congressional leaders in their dealings with Communist officials both in Washington and

Eastern Europe, it seemed to me that many U.S. representatives have proven easy prey for well-trained, experienced, Communist professionals.

United States Information Agency Director Charles Z. Wick, Director of the United States Information Agency (USIA, but referred to as USIS abroad) spent one of the lengthier stays in Romania for a high ranking official. He visited Romania from October 3rd to October 7th, 1984. In the fall of 1984, during his visit to Romania, Charles Wick specialized more in candor than in State Department "diplomacy."

I had met with Wick back in 1982, at his request and had presented him with my recommendations for better projecting America's values and image in places like Romania. I noted that most Romanians had long questioned and wondered why the U.S. presented such an emphasis on negative news. They felt that such overwhelming daily self-denigration reflects weakness in American government and society, not the strength of "objectivity and diversity" aimed for by USIA-Voice of America (VOA) broadcasters. Since it seems self defeating for the U.S. to emphasize the worst parts of American society, I recommended accentuating the positive even while presenting all the relevant news in an objective manner. It is not necessary to present biased news reports but rather to explain the values, principles, and motivations responsible for outstanding American achievements, e.g. the great productivity of farmers and creativity of scientists in terms of technological advances. I continued by saying that our strategy in VOA broadcasting and representations of U.S. society and government via libraries, publications, films, and speakers, would be made more effective by a great nation unashamed to express pride in its distinctive government system with freedoms, opportunity, and comparative wealth.

We should proudly proclaim that with all of its flaws, the U.S. is still the beacon of freedom and hope for enslaved and persecuted people everywhere desirous of liberty. As President Reagan has done so articulately we should unapologetically be positive advocates of our way of life and government. This will be viewed as a strength—not weakness—of a confident U.S. determined to preserve its unique inheritance and economic and political systems. I said that it was my sincere hope that the newly appointed VOA Director will complete a shift in emphasis in the way we present news and information to the rest of the world, in particular to the Communist countries.

A few specific items I suggested for the USIA in the Communist world of Eastern Europe include: (1) sending speakers and exchangees who are not virulently anti-American or negative in approach; (2) attempting to get USIA officers out to meet a broad spectrum of society, not only the new class elite of the Communist Party plus its supporting intellectuals in the capital city; and (3) broadcasting and reporting some positive elements of American society and government.

Wick responded positively to my recommendations in a letter. He agreed with my suggestions for the Voice of America and shared them with the VOA leadership. Wick said that the USIA would continue to move in the direction of projecting in every way possible "the principles of freedom and democracy to foreign audiences" and not lose sight of the "many positive attributes of the American way of life."[4]

Tiring of the mounting frustrations in dealing with the cultural and education officials of the Communist regime and the increasing obstacles they put in the way of Americans operating in Romania, we fully catalogued these for Charlie Wick in a briefing after his arrival in Bucharest. The irony was that most of the exchanges culturally and educationally benefitted the Romanians much more than the Americans. And the U.S. government went out of its way to help the Romanians help themselves. But fear of outside influences and paranoia took precedence over the more beneficial course for them. An especially praiseworthy action of Wick was his questioning of a Romanian who had recently benefitted from a USIA grant to travel through the U.S. Most Romanian Communists who visited the U.S. under the auspices of the USIA subsequently speak and write glowingly of their experiences. The grantee, Mr. Lazar, did the opposite to please his bosses in Bucharest. Lazar wrote a virulent propaganda tract attacking the U.S. According to many American eyewitnesses, Lazar fabricated tales of horror, misery, and non-cooperation. Wick asked him why he was unhappy about his visit.

Perhaps in part because of our briefing, Wick told the Romanians in a frank, direct, and to-the-point manner that their Ministry of Education officials were not treating the Americans well.[5] Wick also took a tough line at the Foreign Ministry, where he talked with

Deputy Foreign Minister Maria Groza. Word filtered back to Ceausescu, who in a typical fit of pique, decided not to see Wick. In addition to the Ceausescu rebuff the Foreign Minister decided not to serve as host for a dinner for Wick as was previously scheduled. The Romanian officials figured that the tough stand taken by Wick in looking out for U.S. interests came from the embassy. Ceausescu and Andrei wanted to make it clear that they expected the old way of U.S. officials only saying nice things and giving attention to Romania's whims. This is one legacy of past U.S. foreign policy actions *vis-à-vis* Bucharest.

Wick supported the positions and concerns of the embassy as much as any high level visitor. The USIA Director handled the Foreign Ministry and Education Ministry meetings toughly and bluntly, causing his USIA chief in Bucharest—Public Affairs Officer (PAO) Edward McBride—to backpedal and get cold feet. While McBride was a real improvement over his predecessor Alvin Perlman, who seemed to defend actions of the Bucharest regime, he nearly panicked when he saw the Romanians get upset at Wick's remarks. McBride scurried around, subsequently trying to get Wick to soften his approach and smooth the waters.

Arms Control and Disarmament
Agency Director Kenneth Adelman

One of the last official visitors to Bucharest during my watch was Arms Control and Disarmament Agency (ACDA) Director, Ambassador Kenneth Adelman. The Adelman party included Robert Fischer of the ACDA, Paula Dobriansky of the NSC and Tom Simons of the Soviet Affairs Division at the State Department. Meetings took place with the Foreign Minister, and General Ilie Ceausescu—Defense Ministry official and brother of the President. As was the custom, embassy officials privately briefed the American visitors. Along with other principal officers, I candidly expressed the record of Romanian tyranny and collaboration with the Soviets, and U.S. interests in the area. Later Tom Simons of the State Department described the briefing as passionately held views representing a small segment of opinion. While the Adelman-Andrei meeting was uneventful, there were some fireworks during the session with General Ilie Ceausescu on January 18th, 1985.

Ilie Ceausescu was shown a copy of ACDA figures printed in

Business Week magazine showing Romania with more than one billion dollars in military arms exports in 1982, ranking fifth in the world.[6] Ceausescu laughed saying that: it would be nice if that figure on Romania were true. He went on to say that since Romania's total exports were only two billion dollars, such a figure was not true. After all, he said, Romania only exports such things as cement, clothes and bicycles. For those of us who had seen reports detailing extensive Romanian arms exports, Ceausescu's total denial was preposterous. The performance of State Department official Tom Simons was even more incredible, as Simons tried to ingratiate himself to Ceausescu. Simons apparently did not want Ceausescu to be upset about having to see such ACDA figures on Romanian arms exports and deny their validity. Simons said that he wanted Ceausescu to know that all of the Americans present considered the Romanian leaders good friends. The obvious efforts of Simons to curry the favor of Ceausescu constituted a sad example of State Department "diplomacy."

Chairman of the Joint Chiefs of Staff General John Vessey Jr.

The last major American official to visit Romania during my stay as ambassador was General John Vessey Jr., Chairman of the Joint Chiefs of Staff. Vessey's visit was no different than the other official ones in that it was an element of the State Department's policy of frequent high level visits between the two countries. Vessey had told me earlier in Washington that he was going at the behest of Secretary of State Shultz who considered such a visit to be in the national interest. The differentiation policy as interpreted by the State Department required a steady march of government leaders to reaffirm American policy of rewarding Romania on a regular basis. Some of us at the embassy expressed reservations about a Vessey visit. But in view of the State Department's determination to send Vessey, we could only hope for the best during his visit.

I had mentioned to Vessey that the visit could serve a meaningful purpose if he used the occasion to strongly affirm American values and beliefs, concern for human rights, and national security concerns. Otherwise, it only boosted Ceausescu's stock and sent the wrong signals to everyone. Vessey expressed awareness and appreciation of those concerns and said that he would be going to

Bucharest with his eyes open—not to be used for their purposes. For reasons of his reputation as a man of principle and knowing his son, I had to take him at his word.[7]

Vessey, who came officially as the guest of the Romanian Minister of Defense Constantin Olteanu, met with him on March 27th, 1985. During the Olteanu meeting the Defense Minister repeated General Ilie Ceausescu's claim that Romania does not export military arms even though ACDA figures for 1982 placed Romania fifth in the world with over one billion dollars in actual military arms deliveries. Olteanu, who did not last long after this as Defense Minister, seldom if ever said anything that was not in his prepared statements. This time was no exception. In a subsequent meeting with President Ceausescu on March 29th, General Vessey handled himself rather well. There were no surprises in these meetings.

Minor Players

There were many other important figures to visit Romania for political, economic, and religious reasons. These ranged from a stop-over by former Treasury Secretary David Kennedy, trying to get official status for the Mormons, to a private trade mission by former Congressman Charles Vanik, to a mutual admiration society reunion of former President Richard Nixon with Ceausescu. There were many lower level U.S. government representatives— probably the most notable of which was former Congressman Ed Derwinski, Counselor of the State Department. Derwinski's visits did little but give the Bucharest regime an extra measure of assurance from Washington that things would work out all right. I had to wonder when I saw Derwinski in action in Bucharest, at the State Department, and in later Congressional hearings on MFN for Romania, if he was really comfortable—politician aside—in an advocacy role for Ceausescu. Perhaps one State Department way of countering right wing opposition was to put forth a former Congressman of ethnic Eastern European origin with a reputation as a tough anti-Communist, as the government spokesman on matters such as MFN for Romania.

One of the intriguing aspects of the State Department's policy of rewarding Bucharest with high level visits was the parallel activities of the minor "non-government" players. The minor players, perhaps best represented by Milton Rosenthal, Jack Spitzer and Arthur Schneier, had as their paramount concerns, issues of Jewish emigration, business, and trade. Some American businessmen and Jewish leaders played a political role in addition to their other interests. They could play a special role because they had access to Ceausescu. From time to time they were used as intermediaries by the State Department to pass messages, mend fences, and play up to Ceausescu's mammoth ego. On occasion they slipped into Bucharest without contact with the American embassy and were given near royal treatment by the Romanians. During an early visit by Rabbi Arthur Schneier in July 1982, Schneier praised Ceausescu's foreign policy while virtually ignoring the persecution and repression internally. I mentioned to him that some concern shown by him for all people and groups suffering in Romania would afford greater credibility. Subsequently he inquired about the human rights violations of Baptists, Catholics, and Hungarians. Visiting Romania again in December of 1982, Schneier reported that Ceausescu wanted some face-saving compromise on the education tax measure.

In April of 1983, the embassy was bypassed by the State Department when Milton Rosenthal, carrying an Eagleburger message, met for some eight hours over a two day period with Ceausescu. It was unknown to us at the time, but the message included concessions to Ceausescu as part of a deal. It was another example of the State Department not informing the American Embassy in Bucharest of negotiations directly involving the embassy's *raison d'être*. The Romanian Foreign Minister would visit Washington, the State Department would present a package of concessions to the Romanian government in order to salvage MFN for Romania, and the Vice President would personally carry the package to Foreign Minister Andrei. That apparently was the essence of the Eagleburger-State Department plan transmitted through Rosenthal.

In November of 1983, another of the non-government individuals playing at policymaking in U.S.-Romanian relations arrived in Romania. In the words of a colleague, Jack Spitzer—former President of B'nai B'rith—was "a real arrogant ass." The Israeli ambassador volunteered that Spitzer was easily manipulated and naive. During his visit, Spitzer was upset over getting no high level embassy representative to meet him at the airport. We were not aware of any special mission or government status. He showed no interest in the plight of the Romanians, but appeared to flaunt his access to Ceausescu and red carpet treatment by the President. Spitzer advertised: "I will be on the 8:15 television news" with Ceausescu.

Each of the visits by the minor players was highlighted in the Romanian press.

Finally the presidents of American companies doing business with Romania visited Romania from time to time. Originally the State elite had enlisted these business leaders in the favor-Romania game. Since the beginning days of the U.S.-Romania Trade Agreement and MFN, American company presidents have testified for Favored Nation Status for Romania. At the same time they have benefitted from trade with Romania. Many American businessmen appear overwhelmed by the opportunity to meet President Ceausescu and to be photographed with him. Others serve as promoters for Ceausescu, conveniently overlooking the low wages, required labor, poor work conditions, and government repression. George Gellert of Atalanta Company in New York City, for example, has relished the connections as well as the profits. And Howard Goodman of Florida, utilizes Romanian labor to finish construction of shoes, which do well in the American market. Goodman is not atypical of the businessmen who support political positions in order to preserve a good money making opportunity. When I mentioned the actual plight of most Romanians to Howard Goodman, his wife Bobbie offered to include our son in a film depicting the good life of young people in Romania.

There is, then, an alliance between the State elite and American business leaders which has proved useful to Ceausescu.

Epilogue

Contrary to several published accounts I did not abruptly resign in protest. Instead I took the occasion of my resignation and departure to speak out in opposition to U.S. policy toward Romania and to help publicize the plight of the persecuted Romanians.[1] Actually I made arrangements to return to Campbell University which I had left on a leave of absence. Between August 31 and November 6, 1984, I either corresponded or talked in person with Campbell President Norman A. Wiggins, who offered an endowed chair and the departmental chairmanship for me to return. Our family wanted to return to North Carolina and the United States after an absence of almost four years.

Prior to making a definite commitment to return to Campbell and North Carolina, I talked with White House Personnel Director John Herrington who had posed as a conservative. Herrington told me: "you are one of the few ambassadors over there in the State Department we have not changed; I will fight to keep you there." More interestingly he said: "we need you; stay there until June or midsummer when we will possibly have a new Secretary of State and bigger things should be in store for you."[2] I did not feel I could wait in Bucharest until then without any definite on-going plans since I intended to return to the states in any event. Therefore I signed a contract during the fall of 1984, to return to Campbell for the fall semester of 1985.

In all candor I looked forward to leaving the tragic atmosphere in Romania. In a September 1986 conversation with a former administrative officer at the embassy in Bucharest who had subsequently served in Manila and periodically throughout mainland China as an inspector of the new consulates, he said that conditions in Romania were worse than in the Soviet Union, China, and the Philippines. From the perspective of the Foreign Service he said that Romania should have the higher post differential as a hardship post of those countries mentioned. The depressing stories from Romanians, the hardships of everyday life, the sadness and pessimism, all combined to make it grueling. Perhaps most disheartening however was the State Department policy which seemed to help perpetuate the misery. The regime in Bucharest remained the chief beneficiary of the U.S. policy.

One aspect of relief in departing was to leave behind the polluted air in Bucharest and the generally unhealthful atmosphere. In my own case there was evidence of the embassy being radiated by waves sent out by the Romanians to several offices in the embassy complex. Such radiation could very well have contributed to the lower back problems I developed while in Romania. When entering the job as ambassador I was x-rayed without any discernible back or bone problem. X-rays of February 15, 1985, showed according to State Department physician, Dr. Antal: "a narrowing of the disc at the base of the spine/pelvic/sacrum joining, with beginning arthritis at that point." And on March 1, 1985, Dr. L. Ottenritter also of the State Department medical staff said that "the last disc base had narrowed and degenerated. There is a diminution in volume of the disc base. A problem in the lower back could include numbness and backaches." All of this was happening to a 40 year old male in good health with no history of medical ailments or difficulties.

At the same time I did not mind leaving behind the tapped telephones, the electronic surveillance in hotels, restaurants, apartments, the semi-armored limousine chauffered by a Romania driver who worked for the Securitate (KGB-equivalent), and the official residence surrounded by walls and guarded twenty four hours a day by Romanian soldiers carrying Russian machine guns.

Nevertheless, I felt that I was returning home more than departing "our second home of Romania." It was not so much leaving the bad things about the Communist system behind, because the real people could not be left in our thoughts and prayers. But it was time to return to our homeland, our home state, and our families and friends in the U.S. It was time for our son to go to college in North Carolina, for our daughter to return to school in America, to see Betty's parents (our children's only living grandparents) and sisters, as well as my sisters more often, and to work in careers seeking to help those without freedom while preserving our own.

After several letter drafts over a period of several months, I sent a letter of resignation to President Reagan followed almost simultaneously by one to Secretary Shultz. In the letter to the President I stressed the objectives I had worked to attain. Specifically I tried to "demonstrate American concern for fundamental human rights, free emigration and individual worth and dignity," and "to help protect the national security interests of the United States." I also described the ways in which the Romanian government demonstrates its non-independence of Moscow. I expressed my gratitude to the President and said that I would like to end my ambassadorial tour and return to North Carolina for personal and family reasons during the summer of 1985.[3]

I received a letter from the President dated April 29, 1985, accepting my resignation "with deep regret." The President mentioned in particular "efforts to improve the human rights situation in Romania," and "support of our national security interests in Europe."[4]*

After my return to the U.S., the Secretary of State met with me on May 21st during the process of de-briefings in Washington. Shultz said nothing about my resignation. He no doubt was mindful of my interview with *Washingon Post* correspondent Bradley Graham during my return from Bucharest to Washington. He did not express any appreciation or wish me well in the future. His main concern in the discussion seemed to be the cable sent from the American Embassy in Bucharest to Washington just prior to my departure. The cable summarized my concerns about the direction State Department-implemented-policy was taking the U.S., and the need for a reevaluation of American policy *vis-à-vis* Romania. Unlike the previous discussion we had, this time Shultz had obviously taken the time to read up on the situation in U.S.-Romanian relations and Romania itself. Nevertheless, his expressed knowledge was the Kissinger-Eagleburger-Palmer line which held sway in the State Department's European Affairs Bureau. He asked me to elaborate on the questions raised in the cable. Shultz's questions all related to what policy would be best in dealing with Romania and what choice the U.S. had in this regard.

Not long after my departure from Bucharest it was business as usual in U.S.-Romanian relations. In the State Department and other offices of government which actually direct the day to day policy toward Romania, there was no doubt a sigh of relief at my departure. The establishment elite moved quickly to return the relationship to its pre-1981 norm. Some of the principal actions which signalled this restoration were: the appointment of a compliant career officer as the new U.S. ambassador to Bucharest; the sending of

*See Appendix II.

Senator Robert Dole to assure the Romanians everything was back
to normal; and the more urgent visit of Secretary Shultz whose trip
had been long planned.

Roger Kirk is a career member of the Foreign Service elite who
has obviously paid his dues and has done what the State Department wanted. He was designated as my replacement in Bucharest
before I departed but did not actually arrive in Romania until
November 1985—some six months later. When I spoke with him
in Washington after my return from Bucharest he seemed like a personable fellow. His interest as reflected in questions to me appeared
to be oriented toward what the tennis playing possibilities were, and
how the cocktail circuit of the diplomats was, more than anything
else. He had no background experience related to Romania or
Romanian language knowledge at that point. The State Department
probably planted articles in the Washington newspapers which said
a new tough ambassador was being sent to Romania, so that any
potential opposition by conservatives could be defused. However,
from every report I have received the new ambassador has turned
out to be a good advocate for the Romanian government to the
United States. He was reportedly in Washington in late August-early
September 1986, lobbying for Romania's case before Congressmen,
businessmen, and others concerned with Romanian affairs. The
State Department again has in place an ambassador who will help
perpetuate differentiation and a pro-MFN policy toward Romania
which overlooks Romania's tyranny and neglects U.S. interests. I
know that some religious and human rights groups have expressed
frustration that the embassy is showing little concern and interest
in pursuing reports of persecution. There are no more reports from
the embassy which question Romania's so-called independent foreign policy. But a tennis court was recently built at the American
ambassador's residence.

Senator Robert Dole was sent to Romania as soon as possible
after my departure from Romania to assure Ceausescu that everything was all right in the relationship and that basically the Romanian Communists had nothing to fear from the U.S. government.
From friends inside the embassy I learned that Dole went to
Bucharest to let Ceausescu know that the departing blast from Funderburk did not really represent the view of the American government which wanted to restore the business-as-usual association.
MFN would not be taken away from the Romanians but perhaps
a few symbolic gestures on Bucharest's part—which were annually

made anyway prior to summer MFN debates—would sweeten the pot and enable Washington to present the best case for the Romanians.

Secretary of State Shultz's visit to Romania had long been in the works, but was delayed for some time. Perhaps it was postponed until the arrival of a new ambassador in the fall of 1985.

Shultz's trip to Romania was notable for its lack of toughness on Romania, even though published reports maintained that Shultz lectured Ceausescu on religious concerns. Shultz actually mentioned concern about the situation of minor nonrecognized sects such as the Church of Jesus Christ of the Latter Day Saints (Mormons), Nazarenes, Jehovah's Witnesses, and an unofficial Baptist group. The mention of these unofficial religious denominations which are minuscule in size, was hardly threatening to the Romanian regime. Not mentioned were the Uniates, the most important nonrecognized religious group in Romania with a membership of perhaps one and a half million. The Uniates, who are principally of ethnic Romanian origin and concentrated in Transylvania, continue to be highly significant despite having been banned during the past three decades. Shultz also failed to address the major human rights concerns in Romania: the government's treatment of the Romanian people and of practicing believers of all faiths (including the majority Romanian Orthodox Church).

The chief purpose of the trip was clearly to return the U.S.-Romanian relationship to business as usual by continuing to praise the "courageous Ceausescu" for his "independent foreign policy." Shultz said on the eve of his trip to Bucharest that the visit was to show support for the individual "identities and aspirations of Romania, Hungary and Yugoslavia."[5] Simultaneously the U.S. Embassy in Bucharest let it be known that loss of MFN for Romania would take away any leverage they have in trying to solve human rights cases.[6]

One of the worst things the Reagan Administration could do in terms of Romania would be approval of a Presidential visit. If President Reagan agreed to visit Bucharest or to host Romanian President Ceausescu in Washington it would erase much of whatever else was accomplished in U.S.-Romanian relations during the Reagan Administration. A measure of realism was introduced in the equation to the degree that many officials in Washington and others look on Romanian foreign policy independence with skepticism. Also greater pressure was applied on the Romanian government to improve its human rights record. Despite the fact that business has pretty much returned to normal, for four years the Reagan Administration had been constrained to look again at the real face of Bucharest.

A Presidential exchange allowing either Reagan to visit Bucharest or Ceausescu to go to Washington would put the Reagan Administration in the same historical boat with the previous administrations of Nixon, Ford, and Carter. During those administrations either Ceausescu came to the U.S. or the U.S. President—in the cases of Nixon and Ford—went to Romania. Such visits under Reagan would again signal Romania and the world that the U.S. puts "favored treatment" friendship with Ceausescu above the U.S. national security interests and above the plight of the politically and religiously persecuted people in Romania. The Romanian people would not understand what the U.S. actually stands for or believes in. And many knowledgeable Americans and Europeans would not fathom why the U.S. government continues to play ball with Bucharest.

During my stay in Romania, I was worried that the State Department would any day recommend a Presidential exchange to help shore up the relationship and confirm differentiation. But the State position during my stay in Bucharest was to profess nonsupport for such a visit in the hope of getting a consensus on other visitors. If those of us in the American Embassy would agree to support visits to Romania by the Vice President and Secretary of State, then the State officials would claim non-support for a Reagan visit.

What has come out of this struggle, of a conservative ambassador in the Reagan Administration caught between the State Department and an anti-U.S. tyrannical Communist regime in Eastern Europe? If nothing else there is today a greater realism in the way Americans view the government in Bucharest. The news media to a limited extent, Congressmen to a greater extent than before, and even those policymakers in Washington's Foreign Service apparatus, have been challenged to reassess U.S. policy toward Romania and Eastern Europe and the sick reality of life in Romania today. It is unfortunately true that Romania again got MFN in 1985 and 1986, but each time it was more difficult and the Bucharest regime paid a higher price in terms of world-wide condemnation. A July 29, 1986, House of Representatives vote favored Romania by the closest-ever 216 to 190 margin. A Senate resolution sponsored by Senator Paul Trible in 1986, denounced the Romanian government's: "continued hostility to the exercise of religious, political, and cultural rights," and asked the U.S. government to find out if the Romanians are allowing (as they promised) the printing of several thousand Bibles, and the preservation of churches and synagogues.[7]

The most encouraging action to date was the vote in both houses of Congress in 1987, to suspend MFN for Romania for six months. The House of Representatives voted on April 30th, by 232-183, for Congressman Frank Wolf's amendment to the trade bill, which would suspend MFN for six months until the President certified that progress was made on human rights. Senators William Armstrong and Christopher Dodd sponsored a similar amendment which passed on June 26th by a vote of 57-36.*

The change in how Bucharest is viewed was described in an article in the Swiss *Journal De Geneve* of December 1985:

> For years, the United States has been giving Romania velvet-glove treatment because it dared to stand up to Soviet 'Big Brother'—never mind how Marxist-Dictatorial its regime was internally.
>
> Romanian leader Ceausescu has benefited from the deal. Especially from Most-Favored-Nation treatment by the United States. And he has repaid his debts to the IMF and American banks on the DOT. What more could one want?
>
> But in recent months the resignation of the U.S. Ambassador to Bucharest, and revelations by the media, have opened Americans' eyes at last to the real nature of the Romanian regime: its persecution of dissidents, [. . .], the misuse of psychiatry against opponents; Bibles confiscated and used as toilet paper—and so on ad nauseam.
>
> It is all very well for Secretary of State Shultz to warn Romania during his recent visit to keep its promise to respect human rights. The damage has been done: Romania has taken everything—and given nothing.[8]

Media accounts in the U.S. during the past two years have been a mixed bag. Conservative publishers such as *Human Events*, the Heritage Foundation and *Conservative Digest* have expectedly printed accounts critical of State Department policy.[9] The *Reader's Digest* published an article which portrayed a more realistic story

---

*A second Senate vote occurred on July 15th, rejecting pressure to change the amendment to the trade bill by a vote of 53-44. No word has yet come regarding a possible Presidential certification.

of the harshness of Ceausescu's rule.[10] More surprisingly, Bradley
Graham and Jackson Diehl of *The Washington Post* have published
balanced articles which shed more light on both the limits of any
Romanian independence and Bucharest's treatment of its people.[11]
But for every such article which attempts to give a clearer picture
of Romania in the 1980s, there is one which repeats the miscon-
ceptions of the past and the State line. The most blatant whitewash
which could have been produced by the Romanian Communist
Tourist Bureau (O.N.T.) was a week long series on CNN Television's International Hour called "The Iron Curtain Rises." Watching
the whole series on Romania with the Mircea Tatos family (immigrant Romanians), we were convinced that scarcely a glimpse
of the reality of Communist Romania was shown. CNN Diplomatic
Correspondent Stuart Loory's account closely reflected State
Department-U.S. Embassy (Bucharest) arguments and Ceausescu's
wishes.[12]

During the month before departure from Bucharest, Frank
Corry—the Deputy Chief of Mission— returning from a DCM
Conference in Berlin said that perhaps all of our efforts were not
in vain as far as U.S. government policy was concerned. Corry said
he heard privately that our efforts had had an impact on the White
House and NSC, and even to some extent Shultz. They were more
skeptical of Ceausescu and the Romanian government after our
reports. A NSC official told Corry privately that we were being
listened to, and that there was no enthusiasm for Romania in the
White House. We were to some extent successful on the issue of
sensitive technology transfer. Also we had scored points in remind-
ing American officials that Romania is a loyal member of the Warsaw Pact with no real independence and a terrible human rights
record.

Actions by thousands of Romanians outside Romania have made
it clear that most émigré Romanians oppose the Western policies
of favoring Ceausescu's government. The World Union of Free
Romanians headed by Ion Ratiu, and the Faith and Liberty Institute in the U.S. led by Victor Gaetan, have strongly expressed their
opposition to MFN for Romania, and their support for a realistic
appraisal of Romanian foreign policy and human rights abuses. Radio Free Europe broadcasters told me that hundreds of letters
received by RFE were overwhelmingly supportive of my stand.
Similarly, proclamations by various émigré Romanian groups, and
hundreds of letters and telephone calls to me, have supported my

recommendations for U.S. and Western policy *vis-à-vis* Bucharest, as well as for helping the Romanian people.[13]

Following my departure from Bucharest, Bradley Graham of *The Washington Post* immediately printed the account of my resignation. It also appeared in *The International Herald Tribune* and was followed by subsequent articles and editorials in various newspapers. MFN testimony reflected a lot of what was said. Many who had been fighting long and hard for getting the truth out were now listened to by more influential people. Juliana Pilon of the Heritage Foundation, former Congressman Mark Siljander, Congressmen Philip Crane and Frank Wolf, former deputy chief of Romania's Securitate Ion Pacepa, Father Calciu, and many others, helped expose the truth of the sick man of Europe and the failure of U.S. policy there.

By the summer of 1987, it seemed that the U.S.-Romanian relationship had altered somewhat. Under the new embassy officers and the Shultz administration at State the differentiation policy proceeded as usual, even if slightly crippled. What had changed was the increased scrutiny on Romania and Ceausescu by Congress, concerned religious and human rights groups, and other individuals. This led to a heightened awareness and accelerated questioning of U.S. policy toward Romania. The House-Senate votes to suspend MFN for Romania, evidenced the changed way of looking at Ceausescu's Romania.

The official terminology to describe the relationship has changed. During the 1970's it was Romania's independent foreign policy. By the 1980's it was referred to as a *relatively* independent foreign policy. But as my DCM in Bucharest—Frank Corry—liked to say: "relative" is like saying that an expecting woman is relatively or partially pregnant. Romanian independence is a term used less and less to denote Romania's foreign policy. State Department spokesmen before Congressional hearings have become increasingly defensive about the relationship. More and more they are admitting a few aspects of the terrible human records in Romania and Ceausescu's "cult" reign. And they have found new rationalizations for keeping MFN for Romania beyond any Romanian independence. As Nestor Rates of RFE has pointed out, the most recent State Department line is that MFN should be preserved to give the U.S. leverage in terms of human rights, and to put the U.S. in a position to capitalize from the inside on the approaching post-Ceausescu period.[14]

My argument of U.S. differentiation benefitting Ceausescu's regime and not the Romanian people, as well as being detrimental to U.S. national security interests, has now been joined by Romanian dissidents such as Mihai Botez. Botez has stated that the "ordinary Romanian is less and less inclined to hope for support from those in whom he had placed his hopes, namely the Americans, but who are 'betraying' him by allying themselves with his oppressors."[15]

Perhaps some of the best indicators of our getting close to home uncovering the truth was the level of esteem we were held in by both the State Department leadership elite and the Communist leaders in Bucharest. I learned from various sources that Ceausescu considered me less helpful to the Romanian Communists than the previous two U.S. ambassadors. Also Ceausescu ranked me as the Romanian Communist's number one enemy working inside the American embassy. One source that can be quoted is University of Colorado History Professor Stephen Fischer-Galati, who frequently visits Romania and talks with Romanian leaders. In a January 1985 session with the professor, he related conversations he had with the Deputy Defense Minister Ilie Ceausescu.[16] Fischer-Galati said that Ilie Ceausescu tried to enlist him in an effort to discredit me. It is not coincidental that the State Department has made similar efforts to discredit me, witness *The Charlotte Observer* article of March 16, 1986, and its nearly identical counterpart in the *Foreign Service Journal*. Fischer-Galati said that Ceausescu stated their main concern was in protecting their maverick image and getting an improved reputation in the U.S. both from the "independent" foreign policy and human rights points of view. He said that Ambassador Funderburk was not helpful to the Romanian Communists in these endeavors. Romanian dissident intellectuals told both me and Fischer-Galati that two of the three previous U.S. ambassadors during the 1970s were disasters from the "Western" point of view who knew nothing of the reality. And the other one who had had prior experience in Romania knew something about the situation but turned out to be not what was really needed. But when Funderburk was appointed, the Romanian government expected nothing but eventually got something they were not expecting. Dissident intellectuals said the 1981-85 embassy was what was needed from their point of view. Finally, Fischer-Galati mentioned that neither Ceausescu nor the State Department elite liked me. The pinstripers and Romanian Reds again had a commonality of interests on the subject of the U.S. ambassador.

State Department efforts to discredit me did not end with my departure from the ambassadorial post, but were much in evidence in my Republican primary campaign for the U.S. Senate from North Carolina during the fall of 1985 and spring of 1986. The foremost example of the State Department attacks came in a feature story in March 1986, in North Carolina's largest newspaper, *The Charlotte Observer*. One Washington based staff writer spent two or three months interviewing State Department employees who had worked with me at the American Embassy in Bucharest, Romania, between the fall of 1981 and the late spring of 1985. The newspaper article included comments by over 20 "unnamed" State Department officials. The fact of our playing the national anthem and patriotic music on the Fourth of July was mocked by State elitists. Accounts by the unnamed sources were replete with errors. Examples include the items about the secretaries and the American Club. And one official as in condemnation said that Funderburk "had grave reservations when he arrived so far as the career people were concerned . . . and skepticism about U.S. policy towards Romania." If I did not have such reservations I should have had them. Otherwise I would not have been doing the best possible job of trying to look out for U.S. interests. There were a few accurate quotes in the account. One official correctly noted that Funderburk "was cursed before he ever got there because Jesse Helms was his patron. . . .He simply wasn't told things. He was treated very shabbily." And Juliana Pilon of the Heritage Foundation said that "the conclusions he came to made the State Department a bit uncomfortable." One embassy official said that Funderburk "was no wimp, if he was, they [Romanian Communists] would have crapped all over us."[17]

Some progress has been made in getting out the truth about the Communist Romania-State Department collaboration. But much remains to be done to actually change the State Department policy *vis-à-vis* Eastern Europe. A few suggestions are herewith advanced for establishing a pro-freedom foreign policy.

We can challenge the convergence of interests of the pinstripers and Reds by a new U.S. policy toward Eastern Europe. Presidential selection of several dozen competent leaders to top positions at the State Department would be a necessary beginning. The new appointees must be qualified in terms of area studies, language, and overseas experience as well as leadership in non-government occupations in society. Additionally they should have demonstrated awareness of the need to put America's interests first. This would help counter the institutional tendency at State to emphasize the concerns of the country in which Foreign Service officers are serving. Leaders outside government are often in a better position to monitor the obsessive conformity and loyalty to the system and its elite, found in the State Department. A more effective mix of non-career appointees and careerists to the top positions at State should be made, which reflects a recognition by State of the necessity and value of political involvement in the foreign policy making process. Elected officials have the right and duty to participate in the process by appointments at State. These appointees should bring the elements of common sense, current American opinion, and a detachment from bureaucratic requirements. State Department diplomats excel in reporting what they have heard other officials say, and in the carrying out of policy instructions. Non-career appointees add the qualities of reflecting domestic and foreign policy concerns of the American people and politicians, and the initiative, boldness and courage needed to help formulate policy—which looks out for America's interests.

In formulating a new policy toward Eastern Europe, we have to consider the historical, ethnic, linguistic, cultural, and other differences among the individual nations and peoples of Eastern Europe. We have to keep in mind that the Soviet Bloc countries are subject to the Brezhnev Doctrine which prevents their voluntary escape from the bloc. Similarly they have mandatory membership in the Warsaw Treaty Organization and COMECON. There are agreements and treaties which bind the bloc states and require them to share sensitive technology and intelligence information acquired from the West.

Current U.S. policy says that a country making efforts to carry out a foreign policy independent of Moscow or efforts to make internal improvements including human rights and emigration, merit favored treatment. U.S. policy does not specifically spell out what constitutes foreign policy independence of Moscow or where the line is drawn in terms of internal reforms. Furthermore, U.S. policy does not in actual practice factor in the degree of the country's involvement in terrorism, drug shipments, military arms exports, and aid to Communist forces fighting against American allies or interests. Present U.S. policy only artificially divides the Eastern European states and in the process misleads many in the West into considering them as virtual non-bloc countries. The leadership elite at the State Department tends to come down on the side of Western bailouts for Eastern Europe and even the U.S.S.R. Present policy does not take into account that the bloc governments have far greater similarities than differences. Neither does current policy keep in mind that we are dealing with Communist regimes that are not free, not democratic, not capitalistic, and not pro-individual (or pro-human rights). State Department policy operates on the assumption that the Eastern European governments are not wed to the Soviet Bloc and thus disintegration can occur via American tweaks of the Russian bear and aid to the favored states. U.S. policy has not advanced the process of splitting the satellites.

As a minimum set of principles underlying a new U.S. policy, we should consider what most benefits the U.S. morally, politically, strategically, economically, and in terms of national security. Concomitantly we should keep in mind our obligations to seek improved measures of spiritual and material well being for the peoples of Eastern Europe. There can be no permanent abandonment of the people of Eastern Europe as far as freedom is concerned. It is questionable whether our policy should be geared toward making the world safe for Titoism, Ceausescuism, or Kadarism, when our first focus should be the pro-capitalistic, pro-democratic, and pro-human rights governments that are free. It is more important symbolically and practically that we first extend aid, trade subsidies, and/or technological and political benefits to free democratic countries which are allies.

U.S. policy should not extend important technology, military or security items to Soviet Bloc countries. U.S. subsidized loans, credits, and other forms of assistance through the World Bank, IMF, Eximbank, and individual American banks, should not be granted. There may be a determination that non-strategic, consumer-oriented trade, as well as closely monitored scientific, cultural, educational, and touristic exchanges, can benefit both U.S. interests and those of most of the people in Eastern Europe. Minimum criteria for such a determination should include governments which do not destroy churches, imprison pastors or priests, or persecute religious or political dissidents; which do not have anti-emigration policies; and those which do make progress in improving the general conditions of life for the people—including better work conditions, food, hous-

ing and energy, and cultural-religious opportunities. Basic human
rights are central in importance because they reflect how the Communist societies respect their own citizens, and whether they recognize any of the fundamental values for individuals that underlie our
society.

It is essential for the U.S. (with its traditional values and beliefs)
to have a convergence of interests with the people of Eastern Europe. If the Soviets are more likely to allow change only when they
are pressured to do so, we should remember our duty to assist those
elements working for change in the Soviet satellites. There are many
ways the U.S. government can both assist and encourage such forces
seeking change in the direction of freedom and self-determination.
We have to continue to strongly espouse our support for the right
of the peoples in Eastern Europe to a freer internal order, to improved conditions of life, and to open religious and political expression.

The U.S. government must be more courageous in its espousal
of a pro-freedom policy via agencies such as USIA. Our values and
principles, and solid support for the common aspirations of the peoples in Eastern Europe, should be firmly enunciated over the Voice
of America and Radio Free Europe. Beyond radio broadcasting,
there are opportunities in television, videos, books, and other publications. It should be made clear that the genius of America is not
its economic and material wealth alone, but its spiritual underpin-
nings, individual worth, and opportunity. Furthermore, the perception around the world that the U.S. prefers the status quo in Eastern Europe must be changed. It should be made clear that our
national interests are not served and security is not advanced for
all in Europe, until the legitimate aspirations of the peoples of Eastern Europe for freedom are recognized and granted.

Finally our government and nation should encourage assistance
on a private basis for our freedom allies in Eastern Europe. Both
the political dissidents and active religious believers of the bloc
states constitute groups seeking change. These indigenous forces
are the allies of freedom and democracy behind the Iron Curtain.
In the past American labor unions, churches, and humanitarian
groups have taken the lead in aiding such groups. Additionally,
hundreds of small organizations have participated in the channel-
ing of assistance to these groups. Food, vitamins, aspirins, and other
needed items (including Bibles and religious literature) in addition
to money, have been delivered privately to people in Eastern Europe.

There is no question about the Communist fear of religion. The Romanian Communist Party held a meeting on atheism during the spring of 1987 at the University of Bucharest. On the one hand, the meeting applauded the declining influence of religion in day to day life. On the other hand, participants were warned of the "social dangers of the proselytism [being carried out by] some neo-Protestant sects" (i.e. Baptists, Pentecostals, Brethren, and Adventists), and of the need to improve atheist (scientific-materialist and revolutionary-humanist) education.[18] In assisting such activist groups as the ones mentioned along with the "dissident" Orthodox, Catholic, and other groups, we are helping our allies and adding to the woes of the Communist regimes.

Political and religious dissidents have shown above all the weakness of the Communist system in the face of courage and faith. Where there is an indomitable spirit which is impervious to fear and terror, the Marxist-Leninist rulers appear helpless. Former Yugoslav Vice President under Tito, Milovan Djilas, has said that "Poland's opposition is the incurable cancer of democratic resistance within the body of the Eastern bloc."[19] Even beyond Djilas's valid observation we can add that the religious believers in God and the political believers in freedom and democracy, are the persistent, unconquerable thorns in the flesh most feared by the Communist elites. The least we can do is give such believers our support and prayers.

During the last weeks and months of our stay in Romania, hundreds of Romanians came to the residence for receptions and other occasions. Aware of our departure many asked that I never forget what was seen. "Never forget what the Romanian Communist Government is doing to destroy us, and never forget what the United States is doing to help the Bucharest regime keep us in this situation," one said. I will never forget.

One day the complete story of misery, gulags, and death under Communism will come out. Americans will hold the State Department elite accountable for perpetuating a misconceived policy that is a threat to the United States and no help for the captive peoples. And the danger of Communist slavery and Soviet expansionism will be laid bare for all to see. Until that day it is our duty to weaken and break the "convergence of interests" link between the State Department leadership and Eastern European Communist regimes like Romania.

APPENDIX I:

Presidential Letter of Ambassadorial Duties

THE WHITE HOUSE

WASHINGTON

October 2, 1981

Dear Mr. Ambassador:

I want to extend to you my personal best wishes
for the success of your mission in the Socialist
Republic of Romania. As my personal representative there, you, along with the Secretary of
State, share with me the responsibility for the
conduct of our relations with Romania. I know
we share a mutual conviction that carrying the
American message of hope and freedom and advanc-
ing United States' interests abroad reinforces
the foundations of peace. Together we are
pledged to work for national strength and
economic growth and to promote the values
undergirding our Nation's unity and security.

I give you my full personal support as Chief of
the United States Mission in Romania in the exercise of your strong statutory mandate under
section 207 of the Foreign Service Act of 1980
(22 U.S.C. 3927). I charge you to exercise full
responsibility for the direction, coordination,
and supervision of all United States Government
officers and employees in the country or organization to which you are accredited, except for
personnel under the command of a United States
area military commander, personnel under the
authority of the Chief of another United States
Mission (for example, one accredited to an international organization), or personnel detailed
to duty on the staff of an international organization. I expect you to oversee the operation
of all United States Government programs and
activities within that responsibility. I have
notified all heads of departments and agencies

accordingly and have instructed them to inform
their personnel in the United States and abroad.
So that you can ensure effective coordination of
all United States Government activities within
your responsibility, I ask you to provide strong
program direction and leadership of operations
Mission-wide. Please instruct all personnel
under your charge: it is their duty to keep you
fully informed at all times about their activities so you can effectively direct, coordinate,
and supervise United States programs and operations under your jurisdiction and recommend
policies to Washington.

You will receive policy guidance and instructions from the Secretary of State, who is my
principal foreign policy spokesman and advisor,
or from me directly. I expect you to report
with directness and candor. I want to emphasize

that the Secretary of State has the responsibility not only for the activities of the
Department of State and the Foreign Service but
also, to the fullest extent provided by law, for
the overall policy direction, coordination, and
supervision of the United States Government
activities overseas. There may be developments
or decisions on which personnel under your
authority disagree. The Secretary of State and
I will always welcome the opportunity to consider your recommendations for alternative
courses of action and policy proposals.

As you assume your duties, I know that you will
do so with a strong commitment to impartial and
equitable treatment of all U.S. Government personnel under your jurisdiction. Should any
perceived inequities be amenable to elimination
or mitigation by appeal to or negotiation with
the host government, I urge you to pursue this
course in a manner consistent with your authority and with international law and established
customary practice. Recognizing that various
agencies operate under different legislation and
regulations, should you consider legislative or
executive policy changes to be desirable in this
connection, you should recommend such changes
through the Secretary of State. Additionally,
fair treatment of all U.S. Government personnel
regardless of race, color, creed, sex or nation-

al origin epitomizes our belief in and adherence
to the principles of equality of opportunity, a
value and concept that form an important element
of the American democratic tradition.
As Commander-in-Chief, I have authority over
United States military forces. On my behalf you
have responsibility for the direction, coordination, supervision, and safety, including security from terrorism, of all Defense Department
personnel in Romania except those forces under
the operational command and control of a United
States area military commander and personnel
detailed to international organizations.
Defense Attache offices, units engaged in security assistance, and other DOD components attached to your Mission, as well as other Defense
Department activities which may have an impact
upon the conduct of our diplomatic relations
with Romania fall within your responsibility.

It is imperative that you maintain close relations with concerned United States area military
commanders and Chiefs of Mission accredited to
international organizations. A copy of this
letter is being disseminated to them. You must
keep each other currently informed and cooperate
on all matters of mutual interest. Any differences which cannot be resolved in the field
should be reported by you to the Secretary of
State; unified commanders should report to the
Secretary of Defense.

I expect the highest standards of professional
and personal conduct from all United States
Government personnel abroad. You have the authority and my full support to take any action
required to ensure the maintenance of such
standards.

Your mission is to protect and advance the
United States' interests abroad, and you will
receive the resources necessary to accomplish
that mission. At the same time, I expect that
these resources will be used in an effective and
efficient manner, and that they will be directly
and carefully related to priority policy and
program activities. You should inform the
Secretary of State when you believe that staf-
fing of any agency is either inadequate or
excessive to the performance of essential
functions.

I am confident that you will represent the
United States with imagination, energy, and
skill.   You have my full personal confidence
and best wishes.

Sincerely,

Ronald Reagan

The Honorable David B. Funderburk,
American Ambassador,
Socialist Republic of Romania.

APPENDIX II:

Presidential Letter of April 29, 1985

THE WHITE HOUSE

WASHINGTON

April 29, 1985

Dear David:

Thank you for your thoughtful letter of March 14 advising me of your intent to resign your current position as Ambassador to the Socialist Republic of Romania. It is with deep regret that I accept your resignation effective upon a date to be determined.

Your ambassadorship has been marked by a firm commitment to upholding democratic ideals. In particular, your efforts to improve the human rights situation in Romania have exemplified this Administration's strong dedication to the cause of freedom and they have helped to strengthen our ties with the Romanian people. I appreciate your role in encouraging this process, which I believe serves the fundamental interests of the Romanian people and all others in Eastern Europe seeking to shape their own destinies. You are also to be highly commended for your steadfast support of our national security interests in Europe. During your tenure, you have made an invaluable contribution to the goals of my Administration in this and many other areas.

As you return to North Carolina and Campbell University, you take with you my deep thanks for a job well done and my very best wishes for all success and happiness in the days ahead.

Sincerely,

Ronald Reagan

The Honorable David B. Funderburk
American Ambassador
Bucharest

NOTES

Prologue

[1]The following is a list of U.S. companies with offices and/or multinationals headquartered in Romania as of mid 1984: (1) Manufacturers Hanover Trust, headquartered in New York with a branch office in Bucharest; (2) American House, headquartered in Charleston, South Carolina with an office in Bucharest; (3) Dow Chemical with centers in Horgen, Switzerland, and Midland, Michigan, and an office in Bucharest; (4) DuPont de Nemours International, with centers in Geneva, Switzerland, and Wilmington, Delaware, and an office in Bucharest; (5) Eli Lilly Elanco, with headquarters in Vienna, Austria, and Indianapolis, Indiana, and an office in Bucharest; (6) General Electric Trading Company, with its main office in New York, New York, and a branch office in Bucharest; (7) Hewlett Packard, headquartered in Vienna, Austria, and Palo Alto, California, and an office in Bucharest; (8) I.C.E.C., with main offices in London, England, and White Plains, New York, and an office in Bucharest; (9) Ingersoll-Rand, headquartered in Milan, Italy, and Woodcliff Lake, New Jersey, and an office in Bucharest; (10) Martin Engineering, centered in Wiesbaden, West Germany, and Neponset, Illinois, with a branch office in Bucharest; (11) Merk Sharp and Dohme, headquartered in Zug, Switzerland, and Rahway, New Jersey, with an office in Bucharest; (12) Monsanto, centered in Brussels, Belgium, and St. Louis, Missouri, with an office in Bucharest; (13) Pan American Airways, headquartered in New York, New York, with an office in Bucharest; (14) Phibro-Salomon Inc., centered in New York, New York, with an office ln Bucharest; (15) Pioneer Overseas, headquartered in Johnston, Iowa, with an office in Bucharest; (16) Prudential Lines Corporation, headquartered in New York, New York, with branch offices in Constanta and Bucharest, Romania; (17) Rank Xerox, headquartered in England and the U.S., with an office in Bucharest; (18) Royce International Corporation, with the main office in New York, New York, and a branch in Bucharest; (19) Stafford International Corporation, centered in New York, New York, with an office in Bucharest; (20) Wang Laboratories, headquartered in Lowell, Massachusetts, with an office in Bucharest; (21) WJS/Moody International, Inc., centered in McLean, Virginia, with an office in Bucharest; (22) Applied Research Laboratories, centered in Vienna, Austria, and Sunland, California, with an office in Bucharest; (23) Pfizer Company, centered in Belgium, with an office in Bucharest; (24) Sperry N.V. Electronic Systems, with a branch office in Bucharest; (25) Stauffer Chemical Corporation, with a branch office in Bucharest; and (26) 3-M Company, centered in Switzerland, with an office in Bucharest. Other companies whose status is questionable and who have not fared well recently in Romania include: Control Data Corporation, headquartered in Vienna, Austria, and Minneapolis, Minnesota, with an office in Bucharest; Felton International, Inc.; and F.M.C.

[2]Bill Arthur and Ken Eudy, "Funderburk's Effectiveness As Ambassador Questioned," *The Charlotte Observer*, March 16, 1986, 1, 16A.

[3]Michael Isikoff, "Reagan's Ambassadors: Too Many Amateurs?", *International Herald Tribune*, March 31, 1983, 7. Also in *The Washington Post* as "The Return of the Political Ambassadors," March 29, 1983, A13.

[4]"Whither Funderburk?", *The New York Times*, March 20, 1985.

CHAPTER ONE:
The State Department Problem

[1]Proclamation 5223 of President Ronald Reagan "Captive Nations Week, 1984," July 16, 1984, White House Press Release.

[2]Notes to the author from Frank Corry, U.S. Embassy DCM, 1984. See also John Krizay, "An Ambassadorial Quota System," Heritage Foundation Issue Bulletin No. 85, June 3, 1982.

[3]James T. Hackett, "Regaining Control of the Department of State," *Mandate for Leadership II: Continuing the Conservative Revolution* (Washington: The Heritage Foundation, 1984). See also John Krizay, "How the White House Can Regain Control of Foreign Policy," The Heritage Foundation Institution Analysis Number 27, March 5, 1984.

[4]"Senior Foreign Service Performance Pay Recipients—FY 1985," *State* Magazine, May 1985.

CHAPTER TWO:
U.S. Policy Toward Romania and Eastern Europe

[1]Speech by Vice President George Bush, "U.S. Policy Toward Central and Eastern Europe," September 21, 1983, Vienna, Austria.

[2]*Ibid.*

[3]U.S. Department of Commerce, "Joint Venture Agreements in Romania: Background for Implementation," Pompiliu Verzariu and Jay Burgess, 1977, pp. 11-12. The Trade Agreement between the United States and Romania of August 1975 provides for the extension of Most-Favored-Nation tariff treatment to each others' products and makes Romania eligible for inclusion in the U.S. G.S.P., granted January 1, 1976.

[4]U.S. Department of Commerce, International Trade Administration, "Study of the Effects of a Termination of Romania's Most-Favored-Nation Tariff Status on Trade and Commercial Relations Between the United States and Romania," Edgar D. Fulton, March 28, 1983.

[5]Testimony by Gary Matthews, Deputy Assistant Secretary for Human Rights and Humanitarian Affairs of the State Department, before the U.S. House of Representatives, Subcommittee on H.R. and International Organizations, May 14, 1985.

[6]Leslie H. Gelb, "State Department's No. 3 Has a Habit of Succeeding: Working Profile—Lawrence S. Eagleburger," *The New York Times*, September 16, 1982.

CHAPTER THREE:
Romanian Foreign Policy:
The Myth of Independence

[1]Robert D. Kaplan, "Rumanian Gymnastics," *The New Republic*, December 17, 1984, 10-12. See also Kaplan, "Communist 'Maverick' Back in the Fold," *The Toronto Globe*, September 8, 1984.

[2]Ion Ratiu, *Contemporary Romania* (Richmond, England, Foreign Affairs Publishing Co., Ltd., 1975), pp.98-100.

[3]Vladimir Socor, "The Limits of National Independence in the Soviet Bloc: Rumania's Foreign Policy Reconsidered," *Orbis*, Fall 1976, Vol. XX, No. 3, pp. 729-730.

[4]Conversations with Researcher at the Romanian Institute of Historical and Social-Political Studies of the Romanian Communist Party, 1983-85.

[5]Socor, pp. 705-706.

[6]Anatoliy Golitsyn, *New Lies for Old* (New York: Dodd, Mead and Co., 1984), pp. 184-185.

[7]Ratiu, pp. 32-34, 97.

[8]Frank B. Corry, "Scinteia Traces of Ceausescu's Postwar Rise to Political Power," unpublished manuscript, 1984, pp. 2-3.

[9]Golitsyn, pp. 184-186.

[10]Ion Mihai Pacepa, "How the West's Secrets Are Stolen," unpublished manuscript, 1984 (with Michael A. Ledeen).

[11]Letter from Robert C. McFarlane to the author, November 21, 1983.

[12]*Ibid.*, pp. 1-38; Pacepa, "The Big Rip-Off," unpublished manuscript, 1982; Pacepa, "The Defector's Story," *The Washingtonian*, December 1985, pp. 168-183; Transcripts of U.S. House of Representatives Committee on Ways and Means Hearings on Most-Favored-Nation Trading Status for the Socialist Republic of Romania, June 10, 1986; and Linda Melvern, Nick Anning and David Hebditch, *Techno-Bandits* (Boston: Houghton Mifflin Company, 1984), pp. 52-54, 135.

[13]Pacepa, "The Big Rip-Off," p. 1.

[14]Pacepa, "The Defector's Story," p. 178.

[15]Interview with Nicolae Ceausescu, President of the Socialist Republic of Romania, July 1984, by John P. Wallach.

[16]"The World's Top Arms Exporters: 1982 Arms Deliveries," *Business Week*, October 22, 1984, p. 36.

[17]See, for example, Pacepa, "How the West's Secrets Are Stolen."

[18]See Theodore Shabad, "Kremlin Lets Factories Reach Out to the East Bloc," *The New York Times*, November 4, 1984, 17, for a discussion of the direct factory links.

[19]See, for examples, *EIU: The Economist Intelligence Unit Regional Review: Eastern Europe and the USSR 1986* (London: The Economist Publications, Ltd., 1986), pp. 92-95; Stephen Fischer-Galati, ed., *Eastern Europe in the 1980's* (Boulder, Colorado: Westview Press, 1981), p. 205; Teresa Rakowska-Harmstone and Andrew Gyorgy, eds., *Communism in Eastern Europe* (Bloomington, Indiana: Indiana University Press, 1979), pp. 161-166.

[20]Pacepa, "How the West's Secrets Are Stolen," pp. 1-38.

[21]Golitsyn, p. 191.

[22]*The Economist Intelligence Unit Regional Review*, p. 93.

[23]See newspaper accounts such as "No. 2 Jordanian Diplomat in Romania Shot to Death" in the *Daily Press* (N.C.), December 5, 1984, A6.

[24]Pacepa, "How the West's Secrets Are Stolen"; and Juliana Pilon, Transcripts of U.S. House of Representatives Committee on Ways and Means Hearings on Most-Favored-Nation-Treaty Status for the Socialist Republic of Romania, June 10, 1986.

[25]Pacepa, "How the West's Secrets Are Stolen," pp. 1-38.

[26]Golitsyn, pp. 183-194; Ratiu, pp. 96-97; and Socor, pp. 720-728.

[27]See, for examples, Juliana Pilon, "Romania Breaks Its Bargain with the U.S. on Trade Favors," The Heritage Foundation Backgrounder, August 1, 1986; Juliana Pilon, "Why Romania No Longer Deserves to be a Most Favored Nation," The Heritage Foundation Backgrounder No. 441, June 26, 1985; Melanie Merkle, "How United Nations Members Voted in 1982," *Human Events*, September 10, 1983, p. 14; and U.N. Voting Record, 38th General Assembly, All U.N.G.A. Plenary Votes.

[28]Pacepa, "The Defector's Story," pp. 177, 1982.

[29]*Ibid.*, pp. 171-182. Pacepa said that Brezhnev personally asked for information on American microelectronics which Ceausescu did his best to acquire. He also noted that Ceausescu considered the "Horizon" operation to be the most "valuable political, financial, and technological benefits in its (Romania's) history" (p. 172).

[30]A conversation between the author and one of the participants (Jeffrey Collins) in the discussion with the Romanian defector, in Austin, Texas, September 5, 1986.

CHAPTER FOUR:
The Communist-Imposed Tragedy in Romania and the State Department

[1]Four poems by Ana Blandiana, originally published in *Amfiteatru*, December 1984, translated in English initially (in rough translation) by Kiki Skagen Munshi, Director of the American Library (USIS) at the American Embassy, Bucharest.

[2]William Echikson, "US-Romanian Ties Under Fire Due to Bucharest's Rights Record," *The Christian Science Monitor* (1986).

[3]Calciu was released from prison and allowed to emigrate in 1985. See Calciu's article, "Persecution of the Orthodox Church in Romania," in *Sources of Human Rights Violations in Romania* (Washington: American Foreign Policy Institute, 1986).

[4]*Ibid.*; and Ion Ratiu, "The Communist Attack on the Catholic and Orthodox Churches in Romania," *The Eastern Churches Quarterly* (July–September, 1949).

[5]See Dr. Alexander Havadtöy, "The Oppression of the Hungarian Reformed Church in Romania," *Sources of Human Rights Violations in Romania*.

[6]See, for examples, Christian Response International (Christian Solidarity International) newsletters during the 1980's; "Sabin Teodosiu—An Industrial Ac-

cident," *A Bible for Russia* (I, No. 9, August-September 1983), p. 7; "A Romanian Tragedy," *The Voice of Truth* (Romanian Missionary Society, Wheaton, Illinois, February 1984); and Letter from the Romanian Committee for the Defense of Religious Freedom and Conscience (in exile), New York, New York, March 7, 1984, signed by Rev. Pavel Nicolescu, Mr. Radu Capusan and Mr. Petru Cocirteu, with an attachment on "Romanian Christians Interrogated, Arrested, Imprisoned, and Persecuted by the Communist Government."

[7]Calciu, *op. cit.*, p. 23.

[8]Letter from Bela Szigethy (of 4620 Taylor Avenue, N.E., Bainbridge Island, Washington 98110) to Congressman Joel Pritchard, U.S. House of Representatives, Washington, D.C. 20515, May 24, 1984. The letter was forwarded to me at the embassy in Bucharest.

[9]Statement of David B. Funderburk at MFN Hearings, U.S. Senate Finance Committee, International Trade Subcommittee, July 23, 1985.

[10]Letter from Romanian Ambassador to the U.S. Mircea Malitza to Mrs. Newberry, July 20, 1984.

[11]Congressional Record, U.S. Senate 10468, "Trade With the Socialist Republic of Romania," Senator Jesse Helms, including a "Voice of America Transcript: Romanian Priest," August 10, 1984. Senator Helms also referred to two broadcasts on Radio Free Europe regarding Palfi on May 7 and July 25, 1984.

[12]"World Meat Consumption Up," *The New York Times*, August 25, 1981, D6L. Romania's annual meat consumption per capita based on 1980 estimates in kilograms was 24.2 compared with the world leader the United States' 112.6, East Germany's 85.9, Hungary's 73.0 and the Soviet Union's 58.3.

[13]Robert D. Kaplan, "Rumanian Gymnastics," *The New Republic* (December 17, 1984). See also *Radio Free Europe Research*, Romanian SR 16 (November 2, 1984), pp. 10-11.

[14]Memorandum on "The City, a Permanent Part of Romanian Civilization," January 1985, to Romanian leaders from Dr. Dinu Giurescu, Academician Dionisie Pippidi, Dr. Grigore Ionescu, Dr. Vasile Dragut, Dr. Aurelian Triscu, Dr. Razvan Theodorescu and Dr. Radu Popa.

[15]Resolution 2508 of the Research Institute of Rubber and Plastic, Bucharest, February 15, 1982.

[16]Resolution 588 of the Inspectorate of Schools, General Inspector of Schools, Bucharest, November 24, 1980.

[17]See Dr. Alexander Havadtöy, *op. cit.* In a letter of January 15, 1986, Havadtöy sent me photo copies of the paper as well as the documentary account of the Bibles turned into toilet paper.

[18]Letter to the author from James E. Andrews, Stated Clerk, Office of General Assembly, Presbyterian Church (U.S.A.), New York, New York, September 17, 1985.

[19]Letter to the author from Mrs. Ted Warren of 928 Briarfield Road, Jackson, Mississippi, December 1, 1982.

[20]Calciu, *op. cit.*

[21]Letter to the author from Rev. Alton H. McEachern, Pastor of the First Baptist Church of Greensboro, North Carolina, and N.C. Baptist State Convention official, November 14, 1985.

[22]"Reflections on Billy Graham's Trip to Romania," *Religion in Communist Lands*, Summer 1986, vol. 14, no. 2, pp. 224-227.

[23]Statement of Elie Wiesel for presentation (by the author) on the occasion of the Holocaust Commemoration, June 15, 1984. We hosted a reception at our residence on the occasion at which Wiesel gave me his book, *Souls On Fire*. In the book he wrote: For Ambassador and Mrs. David Funderburk, who has done so much for all of us, with appreciation."

[24]Letter from Judith Kent to Senator Howard Baker, May 31, 1983, sent to the author by Senator Baker, June 16, 1983.

[25]See, for examples, John Barron, *KGB* (New York: Bantam Books, 1977), photograph; and Brian Freemantle, *KGB* (London: Michael Joseph/Rainbird, 1982), Illustration #55.

[26]Romanian Foreign Affairs Ministry Note Number 8/98.671, January 3, 1985, referring to Note Verbale P.S. 7-2/373, December 21, 1984, declaring American citizen Donald Kyer as "persoana nedorita pe teritoriul Republicii Socialiste Romania" (literally, undesirable person in Romania).

CHAPTER FIVE:
Nicolae Ceausescu—The Mad Man Favored by Washington

[1]See, for example, the A.P. report "Three Get Death Penalty for Stealing Meat," December 21, 1983. The report describes three packing plant employees sentenced to death for stealing meat from a plant in Tirgoviste, Romania.

[2]Franz Johannes Bulhardt, "Sie Sprechen Deinen Namen Aus" ("They Pronounce Thy Name"), *Neue Banater Zeitung* (The New Banat Times), July 19, 1984.

[3]Professor Radu Florescu of Boston College has done the most extensive research on the historical Dracula, publishing such books as *In Search of Dracula* (Greenwich: New York Graphic Society, 1972); and *Dracula: A Biography of Vlad the Impaler 1431-1476* (New York: Hawthorn, 1973). When visitors came to Romania as our house guests, their most frequently requested site to tour was "Dracula's Castle" in Transylvania. We usually obliged by taking them to the touristic Bran Castle, where Dracula perhaps spent a night or two. The authentic Dracula Castle at Poenari lies in rubble but is in the process of reconstruction. An interesting coincidence which Florescu points out is the Evangelical Lutheran Church in Sibiu (formerly Hermannstadt under Saxon-German domination in the Middle Ages) as the burial site for two notable names. Both the son of Dracula, known as Mihnea Cel Rau or "Mihnea the Bad," and the leader of the German Saxons, who was named Frank von Frankenstein (no relation to the Hollywood version), were buried with marker stones close to each other in the church. As one who worked for the USIA as an exhibit guide in the same city in 1975 and who visited it from time to time as ambassador, the strange site was seen several times by the author.

[4]See George G. Potra, "A Name of National Pride," *Romanian News* (November 16, 1984); Roger Boyes, "Romania: Who Will Follow the Conducator?", *The Times* (London), November 19, 1984; Paul Martin, "The Mad Mad Romania of Nicolae Ceausescu," *Reader's Digest* (January 1986), pp. 118-122; Roger Thurow,

"Romania Clings to Cult of Ceausescu as Nation Fast Slides into Decay," *The Wall Street Journal* (January 27, 1986); and Eugen Popa, "Omagiu" in *Romania Literara* (1984).

[5]See "The Bust of Comrade Ceausescu" by Horia Flamindu; "Portrait of Ceausescu" by John Jalea; Wood Icon picture by Bogdan Ion Cociuba; Homage: picture by Corneliu Brudascu; Poem by Viorel Cozma; Cloth art by Eugen Popa (July 18, 1982, *Romania Libera*), except where noted in *Romania Literara*, *Romania Libera*, *Scinteia* and *TeleRadio* between January and March 1983.

[6]See Claire Trean, "Le Parti Roumain Et Sa Femme," *Le Monde*, January 31, 1983.

[7]See "Aniversarea Zileie De Nastere A Tovarasei Elena Ceausescu" (The Anniversary of Comrade Elena Ceausescu's Birthday) in *Buletinul Oficial Al Republicii Socialiste Romania* (Bucharest), January 9, 1984, Vol. XX, No. 2, Part III, pp. 1-3.

CHAPTER SIX:
Dissent by the United States Ambassador

[1]Pacepa, "The Defector's Story," pp. 168-182.

[2]See Presidential Proclamation 5223, July 16, 1984, from a White House Press Release, for example.

[3]See, for examples of the print reviews of the book: Gheorghe Buzatu, *Cronica*, July 29, 1983, "History and Diplomacy From an American Perspective" refers to the book as "a valuable contribution to the study and understanding of the subject"; Cristian Popisteanu, *Romanian Review*, 4-5 (1984), "Fresh Landmarks of Romanian-British Inter-War Relations" says that the work includes "a picture where not only great billows but also the waves of the extremely troubled sea of the time's international relations are clearly seen. Such a picture contains the British consistent and inconsistent actions"; Elisabeta Petreanu, *Anale De Istorie*, Vol. XXXI, No. 2, 1985, concludes that the book brings an important documentary and interpretative contribution to the knowledge of the historic epoch; and Teodor Popescu, *Revista Romana De Studii Internationale*, Vol. XVII, November-December 1983, describes the publication as presenting a new conception in the study of Great Britain in southeastern Europe on the eve of the Second World War which constitutes an excellent example of dialogue between Romanian and American historians.

CHAPTER SEVEN:
Washington Meetings With President Reagan and Secretary Shultz

[1]Letter from the author to Ambassador Faith Ryan Whittlesey, Assistant to the President for Public Liaison, April 27, 1983.

[2]See John Maclean, "I'd Like to Present Our Ambassador, Mr. Klunk," *The Washingtonian*, July 1983, pp. 62-79.

CHAPTER EIGHT:
Washington Meetings with Lawrence Eagleburger, Elliott Abrams and Senator Jesse Helms

[1]During my stay in Romania, I worked closely with the Jewish community and Rabbi Moses Rosen, and had an excellent relationship with the first Israeli Ambassador Aba Gefen. I attended Jewish community receptions and spoke in the main synagogue. Most notably I filled in for Elie Wiesel by giving a talk on the occasion of the Holocaust Commemoration.

[2]Kissinger Associates reportedly has helped market Yugos in the U.S.

[3]Leslie H. Gelb, "State Department's No. 3 Has a Habit of Succeeding," *The New York Times*, September 16, 1982.

[4]Elliott Abrams Interview with Voice of America, October 18, 1982.

[5]*Ibid.*

[6]See Bill Arthur and Ken Eudy, "Funderburk's Effectiveness as Ambassador Questioned," *The Charlotte Observer*, March 16, 1986, 1, 16A.

[7]Letter from the author to Elliott Abrams, February 1, 1983.

[8]*Ibid.*

[9]Letter from Elliott Abrams to the author, February 17, 1983.

[10]See Press Statement of the United States Government on the occasion of the U.S.-Romanian Human Rights Roundtable, issued February 29, 1984, Washington, D.C.

[11]Letter from Senator Jesse Helms to Romanian Foreign Minister Stefan Andrei, June 20, 1983.

[12]*Ibid.*

[13]Letters from Senator Jesse Helms to the author and to Dr. Norman A. Wiggins, October 8, 1984.

[14]Don Phillips, "22 Ambassadors Endorse Helms: Shultz Issues Caution Over Unusual Action," *The Washington Post*, October 26, 1984, 1.

[15]United States Department of State, Office of the Inspector General, "Practical Ethics: A Briefing Book for Chiefs of Mission" (November 1984).

[16]Lucia Mouat, "Rising Tide of Noncareer U.S. Envoys Worries Experts," *The Christian Science Monitor*, November 29, 1984, in the USIA Wireless File of November 29, 1984.

[17]"N.C. Visitors Assist Helms," *Greensboro News and Record*, October 31, 1984, B2.

[18]See "Mr. Helms's Foreign Legion," *The New York Times*, October 27, 1984, 24; James Reston, "Jesse The Helmsman," *The New York Times*, September 14, 1984; Bernard Gwertzman, "The State Department In A Dither Over Helms," *The New York Times*, November 8, 1984, B16; "Undiplomatic Diplomats," *International Herald Tribune*, February 2, 1985, 6; and Flora Lewis, "Independent Envoys Pose Problems For U.S.," *International Herald Tribune*, February 16-17, 1985, 4.

[19]See James T. Hackett, "Regaining Control of the Department of State," *Mandate For Leadership II: Continuing the Conservative Revolution* (Washington: The

Heritage Foundation, 1984); Smith Hempstone, "Choosing Envoys: Career Officers Vs. Political Appointees," *The Washington Times*, November 30, 1984, D1, and "Career Officers Vs. Political Appointees At State," *Human Events*, December 15, 1984, p. 13; John Vinocur, "Galbraith Derides U.S. Career Diplomats As Timid," *International Herald Tribune*, February 14, 1985, 1; and William F. Buckley Jr., "What Galbraith Meant About Guts in the Embassy," *International Herald Tribune*, February 23-24, 1985, 4.

[20]See Bernard Gwertzman, "State Department in a Dither Over Helms," *The New York Times*, November 8, 1984, B16.

CHAPTER NINE:
High Level Visitors to Romania: From Secretary of State Alexander Haig to Vice President George Bush

[1]Alexander M. Haig Jr., *Caveat: Realism, Reagan and Foreign Policy* (New York: Macmillan Publishing Company, 1984), p. 258.

[2]Letter from Frank C. Carlucci to the author, October 20, 1982.

[3]Speech by Vice President George Bush, "U.S. Policy Toward Central and Eastern Europe," September 21, 1982 (Vienna, Austria).

[4]See Charles Humana, *World Human Rights Guide* (London: The Economist Publications Ltd., 1986), and in *The Free Romanian*, Vol. 2, No. 11, November 1986, 2-3.

CHAPTER TEN:
U.S. Visitors to Romania: From Secretary of Commerce Malcolm Baldrige to Chairman of the Joint Chiefs of Staff John Vessey

[1]Malcolm A. Kline, "Commerce Pampers East Bloc," *Washington Inquirer*, December 13, 1985, pp. 4, 7.

[2]Details of the trip including participants, meetings and the full itinerary of activities are part of a confidential Christian Response International Romania Trip Report of December 9-18, 1984, C.R.I., Rockville, Maryland.

[3]*Politics in America: Members of Congress in Washington and at Home* (1984), edited by Alan Ehrenhalt (Washington: C.Q. Press, 1983), pp. 125-126.

[4]Letter from Charles Z. Wick to the author, October 5, 1982.

[5]No doubt as he did in other places for American ambassadors Wick added that

I was one of the most outstanding ambassadors appointed, and much respected by President Reagan.

[6]"The World's Top Arms Exporters: 1982 Arms Deliveries" (Data: U.S. Arms Control and Disarmament Agency), *Business Week*, October 22, 1984. Romania's $1.1 billion in arms exports ranked it fifth behind the U.S.S.R., the U.S., France and Great Britain, and ahead of China, Italy, Czechoslovakia, West Germany, Brazil, Poland, Spain, North Korea, South Korea, Israel, Egypt and Libya.

[7]General John Vessey Jr.'s son, John Vessey III, was the chief of the consular section of the American Embassy at Bucharest during my tenure as ambassador. I considered John Vessey III a quietly competent employee of the U.S. Foreign Service. In one of the most difficult jobs in the embassy as consular chief, he treated the Romanian nationals working there with respect and equality and defended their positions in the face of various charges of spying and uncooperative behavior by U.S. citizens of Romanian and non-Romanian origin. Thus my surprise when he told me a day or two before his departure from Bucharest—less than two months before his Dad came as an official visitor—that he had lost respect for Romanians. He said that of the thousands of Romanians he saw who came into the embassy consular section during his 3½ years there, most seemed to be motivated by "I would rather kill my neighbor's goat than let him be better off than me." He was in part reflecting the concern of some observers who felt that many Romanians desiring to emigrate to the U.S. were motivated by material or economic reasons.

EPILOGUE

[1]See my letter to the editor of *The Washington Times*, "Funderburk Resigned, But Not to Protest U.S. Policy," May 24, 1985, 9A.

[2]Conversation with John Herrington, then White House Personnel Director, in his White House office, September 5, 1984. Herrington, posed as an understanding conservative fighting to keep Reagan conservatives in top positions. Shortly afterwards, he got a Cabinet level position—Secretary of the Department of Energy. I never again heard from him or the Personnel Office.

[3]Letter from the author to President Reagan, March 14, 1985. So that I would have time to complete the move from Bucharest to Buies Creek and prepare for the new job at Campbell University, we decided to push up the departure to mid-May. Following a week or so of de-briefings in Washington, we arrived in North Carolina at the end of May.

[4]Letter to the author from President Reagan, April 29, 1985.

[5]"Shultz Says European Trip Will Show U.S. Supports Autonomy," (L.A. Times-Washington Post News Service), *The News and Observer* (Raleigh, N.C.), December 8, 1985, 21A; and Bernard Gwertzman, "U.S. to Warn Romania to Improve Rights," (New York Times News Service), *The News and Observer*, December 5, 1985, 28A.

[6]"Shultz, Romanian Leader to Meet," *The News and Observer*, December 14, 1985, 6A.

[7]See, for example, Ross MacKenzie, "Why Classify Romania Most-Favored Nation?" in the *Winston-Salem* (N.C.) *Journal*, October 9, 1986, 11.

[8]Editorial by Antoine Bosshard, "Damage Has Been Done" in *Journal De Geneve* (Geneva, Switzerland), December 1985.

[9]See, for example, Connaught Marshner, "An American Ambassador Who Took On State," *Conservative Digest*, November 1985, pp. 73-80.

[10]Paul Martin, "The Mad Mad Romania of Nicolae Ceausescu," *Reader's Digest* (January 1986), pp. 118-122.

[11]See Bradley Graham, "The Big Chill, Romanian Style," *The Washington Post* (National Weekly Edition), April 29, 1985, 18; and "Envoy Quits, Faults Policy: Funderburk Sees Romania Coddled," *The Washington Post*, May 15, 1985, A28; and Jackson Diehl, "Economic Woes Trim Romania's Independence," *The Washington Post*, October 28, 1986, A17, and "Romania Criticized Over Treatment of Minorities," *The Washington Post*, October 25, 1986, A20.

[12]The CNN account by Loory showed an "idyllic countryside," no absence of food for the people, a feature on Dracula's Castle, Ceausescu as the only leader in the world who regularly makes statements condemning anti-Semitism (only part of the picture) and a wedding and feast of plenty. It showed nothing about Ceausescu's solid alliance with the Soviets, his persecution of religious and political dissidents, and the overall plight of the oppressed people under a government with a terrible human rights record in Europe. Loory's unwillingness to present the real picture of life in Romania was also made obvious during my appearance with him on November 6, 1986, on CNN's International Hour. See Cliff Kincaid, "Ted Turner of The Cable News Network Is Quoted As Saying That Communism Is Okay With Him," *Conservative Digest*, October 1986, pp. 25-30; and Cliff Kincaid's research for Accuracy in Media, Inc. The major television networks along with *The New York Times* and *The Washington Post* have often carried water for the clientitis pros at State. A good example is "Romania's Defiance," by Jack Anderson and Dale Van Atta in *The Washington Post*, August 25, 1985, B7. Quoting a CIA profile of Ceausescu's popularity the Anderson-Van Atta column was essentially equivalent to a KGB-Securitate disinformation article. A greater effort is obviously needed to help balance such biased accounts.

[13]Among the tributes from Romanians outside Romania which perhaps meant the most personally was the formation of ROMPAC during my recent primary campaign for the U.S. Senate from North Carolina. Romanian-Americans led by Victor Gaetan set up a Romanian Political Action Committee (ROMPAC) in Washington, D.C. in the spring of 1986, which "supports federal candidates sensitive to and actively involved with issues concerning Romanian-Americans. ROMPAC's immediate priority and urgent task is to support Ambassador David Funderburk in his upcoming Primary Senate Election in North Carolina May 6, 1986. Both Ambassador Funderburk's past record and his potential to become a member of the U.S. Senate are of unique importance to Romanian-Americans. Ambassador Funderburk's demonstrated sensitivity toward Romanian-American concerns would constitute a major asset to the hundreds of thousands of Romanian-Americans." In June 1987, I was unanimously voted an honorary member of the World Union of Free Romanians, in Paris. One of those whose support and prayers have meant the most to me is Virgil Pop of Glendale, California.

[14]Lecture by Nestor Rates at the Eleventh Congress of the Romanian-American Academy, May 8-10, 1986 at the University of Colorado, Boulder. See *Lupta* (The Fight, Providence, R.I.), September 15, 1986, 9-10.

[15]*Ibid.*

[16]Fischer-Galati also noted in the what it is worth category that he, Fischer-Galati, is considered by the Ceausescu clan (read Ilie) the one most indispens-

able person in terms of academia, publicity and prestige for the Romanians—even though he says he has written things very critical of the regime.

[17]Bill Arthur and Ken Eudy, "Funderburk's Effectiveness As Ambassador Questioned," *The Charlotte Observer* (March 16, 1986), 1, 16A.

[18]See *Scinteia* of April 5, 1987, quoted in *Keston News Service*, No. 273, April 16, 1987, p. 11.

[19]See Dennis L. Bark, ed., *To Promote Peace: U.S. Foreign Policy in the Mid-1980s* (Stanford, California: Hoover Institution Press, Stanford University Press, 1984), p. 250.

Index